Gender and Power
in Rural North China

Qing dynasty monument to a "virtuous woman"

Gender and Power
in Rural North China

ELLEN R. JUDD

STANFORD UNIVERSITY PRESS

STANFORD, CALIFORNIA   1994

Stanford University Press
Stanford, California
© 1994 by the Board of Trustees
of the Leland Stanford Junior University
Printed in the United States of America

CIP data appear at the end of the book

Stanford University Press publications are
distributed exclusively by Stanford University
Press within the United States, Canada, Mexico,
and Central America; they are distributed exclusively by Cambridge University Press throughout the rest of the world.

Original printing 1994
Last figure below indicates year of this printing:
04   03   02   01   00   99   98   97   96   95

For Ruth and Allan Judd
and to the memory of
Gladys Ellen Harpell

Preface

One of the abiding mystifications of anthropological writing is the convention that only the fieldworker's name appears on the title page. As with every effort in cross-cultural understanding, the research that produced this work was a shared enterprise. I am most deeply indebted to the residents of the three north China villages—Zhangjiachedao, Qianrulin, and Huaili—who accepted me into their communities and helped me toward an understanding of their lives. Their generosity is the source of whatever may be of value in the book that follows. I hope they will find some pale reflection here of the richness and courage of their lives.

In each village I was accompanied by at least one official representative of a sponsoring body or a level of local government. Each contributed a different perspective—from the profession of sociology, from official woman-work, and from local government—and each was invaluable in facilitating the research. In addition, representatives of the leadership of each village took the time to make arrangements for the daily research process, and often joined in it. All these official companions were helpful and gracious in the face of the inconvenience and added work load my presence caused.

The research was made possible by a series of grants from the Social Sciences and Humanities Research Council of Canada: SSHRCC–Chinese Academy of Social Sciences Exchange Grants, 1986 and 1987–88; a SSHRCC General Research Grant, 1986; a SSHRCC Canada Research

Fellowship at the University of Western Ontario, 1987–89, and at the University of Manitoba, 1989–92; and a SSHRCC Research Grant, 1990–91. The Canada Research Fellowship was supported by matching funds from the university endowment funds of the University of Western Ontario and the University of Manitoba, and by the University of Manitoba Alumni Fund. Within China, the research was facilitated by the Chinese Academy of Social Sciences, the Shandong Academy of Social Sciences, the China Shandong International Culture Exchange Center, the Shandong Women's Federation, and various levels of government in Shandong province.

Within Canada, I was assisted at various stages by a number of research assistants, whose work was made possible through the grants cited above, the Department of Anthropology of the University of Western Ontario, the Ontario Work-Study Bursary Programme, and the Department of Anthropology of the University of Manitoba. These were: Lü Xiuyuan, Suellen Seguin, Fu Xiaojiang, Leo Chan, Fu Mengsong, Liu Dongyang, Brett Waddell, Sharon Gereaux, and François Gaboury.

This work has benefited from the generous advice and comments of many colleagues and friends. I especially wish to acknowledge Myron Cohen, Isabel Crook, Norma Diamond, Graham Johnson, Diana Lary, Sandra Sachs, Rubie Watson, and Martin King Whyte.

Part of Chapter 2 originally appeared under the title, "Land Divided, Land United," in *China Quarterly* 130 (1992): 338–56; and part of Chapter 6 originally appeared as "'Men Are More Able': Rural Chinese Women's Conceptions of Gender and Agency," in *Pacific Affairs* 63, 1 (1990): 40–61. I am pleased to acknowledge the permission of the journals to include this material here.

I am grateful to my family for their support and interest in my work through the years, and especially to my parents and aunt, to whom this book is dedicated. My sister, Janet LeSarge, was able to locate and contact me in China when nobody else could, in June 1989, and has been invaluable in the preparation of this manuscript. Special thanks to Chris Egan for relentless efforts to speed its completion.

The manuscript has benefited from the attention of the editors of Stanford University Press, and I would particularly like to express my appreciation for the work of Muriel Bell, Ellen Smith, and Victoria Scott. The index was prepared by Victoria Olsen.

Finally, if there is a real reason for my name appearing alone on the title page, it is that I accept sole responsibility for the interpretations presented here and for all remaining shortcomings in this study.

Contents

Tables

A Note on Measures
and Family Terms

Measures

jin	1 jin = ½ kg
li	1 li = ½ km
mu	1 mu = ⅙ acre
renminbi (RMB)	US $1 = RMB 3.5 (1986) to RMB 4.8 (1990)

Family Terms

The distinction between stem and extended families is an important one in rural Chinese society. A stem family consists of a nuclear family (husband, wife, and children) with the addition of at least one parent of either the husband or wife. In China this most commonly includes the parent(s) of the husband, but in the case of uxorilocal marriages it includes the parent(s) of the wife.

Extended families in China are found only in patrilocal situations. An extended family, as found in China, consists of at least two married brothers, their wives and children, and at least one of their parents. The extended family ideal is that all sons remain in the family after their marriages and none divides out while either parent is living, but this family form has never been common in China. Where it is found, it is based on a shared estate controlled by the senior man in the family, and it may involve economic cooperation and division of labor among the mature men in the family (see M. Wolf 1972). The more common arrangement is that sons divide out of a household following marriage, but the parent(s) are not left alone (it is often the youngest son who remains after his own marriage).

The resulting distribution of family forms in rural China is a mix of stem and nuclear families, with an occasional and often temporary extended family.

The term aggregate family has been proposed to refer specifically to recent trends in family form in China. An aggregate family, as Croll originally (1987a) proposed the term, refers to a family that has divided into more than one household but retains close economic cooperation and sociopolitical relations. The retention of close ties after division is an important and common aspect of rural social life. In this study I have reserved the term aggregate household for those situations in which such relations are exceptionally close and include ties characteristic of single-household families, such as pooled incomes. These are often situations in which family members describe themselves as having divided, but not "clearly" (see p. 175).

Gender and Power
in Rural North China

CHAPTER 1

Introduction:
On Virtue

"For a woman to be without ability is a virtue" is a view attributed to Confucius but still living and efficacious within the contemporary Chinese polity. It is a paradox in either context—a proposition widely accepted as true by both women and men but practically denied in the conduct of everyday life. Here I will explore this paradox as recreated within the processes of the rural reform program that restructured rural China during the 1980s.

The watershed of transformation that followed in the wake of the Cultural Revolution moved quickly from a denunciation of the ten Cultural Revolution years (1966–76) to a rejection of the collective era as a whole (1956–c. 1980) and of the framework of policy and political philosophy on which it had been based. The rural reform program, as it developed in the early 1980s, included (1) the institution of a "responsibility system" contracting collective resources to individuals, households, or groups of households under terms that came increasingly close to de facto ownership; (2) the dissolution of the commune and of the previous collective system, and its replacement with formal local governments and mixed (private and public) forms of economic organization; (3) the revival of private marketing and of a market for labor power; (4) reduced state control over production and sale of agricultural produce; (5) the adjustment of state purchase prices for agricultural commodities to the advantage of rural producers; (6) the legalization of hiring labor; (7) the growth of rural industry, both private and public; and (8) promotion of production and exchange in a commodity economy.

All these policy changes have had wide ramifications throughout rural society, and none can be viewed as gender-neutral. Each of the policy changes and the program as a whole have been officially presented as changes in political economy without reference to gender or to the specific interests of women. Most subsequent discussion, both within China and abroad, has also focused on the changes as a matter of political economy. At the same time, the substantial literature on women in China has often taken other issues as its focus and has not concentrated on the implications of the reform program for the lives of rural women.

The official choice not to examine the roles of women in rural society in the course of this transformation can be attributed to a variety of sources. The reform program is overwhelmingly oriented toward the narrow economic goals of increased rates of economic growth, and considerations of social policy have not been a priority for policymakers. The shift from the collective system to a reconsidered form of household-based rural economy was a fundamental one that directed most attention toward the collective-household relation, at the expense of considering gender relations internal to households or to collectives and their successors.

It is also implicit within the reform program that the program can proceed *without any need to take the specific roles of women into account.* This is a cultural assumption that obscures otherwise evident contradictions. But, although taken for granted, this assumption is not uniformly or consistently shared. In particular, its validity is constantly put into question by the everyday roles women play in agriculture, rural industry, commodity production, and in the dense networks of social relations that comprise rural life. The gender-specific roles played by women are essential to each of these spheres, and in practice are recognized as essential, even if it is possible and common to deny or minimize their import within official modes of discourse.

In the chapters that follow, I trace the practical roles of women (and men) in several dimensions of rural life. In each dimension, I examine the relation between observable and recounted practical activities and relations on the one hand, and official models of these on the other. In this approach I am following Bourdieu (1977), who has provided the sharpest methodological argument for practice theory. I am also following his observation that anthropological models may replicate official models and so be inadequate and misleading. Each of the substantive chapters of this volume is implicitly structured by models I took with me into the field, and by the contrast between these models and the practices I found there. In this sense, the volume is a summary report on a fieldworker's reflexive critique. The critique is immanent in the following pages and will not be exhaustively previewed here.

There is one caution that should, however, be made explicit at this point, a point where the critique is still work-in-progress. The anthropological models available to me were almost wholly based on research in south China, especially Taiwan and Hong Kong. Sinologists are agreed that there are major north-south and other regional differences, and that the rural north has been relatively little studied. At the present stage many problems with the adequacy of existing models of rural Chinese society derive from their basis in ethnographic work in limited regions of China. The extent to which this is the source of problems with available anthropological models will only be resolved by further ethnographic study in a wider range of regions. Some questions cannot be adequately answered until this work has been done. Nevertheless, I have been struck by the close resemblance of certain aspects of the available anthropological models to the official models, and the official models are generally presumed to be nationally more shared than are local practices. I am referring here especially to elements of the official models that describe and prescribe norms of authority and of relationship in kinship and gender relations.[1] In particular, the official models remain silent about or substantially deny practical, strategic roles for women that women do actively realize. By directing attention toward ordinary rural women as strategic agents—and highly significant ones within their immediate social worlds—revisions can be suggested regarding the lives of women and the understanding of the fabric of gender and social relations in rural China.

The approach I have taken here utilizes practice theory and attempts to do so as much as possible from the perspective of ordinary rural women. Rather than examining the impact of the reform program explicitly or implicitly from above, from the perspective of the makers of policy, I have looked at it from the perspective of those remaking their lives within the somewhat altered framework of possibilities offered by the reform program. Similarly, I have approached the structure of rural social life, specifically kinship and household relations, from the perspective of women within these relations, again making and remaking vital aspects of their lives.

The common human condition of striving for a good life has been complicated in China for many decades by an urgency to resolve persistent and frequently desperate problems of poverty and politics. Much of the past century has been characterized and shaped by the convictions of many people that fundamental solutions, of one type or another, were feasible. The reform program of the 1980s is the most recent of these. I add to the debate regarding this program by examining it from below, by looking at the practices and strategies of rural women, and the changes in these, in the 1980s. I examine some of the possible—including newly possible—strategies for women in economic and social relations, and examine changes in the structure of the social fields in which these strategies are located and realized (see Bourdieu 1988).

The study is not an exhaustive one—it is focused on a selected set of questions and is constrained by the range of possibilities in the three villages studied. The criteria used in selecting the foci of the study were simple and straightforward, although they did sometimes lead in unexpected directions. I focused on aspects of rural social and economic life that were of major importance in everyday life, and that were being significantly changed in the context of the rural reform program. The reform program has allowed a much greater diversity of socioeconomic arrangements and activities than was possible during the collective era, and not all these diverse possibilities could be present in the limited number of sites I could examine. The issues covered are therefore restricted by what was present in these communities. By comparing three different, geographically separate communities, and by consulting the literature in English and in Chinese, I tried to avoid an intensive treatment of issues that might be local anomalies. There are unavoidably many common and important issues that are not highlighted in this study, simply because they were not alternatives emphasized in any of these three communities. The study should therefore be read as an element within the growing ethnographic literature on contemporary China, and it has been conceptualized throughout as part of that larger and growing endeavor.

I also chose to focus, as the study progressed, on those aspects of life in the three villages which offered some new insights or perspectives for the understanding of rural Chinese society. Finally, I chose to focus on what was evidently important in the lives of the women and men in these villages, as it emerged from their accounts or as they coached me in understanding their lives.

At the same time, I particularly attended to critical elements structuring the social field for women and defining the strategies they can realistically and practically pursue at the present time. This standpoint is immanent throughout the following presentation and analysis of data, whether on social and economic organization and practices, on the interpretation of meanings embedded in social life, or on the relation of these to anthropological models for understanding gender and power in rural north China.

The Reform Era

At the end of 1978, China turned decisively away from the path of collective ownership and development in the countryside that people within and without China had for decades thought of as China's unique version of socialist rural development. Policies both before and after this threshold continue to be described in China as "socialist," and there are some genuine continuities, but the profound quality of the shift in direction is acknowledged by all.

Prior to this shift, rural China had been uniformly organized in a multitier collective system of production team (*shengchan dui*), production brigade (*shengchan dadui*), and people's commune (*renmin gongshe*). This structure had come into existence during the Great Leap Forward of 1958 and had been continually modified, but it had also provided a continuing framework for rural Chinese society from the early 1960s to the end of the 1970s. Within this framework, the production teams had effective control over the basic productive resources of the rural economy—people and land. The national state claimed ultimate ownership, and the role of the teams was expressed as that of being the basic "accounting unit" (*hesuan danwei*) in the countryside. Access to and use of land for agriculture, housing, and other local use, management of rural labor, and provision of local benefits were brought together at the level of production teams. These were territorially bounded residential units with clear agnatic biases based on the norm of patrilocal postmarital residence. In different parts of the country, they might coincide either with individual hamlets or with neighborhoods in larger villages. Members of the teams effectively shared ownership of land and of some other resources (draft animals, agricultural machinery, storehouses), and had no access to any of these resources except through membership in such a team.

Several teams, in many cases those which together comprised a natural village, formed a brigade. This was often a relatively empty level with no direct access to either local resources or to higher levels of the state. Under certain circumstances, however, it could be very important. In some parts of the country, especially those with low population density, the team level did not exist, and the brigade level assumed the resources and role of the team. In other cases, teams had been replaced as accounting units by brigades, a step that was especially promoted in 1975–76 as an effort to reduce economic inequities between neighboring teams. The mechanism for accomplishing this was the promotion of rural enterprises (often described as rural industry) at the brigade level. These enterprises, where successful, were much more profitable than agriculture, and brigade growth in this sphere could be sufficient to allow teams to merge their resources at the brigade level without any team suffering an economic loss. The extent of enterprise development at the brigade level was widely variable, but this was one of the major functions of the brigade.

Rural enterprises were also run at the commune level, but the commune had other qualities that made it a distinct type of unit. The commune was the point at which production and membership in collectives merged with the lowest formal level of the government. The commune had some economic roles, especially in running its own enterprises, and provided local government and services to members of all its component brigades.

The economic well-being of people in the countryside was directly tied to their membership in units of this collective system. Every rural resident was a member of a collective at each level in this hierarchy and had corresponding rights of access to resources and benefits, and obligations to contribute labor to the collective. Labor contributions were recorded as workpoints, through complex and locally variable calculations, and the relation of these workpoints to the value of production of the collective determined the member's remuneration. Each member's standard of living was tied directly to the collective to which (s)he belonged. Substantial differences existed among collectives, even among neighboring teams, because of differences in amount and quality of land, size of population, ownership of agricultural machinery and draft animals, and quality of management.

Within teams, too, households varied in their income levels, primarily because of differences (which would change over the course of the domestic cycle) in the ratio of workers to dependents. Customary differences in workpoint levels according to age and gender were factors here, and there were some differences among individuals according to skill, effort, and work accomplished as well. But these latter, individually based material incentives were diluted by membership in a large collective, where leveling mechanisms operated and distribution also took need into account.

Above and beyond the level of the commune, each collective was embedded within a centrally planned state economy. Virtually all agricultural produce was purchased and sold through the state, which controlled production and distribution of necessary agricultural inputs, such as fertilizer and insecticide. Commercial activity was a near-monopoly of the state, as was access to legitimate employment. Both self-employment and hiring labor privately were unacceptable. Migration from rural to urban areas was tightly and effectively restricted.

This set of policies resulted in a rural population firmly tied to localized communities. The structural constraints of the collective-state economy in the countryside were shared nationally, but there was enormous regional and local variation in their impact. In the better endowed localities, the collective system provided assured access to resources and a minimal safety net. The collective era demonstrated real economic growth, although the potential for rising living standards was almost wholly erased by high rates of population increase. Perhaps the chief material benefit for rural people was the survival of their children. Where conditions were less favorable or the economy was managed less well, people suffered from being tied to their collectives and not being able to supplement their livelihoods through self-employment in crafts, petty trade, or migration. Absolute poverty remained an intractable problem in much of rural China through the end of the collective era and beyond it.

The end of the Cultural Revolution in 1976 was followed by a brief interregnum of policy uncertainty. In December 1978, the Third Plenum of the Eleventh Central Committee of the Chinese Communist Party marked the beginning of the reform era. Many reform policies began at a later date (in urban or industrial fields) or are still under debate (especially in respect to the political system), but in rural China reform policies began in the late 1970s and were progressively extended through the early 1980s.

The aspect of reform that has attracted the most attention began with various forms of the "responsibility system" (*zeren zhi*) in the late 1970s. The form that eventually became most widespread in the countryside devolved land and other agricultural resources to households, together with responsibility for delivering a certain amount of agricultural produce and for managing resources. Excess production or profit beyond the contracted levels could be retained by the contracting household. The advantages of the household responsibility system were that direct material incentive motivated higher production and more efficient use of resources. The disadvantages lay in increasing interhousehold inequities and in the possibility that contracting households would choose to maximize their profits at the expense of maintaining the long-term fertility of the soil. Increasing interhousehold income differences have emerged as a result of this policy, and they have been a subject of concern. The negative impact has been cushioned by generally rising income levels in the countryside and the use of some formal and informal leveling mechanisms. The chief thrust of policy, however, remains a willingness to allow uneven levels of prosperity in the conviction that some of the wealth of the most prosperous households will "trickle down" to others. This view is central to contemporary Chinese reform economic philosophy. Concerns about ensuring the fertility of the land have been met by increasing the length of contracts and by repeated official assurances that current policies are long-term and that land will not be recollectivized.[2]

The most dramatic effect of the household responsibility system has been to erode the landed basis of the collective system in the countryside. Nominally, land is still in the hands of local levels of the state—commonly the administrative village—but effective control of agricultural resources and production are now vested in households. The system of collective ownership in agriculture was effectively ended early in the rural reform program.

The implications of the reform program for rural enterprises have been more uneven. Where brigades and communes had viable enterprises, these appear to have continued, and to have done so in a modified form of collective ownership. With the end of the formal collective framework in the early 1980s, these are now attached to levels of formal government—administrative villages and townships—and their management implements some form of management responsibility system. During the early 1980s, it also became possible for households to establish their own enterprises and openly hire labor. Rural enterprises in China may now be either quasi-collective or private, and all operate within the context of a revived rural marketplace combined with continued state regulation of the economy. Rural enterprises grew rapidly from the late 1970s to the late 1980s, and were major sources of increased rural prosperity throughout this decade (see Wong 1988).

At the same time that the collective system in the countryside was being dismantled step by step, the rural marketing system was being revived. The state has maintained some control over the production and marketing of essential goods, such as food grains and cotton, but other agricultural and nonagricultural products, and even some of the essential items, can be legally bought and sold on the free market. This has provided producers with attractive markets for increased production and has provided a channel of self-employment and income for tens of millions of rural people involved in part-time or full-time marketing. The extent of the role of the market in China's current mixed economy has generated some complex questions about the character of China's socialist/postsocialist system, which are discussed in Chapter 4, "Socialist Commodity Production."

The rural economy has been invigorated by the increased opportunities provided by the reform policies, although some of the increase in rural living standards is the direct result of sharp upward adjustments in state purchasing prices for agricultural goods early in the 1980s. The state has not removed itself from the rural economy, but has increasingly used indirect means and market forces to accomplish its policy objectives (see Shue 1984, 1988).

The changes in rural economic conditions have been accompanied by changes in the political structure—indeed, the character of the commune system made it impossible to change one without changing the other. Communes, as well as brigades and teams, were abolished in the early 1980s. Teams had been effectively removed from the landscape almost everywhere by the burgeoning of the household responsibility system. Brigades and communes still had governmental roles, and they were replaced by what were designed as wholly administrative levels of the state—administrative villages and townships—although, in the villages studied here, they continued to be referred to as "brigade" and "commune" long after the formal change.

The more specific changes in this process are discussed in greater detail in later chapters. The starting point is the fundamental nature of the transformation from the state-collective system that characterized

China's recent past to a market-oriented reform system. Some changes have been more apparent than substantial, and there are marked continuities with the past as well as departures, but changed policy at the apex of state power has altered the underlying conditions of rural China's political economy. The chapters that follow trace some of the strategies rural people have developed to respond to these changed conditions and to recreate their lives. Each chapter addresses particular policy changes in somewhat more detail, but the emphasis is on actual everyday strategies.

The effect of reform-era policies has been regionally variable, and no single region can represent the country as a whole. The three villages presented here are all located in Shandong Province and represent a range of possibilities within that province. Shandong is a northern coastal province that enjoys generally favorable natural conditions and that has a diverse and strong economic base.[3] Shandong is highly commercialized and reasonably affluent, but it has not been one of the major early beneficiaries of reform-era policies of opening toward foreign business. The villages presented here are located in areas of modest or moderate affluence, and represent domestic possibilities and choices about the shape of rural communities in reform-era China.

Three Villages

The research reported here began in the summer of 1986 in the village of Zhangjiachedao. Zhangjiachedao is an essentially single-surname village of 175 households, located in Changyi County in the north of Weifang Prefecture in Shandong. In 1986 its economy was centered on a thriving weaving and dyeing factory that was one of the first such factories in the area and that was benefiting from this headstart. Prior to its industrial development in the early and mid-1980s, Zhangjiachedao had been an agricultural village, but one with less than 1.5 *mu* of poor-quality land for each of its 700 residents. The village is on the edge of the coastal salt flats, and even with the additional investment in agriculture made possible by the village's industrial development, the land remains poor.

As was common for poor Shandong villages, Zhangjiachedao had supplied large numbers of out-migrants, especially for the northeast provinces, and this pattern continued as late as the 1950s. If the village had previously had any source of wealth, it consisted of a body of comparatively educated men (and a few women). The village had a modest but valued tradition of educational success, and ties through a student from this village brought an underground Party cadre training school to the village in the 1940s. When the Communist forces moved south at the end of the 1940s, they took with them local men and women they had trained. A few of these cadres and teachers returned to Zhangjiachedao in the difficult years following the Great Leap Forward, or later, upon retirement. Still, the general pattern was a drain of migrants out of this poor village and continuing economic stagnation because the village lacked the means to prosper in agriculture.

The development of village-level industry in the 1980s transformed Zhangjiachedao's economy. By 1986 the village was dominated by the clacking of looms at work around the clock, and Zhangjiachedao was officially considered a model of the "shared prosperity" (*gongtong fuyu*) route to rural economic growth. It did not become a well-known model, but this aspect of its history is unique among the three villages studied. In 1986 some men in the village had employment in nearby towns or more distant cities, but good jobs were also available for both men and women in the village weaving and dyeing factory. Many women from nearby villages also worked in the factory. The village had considerable contacts with the world beyond its boundaries and was looking forward to a future of more expanded and diversified rural industrialization. The atmosphere regarding traditional and disappearing kinship practices, such as small daughter-in-law marriage and matrilateral cross-cousin marriage,[4] was relaxed and accepting, but the trend and official interest were in promoting the new institution of collective weddings and in resolving potential problems in the care of the elderly by encouraging intravillage marriage and establishing a village home for the elderly.

As far as women were concerned, Zhangjiachedao made no special claims, and the prime concern of the village women's head, who was also its paramedic responsible for women's health, was the promotion of the single-child family policy. Nevertheless, some of the village's policies, such as those for education and employment, were distinctly helpful to women. Indirect factors, some of which were connected with the village's prosperity, made Zhangjiachedao a relatively conducive setting for women who wished to pursue quiet strategies of their own.

Qianrulin, in Anqiu County in the south of Weifang Prefecture, resembles Zhangjiachedao in being a virtually single-surname village and in relying on several village-run industries, which were doing well at the time of fieldwork in 1987. This village also has a land shortage and has had many out-migrants. However, these left for the most part to open new lands in the northeast provinces or in Inner Mongolia, and have neither returned nor preserved close contact with their former home. Some Qianrulin residents work elsewhere on contract, young women from nearby villages work in the Qianrulin felt-mat factory, and technical personnel from a furniture factory in the Northeast industrial center of Shenyang spend time in a linked factory in the village.

Qianrulin nevertheless lacks Zhangjiachedao's marked orientation toward the outer world and is more concerned with its own affairs and traditions. This may be related to the influence of the nearby model village of Shijiazhuang and is definitely connected with the tight nexus of village organization. The small village of about 140 households in three teams is one of the relatively few in the country that has remained collective, and it had no plans to decollectivize. Qianrulin is one of the villages in China where the standard of dress is still the high-buttoned Mao jacket, and except for the very high level of industrialization in the village, it is strongly reminiscent of rural China in the 1970s.

Qianrulin began its move toward industrialization earlier than Zhangjiachedao, within the framework of the collective system when it was still the national norm, and its industry grew and diversified smoothly in the conducive economic conditions of the early and mid-1980s. The atmosphere regarding kinship practices is a conservative one of adhering to customs of which the community is proud. Intrasurname marriage is considered unacceptable, and collective weddings are not contemplated.[5]

Women in this village describe its woman-work—the work of the official women's organizations—as "ordinary" (yibande), and this appears accurate: the recommended formal structures are reported to exist, but there is little or no activity apparent.

Huaili, in Ling County of Dezhou Prefecture, is a much larger multisurname village of about 230 households. At the time of fieldwork in 1988, 1989, and 1990, Huaili had a diversified economy of agriculture (grain and cotton) and a wide range of small-scale household productive and commercial sidelines. The village has long been successful in agriculture but had its land base severely reduced by an expropriation for water control purposes in 1986. The pressure on land that this generated, together with the changed economic milieu, sparked a shift in Huaili's economic direction toward more widespread and direct involvement in the rural commodity economy. Seven households qualified as state-recognized specialized households in early 1988—nine by mid-1989—and the majority of Huaili households have some household-based commodity-production project (see Chapter 4).

Village enterprises have grown since decollectivization in 1984, but are modest in scope and have had no prospect of growing in the deteriorating economic conditions of the late 1980s. Few Huaili residents work elsewhere, and there are no nonresidents employed in the village. Huaili has not rebuilt in the row-house style of Zhangjiachedao or Qianrulin but retains a housing pattern of detached single homes within walled enclosures lining the sides of a network of narrow lanes. The village continues traditional wedding practices, albeit in a modified form.

Of the three villages, this is the one that is most representative of contemporary rural China. Possibly its most distinctive quality is that its women's organization is more than usually active, and even received some support in 1987 from the county Women's Federation to promote women's involvement in commodity production.

None of these villages is exactly average, although all are truly in the countryside and beyond the immediate reach of cities or the direct impact of the open coastal regions. All are more affluent than the norm and less heavily involved in grain production than many Chinese villages. Together they represent various aspects of what has been both proposed and implemented in China's countryside in the 1980s—increased commodity production for a more open market, and increased activity and scale in rural industry. Their differences also allow some insight into the range of possibilities and actualities: seeking prosperity through rural industry, or through household-based production; collective ownership and management, or decollectivization; and very limited organization for woman-work, or experimentation in organizing women's economic work under the reform policies of the 1980s.

The Study

The study reported here took place, and took form, during a series of fieldtrips in 1986, 1987–88, 1989, and 1990. As originally formulated, the study was intended to examine the implications of the rural reform program for rural household composition and division of labor, with particular attention to rural women. My concerns in 1985, when I made these plans, were concentrated on the potential dangers of decollectivization for the more vulnerable rural residents, and especially for women. I therefore proposed a study of practical responses that rural households were making to the transformations in their communities instigated by the national reform program. The study shifted in many respects as I learned about the everyday world of reform in these three villages, but attention to household structure and to intra- and inter-household division of labor within these communities remained central components of the study from beginning to end.

The most important change in focus happened early on, in response to findings during the initial fieldtrip in 1986. Partway through that fieldtrip, it became evident that the most interesting and unexpected findings were those related to women's activities and agency, and to the place of these in the microdynamics of reform-era social structure. The focus of the study shifted decisively to gender.

Studies of the rural economic reform have reflected and shared the official stance of the Chinese authorities, who see the reform program as a matter of political economy and in terms which assume that the reforms are gender-neutral. The focus has similarly been on the enhanced role of the rural household as it regained a large degree of de facto control over productive resources and the production process, and, to a lesser degree, on the revived forms of local government that replaced the collectives. These views are largely shared here. I have focused on the three critical areas in which the political economy of these villages has been transformed: agriculture, village-level enterprises, and household-based commodity production. I have given close attention to the restructuring of the political economy of the rural household, including attention to household economic strategies and the practices of household boundary maintenance that make the households appear as economic actors in the Chinese countryside. I have also attended to the implications of the (partial) dissolution of the collective structures and their replacement by reconstituted administrative villages on the basis of the previous production brigades.

This study differs from others in that it introduces the element of gender within every aspect of changes in the political economy, in household structure and relations, and in suprahousehold community relations. As usual when gender is introduced into a field of analysis, this is not a matter of addition but of rethinking. In each of the specific studies that comprise this book, the question of gender has reproblematized the field of analysis. This reproblematization is addressed in specific detail in close connection with the substantive material in each of the following chapters.

The study is also situated within an active milieu of research regarding Chinese women. A large portion of this research has been concerned with movements affecting the status of Chinese women during the course of the twentieth century. The prolonged period of limited or nonexistent field access has meant that, as far as the People's Republic (1949–present) is concerned, this work has been largely based on historical and documentary materials (e.g., Andors 1983, Croll 1978, Johnson 1983, Stacey 1983) and, more recently, has concentrated on urban and intellectual women (e.g., Honig and Hershatter 1988). With a few important exceptions, very little of the recent literature on Chinese women has addressed questions affecting the contemporary lives of rural women. The present study is situated within, and is deeply and broadly indebted to, this entire scholarly field.[6]

This study has been enormously facilitated by a handful of contemporary studies provided by some of the same scholars who have defined the field. The implications of policies creating the household responsibility system were comprehensively addressed by Elisabeth Croll (1987b, 1988), both within the context of the history of the Chinese women's movement (Croll 1978) and within the context of the implications of policy at the most immediate levels of rural social organization (Croll 1981). Delia Davin, working also from the perspective of the history of the women's movement and the official construction of "woman-work" (Davin 1976), has drawn attention to the problematic silence of the rural reform program on issues affecting women (Davin 1988). Working specifically in Shandong, Norma Diamond early identified some of the important lines of the reconstruction of gender in contemporary China (Diamond 1983a), although this work preceded the full development of the reform program. This, and her work identifying residence as an overriding practical element in the construction of women's lives and agency in the Chinese countryside (Diamond 1975), have made major contributions to understanding persistence and change in the everyday lives of rural Chinese women. Margery Wolf's influential studies of Taiwanese women's informal strategies (M. Wolf 1968,

1972), especially for the building of uterine families, opened the field of Chinese kinship studies to an understanding of practical kinship and to the efficacious role of women in unmarked and unofficial dimensions of everyday social relations. Her subsequent study, carried out in 1980–81, of changes in the lives of Chinese women in various locations (including Shandong) in the People's Republic (M. Wolf 1985), made effective use of this approach in analyzing the lives of Chinese women, rural and urban, from 1949 to 1981.

Wolf 1985 is also one of several large-scale projects that have aimed at recovering the history of social change in China during the decades before China permitted foreign fieldwork. It is one of several landmark studies built on contemporary interviews and documentary research of periods that still have force within the living memory of people throughout China (see Friedman et al. 1991, Parish 1985, Potter and Potter 1990, Siu 1989). The present study assumes this research and places its emphasis on the microdynamics of social and cultural transformation within the period of the contemporary rural reform program. The study reported here is designed to examine the immediate consequences of the reform program and the shape of rural society as it was redefined by this transformation. Although it makes reference to previous circumstances, primarily the immediate past of the collective era, it is historical only in the sense of attending to processes of change. The study is a contemporary one, and it directly addresses only the situation obtaining in these three villages at the time of the reported fieldwork, 1986–90.

The conditions under which such fieldwork is done in contemporary China have previously been addressed in the literature (M. Wolf 1985), and the close connections between Wolf's fieldwork conditions in Shandong and my own make a further detailed description superfluous. I will, however, outline some aspects of the fieldwork situation that have changed or that seem particular to the way in which this study was done.

All the research reported here took place through official channels and was subject to official observation on the Chinese side. The first two fieldtrips, in the summer of 1986 and the winter of 1987–88, were carried out within the framework of a bilateral exchange between the Chinese Academy of Social Sciences (CASS) and the Social Sciences and Humanities Research Council of Canada (SSHRCC). In my case, the actual local arrangements were in the hands of the Shandong Academy of Social Sciences (SASS), although CASS, various levels of the Foreign Affairs Office (*waiban*), the Women's Federations, and local government were also involved. This pattern of multiple levels of official and quasi-official involvement continued during the following two field-trips, which took place after the CASS–SSHRCC exchange program had terminated. The official host channel was then the China Shandong International Culture Exchange Center, a quasi-official body representing the official interests of the Shandong provincial government.

None of the host institutions had an active interest in facilitating foreign research in the Chinese countryside, although SASS asked me to provide some field training for the junior sociologist who accompanied me in 1986, and many of the official bodies involved in hosting my research asked for (and received) written or oral research reports from me. In some cases, they also kept extensive records on the field data, either by making their own notes during interviews or by copying out household survey data. All the material was collected with official support and active involvement. At the beginning of work in each location, this meant doing interviews with a rather formidable audience of official observers in attendance—at least one from each interested official or quasi-official body. In each case, quite early in the research process most of these representatives would decide that they had observed enough and would depart.

Most of the research was then done in the presence of, and largely in collaboration with, one person designated to accompany me. This person carried the responsibility of all the various official bodies involved to ensure that I and my research were observed, that I was kept reasonably satisfied and healthy, and that no untoward incidents occurred. Village officials—often but not only village women's heads—were involved in making local arrangements, such as scheduling interviews. As the project proceeded, the involvement of national levels of government disappeared (with the end of the CASS–SSHRCC exchange) and provincial involvement receded somewhat. I was increasingly working with local officials and with people I had come to know over the course of repeated visits. In this respect, the research atmosphere during the late 1980s was somewhat more relaxed than that described by M. Wolf for 1980–81.

Nevertheless, all the research was carried out under some degree of official scrutiny, however relaxed and local. This meant that all interviews were public events in which interviewees were definitely making statements for the public record, at least—but for them, most importantly—within their own village. This had several implications for the study, but none of these was unexpected and the study was designed from the beginning with an eye to what was possible. My years as a student in China at the end of the Cultural Revolution (1974–77) had prepared me for these constraints and even allowed me to feel much less constrained than I had been in the past.

The official presence throughout the research process meant that politically sensitive subjects, such as the state's birth-limitation policies, could not be part of the research project. That did not mean that these subjects could not be or never were mentioned, but it did mean that a research project focused on such topics would not have been possible and that I could not—either practically or ethically—ask informants to provide me with information or views clearly contrary to current official policy. The extent to which this was constraining varied. It has also required some discretion in the writing of this study. The material in the following chapters consists wholly of public information that informants were comfortable about providing.

Similarly, the public nature of the research placed constraints, again both practical and ethical, on the elicitation of more personal or delicate material. I am grateful to those people who did offer their help in understanding the personal aspects of life in contemporary rural China, both joyful and painful. This has enhanced my understanding of the more public processes discussed in this study, but I did not press for such information, and even where it was publicly offered, I have not considered it appropriate material for publication here.

The course of the study was one of constant negotiation, primarily in terms of locating appropriate field sites. Several sites were discussed or visited briefly apart from the three that finally provided the material for this study. Research at every one of the three sites was the result of extended negotiations. Ultimately, it was the third site visited that provided the most representative view—to the extent that a single village possibly could—of the shape of decollectivized rural China. But by the time I began work in Huaili, I was well aware of the advantages of comparison among several sites and had framed the study as one based on comparison between sites.

I initially sought to live (and succeeded in living) in households in the village being studied, and at one time or another I have lived in all three of these villages. I did, however, eventually abandon my earlier insistence on this arrangement as one necessary for my research, because it evidently could only be made in more affluent villages or with an unacceptable degree of imposition on my hosts. Even when I was living, as I usually was in the case of Huaili, in a township building a short walk from the village, it was still possible to maintain close contacts with the village people who regularly facilitated my work, and with many informants whom I made a point of visiting socially on each return visit, even after the conclusion of this study.

Each fieldtrip was short, never more than eight weeks. This was a pattern initially determined by the limits of the CASS–SSHRCC exchange program, but it was one that I continued to use after that program terminated because I found it effective and efficient. It is dependent on a high level of local cooperation in running a very heavy and tightly scheduled program of research during each visit, and I am fortunate in having received such cooperation in each of the three villages as well as on the part of the various people officially responsible for my research. The research was always a group effort carried out at an exhausting pace for all concerned, a pace that could be maintained because the end of each fieldtrip was in sight.

The material on which this study is primarily based was gathered in the course of semistructured interviews in households in the three communities. In Zhangjiachedao in 1986, I first organized a larger survey carried out by assistants hired from the village, then followed up with visits to households selected on the basis of the initial survey. The survey covered 84 of the households in the village, and I carried out 27 household visits. The survey provided a useful data base, but I found that the household visits I did myself were the most valuable sources of information. Therefore I later abandoned the use of surveys done by others and concentrated most of my research time on household visits, all of which I did myself. In Qianrulin, I carried out 33 household visits. In Huaili, I made 7 household visits during my initial stay in 1988, although the core of the material for this village is the 40 household visits carried out in 1989.

The household visits were relatively lengthy, on average half a day in length. Each provided systematic data on the members of the household, relations within and beyond the household, comprehensive economic information on all aspects of the household economy at the time of the interview and during the preceding year, and detailed information on the current work and work history of every member of the household (except those in school or of preschool age). Each household visit also provided the opportunity to extend the interview in the direction of subjects which emerged as prominent issues for that household (such as household division, economic cooperation with other households, or matrilateral kinship ties), or on which members of a household were especially well informed (such as local commercial conditions, the relative advantages of different cropping or animal husbandry decisions, or the history of the village).

The households were selected through a variety of mechanisms. I might request a visit to a specific household on the basis of the village survey or information in the village household-registration book. A village leader might volunteer a certain household as a prime instance of local success, explicitly or implicitly. Households specifically named by either myself or a village leader were all included. There was wider latitude where I simply requested that I visit households in certain categories, and there was a tendency in every village for this to skew the sample in a more affluent direction. I balanced this by requesting households in the full range of possible economic activities in the village, including those that were definitely unrewarding, and each village did provide some households in all the requested categories.

In making my interview requests I aimed either for range—this was the prime concern in the economic dimension—or for exhaustive coverage. In the latter case, I sought to include in my sample all possible instances of atypical household or marriage forms (such as extended families, and uxorilocal and intravillage marriages),[7] all cases of women active in women's organizations or in any aspect of community leadership, and all specialized households. The exhaustive coverage of some atypical household types also had the indirect effect of extending the range of the sample in other directions, including the economic.

I also did interviews on special topics, some extending through a series of sessions on several days. In each village these included interviews on various aspects of the village political economy (with village leaders), the village women's organizations (with present and past women's heads and some women's committee members), and the range of economic activities in each village (with village accountants and enterprise management). Depending on the specific situation, I also conducted interviews on other subjects that had particular importance for a given village and that were accessible. These included the history of local craft specialization and of village-run enterprises, contract labor, decollectivization, taxation, genealogies, lineage affairs, education, house-building, matchmaking, engagements, weddings, funerals, mediation, migration, the registration system, and agricultural and marketing practices.

I consider the material provided in the household interviews to be accurate and complete for the most part, with the exception of reported income. Despite much effort trying to arrive at relatively accurate estimates, I decided that these figures were too unreliable to use. Other problems were occasional (precise information regarding an absent member of the household) or not significant (ages and dates of marriage were often approximations). Special-topic interviews varied in their value, but the most common constraint here was the knowledge or memory of the informant. The informants for these interviews were selected on the basis either of their formal positions, in the case of community or enterprise leaders, or of reliable information (gained directly during household visits or indirectly by recommendation) that they had and were willing to share knowledge on a particular subject. The chief limitation of these interviews was determining the extent of the informant's effective expertise.

Information provided at the village level was more problematic. In every case the initial information provided was inaccurate, incomplete, and misleading, and I expect that this is generally true of the formal introductions given at any level. Most of the difficulties are independent of my or any other investigation, and derive from the formal, public, and highly abbreviated nature of such material. Reported figures and categories are, at best, rough approximations and may be out-of-date or simplified to the point of distortion. I doubt that these reports are actually intended to be accepted literally—they are, rather, formal introductions to a community.

In every case, the introductory report could be used as a starting point and revised following household interviews and special-topic interviews that indicated where the problems or complexities lay. Toward the end of each fieldtrip, I conducted interviews with various village leaders that were designed to clarify these problems. Because I was by that point able to ask precise, locally relevant questions and to cross-check the answers with other information, I believe that I did eventually receive reliable data in most of my areas of inquiry. There are two conspicuous areas of exception, however. Some subjects were too politically sensitive for me to be confident of accuracy under the public conditions of the fieldwork. The economic figures were also a persistently difficult subject—beyond vagueness or generality, there often lurked intransigent and conflicting pressures to report economic success and to hide community assets.

I dealt with the difficulties of obtaining reliable quantitative data on economic matters by focusing instead on more readily verifiable questions of the structure of economic activity that could be confirmed during household visits and in visits to enterprises, shops, and marketplaces. Apart from making efforts to obtain reliable information, I chose to place the weight of my analysis on those elements of the field material which are least vulnerable to either political or economic pressures toward distortion.

The formal nature of the interviews opened them to the participation of my official companions and of the village leaders who would take us to the interview locations. All these might join in the interviews, especially if the subject seemed interesting to them, and our discussions of the issues continued through shared meals and evenings together. The positive side of their involvement in the fieldwork was the insight into official viewpoints that grew out of these conversations.

Throughout the research process, both in the field and later, during analysis and writing, I tried to listen closely to official voices, unofficial voices, and the silent voices that speak in the minutiae of everyday practice. The resulting images are the product of these shared experiences, but are necessarily presented in my own words. They are offered as part of an inclusive and open enterprise that can be started and carried, but never ended, by a written fragment.

CHAPTER 2

Dividing the Land

"When the land was divided" (*fendi shi*) marks a threshold of experienced time in the community of Huaili and shapes the outline of its local history. The date coincides with none of the official historical thresholds of the modernizing decade that began in 1979: it falls well after the series of political events and policy shifts that made it possible, but simply within what is now termed the first stage of the reform. Further and drastic changes followed, but this is the one that marked the move into a fundamentally changed world for the residents of Huaili, and the one to which they constantly refer. Land—its allocation, the work and relations of cultivation, and the harvest—remains central in the life of the entire community.

Once members of a successful agricultural brigade and primarily cultivators of grain, cotton, and vegetables, the people of Huaili are now deeply involved in household-based commodity production, various forms of commercial activity, and employment within and beyond the village. Most households have at least one member primarily engaged in nonagricultural economic activity, and this is essential to even a moderate standard of living in present-day Huaili. Yet very few households have taken the step of relinquishing their allocation of village land. The norm is a continuing close tie with the land, but a tie that is now part of a more diverse household-based economic strategy, and a tie in which substantially and significantly different patterns of access to resources, of division of labor, and of economic partnership, cooperation, and help are being created.

Huaili's economy is relatively concentrated in agriculture, with 51.6 percent of its total production in 1988 being categorized as broadly agricultural, compared with 41.3 percent for rural Shandong in 1988.[1] Although rates of growth and increases in rural prosperity in China have been heavily dependent on the development of nonagricultural economic activity, Huaili's per capita income has nevertheless remained somewhat above the provincial average: RMB (*renminbi*) 721, compared with RMB 583.74 ("Shandong's Economy in 1988" 1989: 5). Huaili shared in the national slowdown in the rural economy in the late 1980s (see Lin Li 1989) and also in the trend toward a worsening ratio of people to land (see Liu Shuzhen 1988).

The case of Huaili raises questions and suggests lines of analysis for the landed basis of relations of gender and power in the contemporary Chinese countryside. For the most part, the relations involved are ones that are not marked, formal, or official in any sense comparable to the corresponding relations of the collective era. The emergent relations are simply legal and possible—and simultaneously flexible and efficacious.

Land Allocation

The land was divided in Huaili in the spring of 1984. This is a notably late date, and one that local officials were initially unwilling to provide. It is, however, not at all surprising. When the rural reforms were introduced and large-scale decollectivization of land began, following the landmark Third Plenum of the Eleventh Central Committee of the Chinese Communist Party (CCP) in December 1978, official policy and expectations were that decollectivization would be most appropriate and most welcome in areas that were especially poor and where collectives had not been successful in the past. This was followed by indications of widespread peasant enthusiasm for decollectivization, followed by official support that accepted and encouraged peasant choices for the radical form of decollectivization in which virtually all aspects of production were contracted to individual households. By early 1982, 50 percent of collectives had adopted this form, and by mid-1982, 74 percent had chosen it, in addition to those in which other forms of decollectivization were implemented (Watson 1984). Although a few collectives have persisted, such as the village of Qianrulin, they constituted no more than 5 percent of the former number of collectives by the end of 1988. As the decade progressed, remaining collectives came under official as well as unofficial and informal pressure to join the trend to decollectivization.

Huaili resisted this for some years, and only one member of the village Party branch was wholeheartedly in support of the change when it occurred. Huaili had been a successful agricultural collective, but it did not have major collective ventures that would be dissolved or adversely affected by decollectivization. The village was essentially an agricultural one with little more than 1 mu of land per person in 1984, and agricultural equipment and draft animals could feasibly be sold or divided without harming agriculture. In fact, some assets, such as threshing machines, were retained by the "agricultural groups" (*nongye zu*) that replaced the collective "production teams" (*shengchan dui*), but the village economy did shift to one based on small-scale production and household-based commerce early in 1984.

This shift was accompanied by a restructuring of village economic organization that resulted in the strengthening of village and household levels at the expense of the former production teams. Prior to decollectivization, what is now the administrative village of Huaili was a "brigade" (*dadui*), and indeed, as with the other villages examined in this study, it is usually still referred to as the dadui by the villagers. The level effectively controlling land and serving as the "accounting unit" (*hesuan danwei*) had been that of the five production teams into which the village was divided. In the course of decollectivization, these teams were dissolved and, although some residue of their former functions was assumed by the agricultural groups that succeeded them, arranging this dissolution was one of the more difficult issues of decollectivization. Since land was to be divided and subsequently managed at the household level, teams lost their most significant economic role. To the extent that the teams held assets other than land, these had to be dealt with in some equitable fashion. None of these was divided among households, and only three threshing machines were transferred to the agricultural groups that replaced the teams. The remaining assets were transferred to the brigade, which had previously had almost no resources or role in the village economy. Most of these assets, including all the teams' draft animals and tractors, were sold; the funds were used for brigade investments, primarily for the construction of a commer-

cial building that was contracted out to village households. One former team leader reported that the teams were not happy about this
reallocation but were powerless to stop it.

The decollectivization process provided a mechanism for adjusting the uneven contributions made by the various teams to the new
village economy. A large ad hoc body was formed to oversee and ensure the equitability of the process of dividing the land and reallocat-
ing team resources. It was described as a "three-in-one" (*sanweiyiti*)
combination, consisting of all brigade cadres (except the only woman,
the women's head), all team cadres (all men), and five "mass representatives" (*qunzhong daibiao*) from each team. The representatives were all
capable, mature men and most had some education, as did many of
the cadres. This body was divided into three groups, each of which put
a value on all the land and other assets that were to be reallocated. The
average of the assessment of the three groups, each of which had
members from all five teams, was taken as representing a fair value for
the assets of each team. An amount equal to the assets of the poorest
team, multiplied by five, was transferred to the brigade. The teams with
greater assets then enjoyed a per capita cash dividend. Members of two
of the former teams received no dividend, while members of the other
three received, respectively, RMB 15, 32, or 36 per person.

Another resource to be reallocated was people. Three agricultural
groups were formed in place of the teams to serve as an administrative
conduit between the village and household levels, and land is allocated through these groups. They have much reduced functions,
especially in a direct economic sense, but do contribute to the management of village affairs, especially through the role of agricultural group
leaders in village government. Members of the two weakest teams were
divided among the other three teams in such a way as to make the new
agricultural groups roughly equivalent to each other in numbers, and
to keep close agnates in the same group. As will be seen below, this
facilitated agricultural cooperation between agnates by making it feasible for them to have land allocated to their households together, if
they so chose.

Judging by the records of the household registry prior to decollectivization, the previous teams showed at least a tendency toward same-
surname concentrations, but the formal grounds for team membership in the past had been the location of a household's residence. The
village was divided into five teams on an east-west grid. This was, of

course, not wholly arbitrary because it reinforced natural neighborhood communities, although it moved in a more arbitrary direction during the collective era. If a household divided and a new house was built in a different part of the village, as might be required by land scarcity and by administrative controls over housing lots, the newly separated households could find themselves in separate teams. The effort to counter patrilineal corporation implicit in this mechanism was consciously canceled in the reorganization that accompanied decollectivization. Allowing agnates to be in the same team, in order to facilitate their working the land together, was one of the considerations in the allocation of members to groups. Nevertheless, group boundaries did not wholly coincide with surname groupings, and this was presumably intentional. The three agricultural groups each have a majority surnamed Kang: the first group is about 60 percent Kang and includes all of the next largest surname, Wang, and also the Meng; the second group is 90 percent Kang; the third is 80 percent Kang and includes most of the Hu.

This organizational restructuring resulted in a strengthening of the levels of the village and the household at the expense of the previously pivotal teams, which were reorganized out of existence. At the same time, a significant opening was provided for agnatically based modes of interhousehold pooling of agricultural resources.

At the time of decollectivization, Huaili had approximately 1,300 mu of land for over 950 residents eligible for land allocation.[2] Persons residing part or all the time in the village but holding nonagricultural residence registration are not included in the 950 and were excluded from the division, but all others were included, although the allocation was not even. The 1984 division of land was soon superseded by a reallocation in 1986, and it is the later arrangement—which appears likely to be long term—that is the subject of the following discussion.

Nevertheless, the essential points of the 1984 allocation are interesting. The land was divided in two rounds. The first round allocated land to persons calculated, by age and gender status, to be full "labor power units" (*laodong li*): each man between the ages of 18 and 55 received 1 mu of land, and each woman between 18 and 45 received 0.5 mu.[3] In the second round, the remaining land was equally divided among all eligible residents. The apparent rationale behind this arrangement was an association between land allocation and the availability of labor power to work the land. However, this explanation falters on several grounds: (1) land allocations are calculated in relation to individuals but are made to households, and there is no necessary or even expected relation between an individual's land allocation and his or her agricultural work; (2) no provision was made for differential allocations for households solely dependent on agriculture in comparison with those for which agriculture was subsidiary to other economic pursuits; and (3) the differential allocation to men and women is not readily explained in terms of availability of labor power in a region such as this, where the customary gender division of labor is that of men primarily growing grain and women primarily growing cotton, that is, where both men and women are well-established components of the agricultural labor force.

The reallocation made at the end of 1986, and in effect from the agricultural year beginning in the spring of 1987, was more complex. It may partly be understood as an adjustment of the previous arrangement, but the decisive factor was external—the expropriation of 250 mu of Huaili land for a water control project on a river bordering the village, together with continuing labor requirements to maintain the project. This expropriation (with no compensation save a reduction in the village's agricultural tax) reduced Huaili's agricultural land by almost one-fifth. This was a heavy blow to the Huaili economy, until then dependent on agriculture, and was critical in setting the village on its subsequent path of diversification into household-based "commodity production" (*shangpin shengchan*) and commerce.

The severity of the economic damage is indicated by the total absence of engagements during 1987 for Huaili young men: residents of neighboring villages were not willing to marry their daughters into a village with an inadequate land base. Huaili's economic diversification succeeded in reviving its economic prospects, and also marriage prospects, by the following year, but the project has had other, continuing consequences. In common with other villages in the vicinity that were also affected (but less severely—Huaili lost more land than any other single village), and that also benefit from the work on the river, each winter Huaili must provide up to a month's labor on the part of every adult male[4] in the village. Compensation for this labor is part of the revised land allocation.

The roughly 1,050 mu of land remaining to Huaili at the end of 1986 was divided into several categories. The scarcity and value of land resulted in allocations being precisely defined to two decimal points. Every eligible woman and man in the village at the time of the reallocation was entitled to 0.67 mu of good quality land, which is referred to as each person's "food grain land" (*kouliangdi*), although it is actually used to grow both grain and cotton. This allotment is subject to taxation, and the village is officially responsible for collecting the aggregate tax on this category of village land. Each person registered in the village is also entitled to a separate 0.1 mu of "vegetable land" (*caidi*). This is a continuation of the "private plots" (*ziliudi*) of the collective era and is usually the same stretch of land.

These two categories of land are the basic land resources to which everyone in the village has access. The township leadership has expressed the general official wish that landholdings become more concentrated in larger holdings, thereby allowing some villagers to specialize in agriculture, invest more heavily in it, and increase agricultural productivity. The leaders can, however, only wish that this should come to pass—the prevailing situation is that villagers are not willing to risk forgoing their land allocations, and in a village such as Huaili, where the small amount of land available can be worked effectively by only part of a household's labor force, there is no advantage in renouncing access to land. The only exceptions to this are the few households that have a prosperous and stable livelihood outside of agriculture and no excess labor power.

The entire village of Huaili, consisting in 1989 of 235 households and 975 officially registered residents, had only four households in which people were eligible for land but had little or no land allocated to them. In one of these households (a nuclear family) only the husband was eligible for land in Huaili, and he and his wife were fully occupied in following the profession she had learned from her father. Two other households had prospered in business, both were hiring labor to carry on those businesses, and they had given up all access to land. One similar household had renounced its food grain allotment but retained the small vegetable allotment. A fifth household without land in 1989 was in a presumably temporary situation in which allocated land was inaccessible to it until a domestic dispute was settled.

Three other households prospering in business were well along the road to nonagricultural status, with most or all of their land rented out, and one additional household was possibly headed in the same direction. There were also two households with thriving small businesses in the village but with no members eligible for land there. This summary of landless households does not, as will be shown below, include all the wealthiest households in the village, for many households in Huaili make a good living in nonagricultural pursuits. This summary serves, rather, to indicate the limited and special conditions under which people are willing to give up land, and its consequent scarcity for the remainder.[5]

Each man between the ages of 18 and 45 is, in addition to the basic allotment, allocated 1 mu of land (*xiuhedi*) in compensation for the month's work each is potentially required to do every winter to maintain the water-control work on the river. This extra mu has a disproportionate value in that it is free from all tax obligations. This allocation is, like the others, continuous, although the actual number of workers required each year is variable. In comparison with the total amount of land available in the village, this additional mu of land may be viewed as very ample compensation for occasional labor. It is not clear, however, that this land allocation is viewed as compensation for public labor—or, rather, as a coercive mechanism to ensure that the unpopular public work is done.

The final major category of land (*baodi*) is that which is optionally allocated to households who "take responsibility" (*chengbao*) for it in return for a rent payment of RMB 40, 60, or 100, according to the quality of the land. This land is in heavy demand—the village has an actual and strongly perceived shortage of land and much more labor available than can be absorbed in agriculture.

Many villagers speak of having been forced into other lines of work, and such a shift is actually the preferred course of action for those able to find attractive employment or to create self-employment opportunities for themselves. Although many villagers have taken this course and their households are the more prosperous ones in the village, not all villagers have this possibility open to them. Villagers are unequally positioned in their ability to make use of the limited opportunities available—many (including a substantial number of young adults) are neither literate nor numerate, some have neither a special skill nor a talent for commerce, and most are short of capital. They all have skills in agriculture, however, and extra land can provide an improved standard of living.

Villagers spoke of grain farming as inadequate for maintaining a good living standard, and cotton prices in the late 1980s were not high enough to have a comparative advantage; villagers involved in market-responsive crop choices reported that there was little difference between concentrating on grain or on cotton in 1989. Choices were, perhaps, made on the basis of guesses about future prices of crops, but considerations of land suitability, crop rotation, fodder supply, and amounts of surplus food grain from previous years all entered into cropping choices.

Where better prices could be had was in vegetable production, and Huaili has a long tradition of encouraging expertise in this area, as well as a location at a reasonable distance from attractive markets, although it does not enjoy the advantage of being near a large city.[6] Vegetables can be grown not only on the designated vegetable land but inter-cropped with grain or cotton, in courtyards, and on extra plots of land. Not all households use this potential to its maximum, but some do cultivate and market multiple crops of vegetables each year on as much land as they have available. The availability of extra land is therefore at least potentially a means to significantly increased income. Although no more than 30 to 40 of the 235 households in Huaili were considered to be purely agricultural, these and others with only minor or back-breaking alternatives to agriculture (as in manual transport or coolie [*kuli*] work) did look to the availability of extra land.

The less than 100 mu of Huaili land not otherwise allocated is at the disposal of the village's three agricultural groups for rental to those households which have little or no alternative to agriculture. This land is divided among the three agricultural groups according to population and then allocated through each group to its members. This constitutes a vestigial remnant of previous production-team control over land resources. Ideally, this fund of land is available to anyone who requests it, and the variation in availability of the land is associated only with the number of requests and with the agricultural group to which a household belongs.

This fund of land is divided among the three agricultural groups; the amounts available in each group, per requesting household, were said to range from 0.5 to 2.5 mu in 1986. The actual amounts available, however, have a higher upper limit. The pattern found in a selected sample of 40 households investigated in the summer of 1989 is consistent with an alternative interpretation that allows larger amounts of land, up to at least 5 mu, to be rented to needy households, and with possible informal pressures against requests for land being made on the part of households prospering in nonagricultural endeavors. In the latter respect, the expressed view is that those doing well in other pursuits do not want extra land and do not request it. This is surely part of the explanation, too, because the most prosperous households either have no excess labor power for agriculture and may be hiring additional labor for their enterprises, or they are more or less conspicuously allowing some members of the household to enjoy exceptional leisure.

Not only will the village rent out land, but it is legal and even acceptable for villagers to rent their allocated land to others. There are occasions when villagers do so—typically, when they are becoming heavily involved in time-consuming nonagricultural enterprises but are not, or not yet, prepared to renounce their household's land allocation.[7] Such land is scarce and much sought after, and will go to a relative or friend of the household either at the standard rent for good quality land of RMB 100; for a lower amount, combined with a share of the crop or the tenant's assumption of tax obligations; or, in a few cases, with no fixed monetary obligation.

The dominant considerations in relation to land allocation are political-administrative ones of government policy regarding land and community decisions regarding its allocation, but these are supplemented by both commercial transactions and (usually kinship-based) gift transactions. These small amounts of land that are rented or loaned to others almost always go to other residents of Huaili; indeed, I have found no exception to this, but there are exceptional cases of women in Huaili who have access to land in other villages. These may include women in atypical postmarital residence who can claim land rights elsewhere.

Although land is nominally state-owned, it is a community resource that is held within the community—the only seepage that occurs is through marriage and the ties women maintain with their natal families. Generally, this seepage takes the form of labor and goods, but the situation of one exceptional woman in Huaili may indicate the finer considerations involved in what has become a very complex web of formal and informal relations in the wake of decollectivization. This woman was born in Huaili and married into a village 25 *li* distant. She is a skilled seamstress; her husband, who holds nonagricultural household registration, repairs bicycles and motor equipment. They have been permitted to take up residence in Huaili, which offers a better commercial location for their businesses, but their only land is 1.5 mu allocated to her in her husband's natal village, where her own household registration is formally located. This land is worked by an agnatic relative of her husband's who provides the nonresident couple with 300–500 *jin* of wheat each year.

In some sense, this woman and her husband benefit from access to the advantages of two communities, but the arrangement is not an unrestricted market exchange. Its feasibility depends on activated kinship relations in both villages, and on the economic contribution and good relations the couple maintain in Huaili. Another married woman in Huaili previously enjoyed the use of land in another village through a matrilateral aunt (*yi*) resident in a village where land is more plentiful and less tightly controlled. This arrangement was short term, but the Huaili tenant said there would have been no obstacle to its continuing for a longer time.

Some smaller amounts of land are also available in Huaili. Land on the slopes leading down to the river is outside the allocations, essentially because it is not considered worth allocating. Those whose allocated land is closest to the riverbanks are considered to have the right to use this land if they wish; otherwise, grass can be collected at will from such areas for fodder. There is almost no wasteland that could be reclaimed in this fertile plain area, but one household that did manage to reclaim 1 mu was allowed to use it for the first year, after which the land was claimed by the village.

The only other available "land" is in the form of deep gullies, which are expensive to fill. Some of these lie close to a highway at the edge of the village and constitute potentially attractive commercial property. Indeed, much of Huaili's recent commercial growth has been accomplished through developing former gullies into a commercial zone, thereby preserving the limited agricultural land in the village. A few of the commercial enterprises are owned by the village and "contracted" (*chengbao*) to households for a fee, but even where the stores are entirely privately owned, village policy is to encourage nonagricultural development, so the village will pay 70 percent of the cost of filling in a gully for commercial development. This subsidy applies only to persons officially defined as Huaili residents, however, and was not enjoyed by the seamstress and her husband. The commercial opportunities available in the village in the mid-1980s, together with this local government support, has meant that there are very few plots of land, even in the form of gullies, that remain available for future development.

There is no remaining fund of land, or mechanism for its creation, that allows for short-term adjustments to population changes. House-holds retain for an indefinite period the per capita allocations and the land rental arrangements that were made with the village in 1986. (Private rentals or loans may be for shorter terms.) There will be a read-justment at some future date, but village leaders decline to specify a date, and ordinary villagers say they have no idea when this will happen. In the meantime, deaths and marriages out result in no loss of land for households, while births and marriages in result in no additional land.

The significant issue here is the effect this has on land rights for women, and this is, in a limited sense, the only aspect of this arrangement that receives comment within the village. In households with new daughters-in-law, members readily commented on the lack of allocated land for this new addition to the household, and they sometimes volunteered the information that other villages in the area did reserve some land for timely allocation to newly married-in spouses.[8] There is a degree of concern about this issue in the village that can be predicted to build as a force for eventual adjustment of land allocation. The perceived issue is that of developing inequality in landholdings among households in accordance with the sex balance in the sibling sets of the generation that is in or approaching marriageable age. Insofar as land-holdings actually are household resources, and because their level affects the economic prospects of all members of the household, this is a significant issue of direct and practical impact on people's livelihoods in cases where household composition is changing dramatically.

In the context of questions of gender and power in contemporary rural China, there are some additional concerns regarding the erosion of women's rights to land. Allocations to unmarried daughters stay with their natal households when they marry, but that does not constitute continued land rights for the daughter.[9] At most, it allows her post-marital visits home to take place without financial strain for her natal family, and hence to be more welcome. The land itself is under the effective control of the household head, who is commonly her father, although her mother may manage or co-manage the household economy. A young woman may marry out of Huaili and into a village that does quickly allocate land to new daughters-in-law, but new daughters-in-law in Huaili have no land allocated to them. In this respect local, informal custom is overriding national policies that indicate—but do not enforce—gender equity in access to land resources.

These arrangements, combined with the preferential land alloca-tion to mature men in the form of xiuhedi for potential water-control work and the continuing, if perhaps decreasing, dominance of the se-nior male in the household economy, constitute an implicit but real gender inequity in access to the basic productive resource in the coun-tryside. It is reinforced by the socio-spatial organization of landhold-ings and the relations of cooperation involved in working the land.

Agricultural Cooperation

Land allocation in Huaili is calculated in terms of individual entitle-ment, but land is effectively held by households and is distributed and worked in accordance with a planned arrangement of interhousehold cooperation built into the 1986 allocation mechanism. Following the view that individual households were not the ideal units for working land, villagers formed themselves into multihousehold units prior to the land division. Each unit so formed held one lot in the land division and could claim an amount of land equal to the total entitlement of its members. The exact division of land within each unit was a matter it handled it-self (compare Potter and Potter 1990: 175, 266), but I am aware of no adjustments in quantity between households within these units. The extent to which households within these groups chose to separate or to cooperate has varied. There was no formal requirement that every-one join in such an arrangement, but this mechanism did facilitate—nor would it be too strong a statement to say that it enabled—multi-household cooperation. The most common form of cooperation within these groups, the sharing of electric or diesel water pumps for irriga-tion purposes, would have been difficult to manage without contig-uous landholdings; and working several households' land together, as chosen by some, would also have been more difficult. One household head said that he and his brothers had not initially taken their land to-gether but that they had later managed to adjust their landholdings so that they were together, for ease of cooperation.

A couple in one household provided what may be taken as the vil-lage image of its land organization pattern in saying that a one-house-hold land group is not practical and that there happened not to be any two-household groups in the village at the time. They said that all the groups were of three to eight households, eight being the largest, and that groups of four or five households were the most common. This

TABLE 2.1

Number of Households per Agricultural Land Group for a Sample of 31 Households in the Village of Huaili, 1989

Size of land group	Number of households reporting membership in a land group of this size (n = 31)
1 household	1
2 households	1
3 households	4
4 households	10
5 households	3
6 households	4
7 households	5
8 households	0
9 households	1
10 households	2

NOTE: The sample consisted of 31 landholding households in Huaili in 1989. A land group consists of a certain number of households that "took a common number" when the agricultural land in Huaili was divided in 1986, and that hence received contiguous land allotments. Land groups usually share irrigation equipment and may cooperate in other ways but are flexible in both cooperation and membership.

image roughly coincides with the pattern I found in a sample of 31 households working the land in 1989 (see Table 2.1). I found slightly greater variation, but this may also have been the result of household divisions and land group adjustments between 1986 and 1989. The land groups are flexible in both cooperation and membership, and the common features discussed below are best seen as similar responses to a shared set of constraints.

The nine-household land group in the sample may serve to raise some of the issues involved. It consists of all the landholding households in the village headed by male descendants of a deceased male two generations above the current young-adult generation or, in other words, an inclusive group of one senior set of brothers and their sons. The group of nine took their land together and share a water pump. They provide some help to each other, but not evenly so. Within the group, a set of four households headed respectively by a father and his three sons work their land in common, and the only division between the households is that each gets the harvest from its own designated land area. The father within this group is considered to be the sole owner of two carts, but they are freely available for the use of all the others in the land group. Aside from generalized neighborly relations, this constitutes the land-based cooperative relations of this land group, but if it were farther from the river, it would most likely be involved in another, larger cooperative group that shared additional irrigation equipment.

When the 31 households in Table 2.1 are examined more closely for patterns of kinship relationship, several identifiable patterns readily emerge. They are so readily identifiable because the villagers themselves described the relations spontaneously in terms of the kinship relations between the heads of the households involved—this is, indeed, a pervasive mode of reference in China's countryside. Nine of the land groups were composed entirely of households whose relations could be expressed *solely* in terms of the close agnatic relations of father, brother, and son. Eight more land groups included the same close relationships but added households with slightly more distant agnatic relations to the referent household, such as patrilateral nephew, patrilateral first cousin (*qin shubai xiongdi*), and more remote patrilateral cousin (*shubai xiongdi*), who might be brothers to each other. If a group did not actually have a form coinciding with a minimal patrilineal descent group, it might still be linked by extremely close agnatic ties. The two land groups in the sample that reported only more remote agnatic ties—with nephews, remote cousins, or simply members of the same *yuan*—were cases where the household head lacked close agnatic relatives but had been able to join with a related cluster. (A yuan is a genealogicially based patrilineal grouping of flexible scope, discussed in the section on "Patriliny" below.)

A second clear pattern in the structure of the land groups is this possibility of composing them flexibly, rather than on the basis of descent rules. Fathers and sons, and sets of brothers, do usually belong to the same land group, although I did find at least one case in which two brothers chose not to do so. Also, men who give up their landholdings effectively remove themselves from their former land groups. But more important than the exclusion of close patrilineal relatives is the possibility of selectively adding to a given land group. Men who lack close agnatic relatives or have few of them (or, in the rare case, choose not to join with them) may attach themselves to another group of kin. Eight cases in the sample showed such a combination of a more or less close agnatic core with unrelated households that were described as neighbors or friends. In two of these latter cases, there was a mix of agnatic kinship and a concentration of village cadre status, indicating another important line of relationship between men in rural China.

The four remaining cases each represent special circumstances that illuminate the patterns outlined above. The single case of a one-household land group is that of a man who has no close agnatic kin. Evidently, although it is possible for a man in such a situation to attach himself to a larger group, it is not inevitable that this will happen. One of the other cases is that of a standard uxorilocal marriage in which the female household head appears to have no close relatives beyond her own household, and instead cooperates with a group of four other households (whose relation to each other is undetermined, and may be agnatic) whose land is located close to that of her own household. The concept of "neighborship" in Huaili now includes two categories—those who live close by (*linju*), and those whose land is close together (*dilin*). This distinction is a salient one in the 1980s, with land returning to the household and the rebuilding of rural homes breaking old and creating new ties of residential neighborhood. The concept of dilin is a significant one in rural agricultural cooperation, and if it is not mentioned more, this is surely because land distribution in Huaili has been arranged to bring this relation into line with selective kinship relations.

The third instance of special circumstances in the sample is that of an atypical uxorilocal marriage—that of a schoolteacher assigned to the village who married into Huaili in an apparent love match, and whose household is in a land group with his wife's two brothers. A final case defies ready classification but is perhaps best viewed as a three-household land group of distantly related agnates. The household head entered the village as an adopted son and took the surname of his adoptive father. At a relatively early age he married the biological daughter of his adoptive father. The couple does not view this as a uxorilocal match, in light of the adoption, and there appears to be no local custom of "small son-in-law" marriage. The arrangement is one that is acceptable but apparently idiosyncratic. The household head is certainly much more integrated into his adoptive/marital family and community than is the usual uxorilocal husband.

The organization into what I have called "land groups" is not referred to in such fixed terms by the villagers. They spoke, instead, of "taking a common number" (*zhua yige hao*) when the land was divided in 1986, or of having land together with a certain number of households. The arrangement is, nevertheless, one that is fixed in the short term, in that sharing irrigation equipment and some other forms of cooperation cannot be conveniently adjusted unless the land to be worked is contiguous. The arrangement of land in this manner, rather than in more ad hoc, dispersed parcels, makes adjustment for demographic changes between households unwieldy in the short term, and this may well operate to lengthen the period of time until the next adjustment. Nevertheless, some adjustments can still be made, as in the case already mentioned of brothers who did not start off with contiguous land but who were subsequently able to adjust holdings so that theirs were together.

A change that is geographically less complicated, although potentially more complicated in social terms, is that of splitting a group or altering the level of sharing and cooperation within it. A drastic reduction in cooperation between close relatives is unlikely to be common, considering the scandal it would create, but adjustments do happen—sons take over the cultivation of their parents' allotted land, or a household that has moved more intensively into nonagricultural pursuits may have its land worked wholly or in part by other closely related members of its land group. The largest change of which I became aware was the dissolution of a large-scale effort at agnatic cooperation, in which twelve or thirteen households comprising one yuan formed a land group on inclusive and formal genealogical lines, but found the problems of cooperation in such a large group too troublesome and soon divided. Some of the households ended up on their own; others formed smaller groups.

This highlights the complexity and flexibility of agricultural cooperation in decollectivized China. Size and level of unit are no longer fixed or uniform, and several different sizes can be used in a multilayered network of cooperation, with scale being suited at each level to varying needs and preferences. Probably everyone in the village considers that some cooperation in landholding and irrigation is desirable, although their views of the ideal arrangement and their capacity to realize it differ. Of the 31 land group cases discussed here, 28 share a water pump. This form of cooperation in reducing fixed investment costs in agriculture is the one that most uniformly suits the land group arrangement implemented in Huaili.

A focus only on what the groups commonly share would, however, miss much of the strength of this socioeconomic arrangement. The land groups facilitate cooperation among member households where that is preferred, but do not impose it. Many households do not report particularly close cooperative relations with other households in their land group. Others actually cultivate their land in common and the only division is that of the product of the harvest. Still others divide the land of the senior generation among the households of the sons, with food grain and other support going to the parents.[10] Such cooperation may characterize either an entire land group or a subgroup within it.

At the other extreme, the formation of land groups does not prevent cooperation on a larger scale. Many households report sharing additional equipment with larger numbers of households or, in rare cases, having a particular partnership with one or two other households for some specific item, such as a donkey or a plow. Sharing of some resources, such as the use of donkeys,[11] is reported as generalized throughout the village, while other resources, such as the use of tractors, are readily available for payment. Each agricultural group has a mechanized threshing machine, either electric or diesel, and households draw lots at harvest time for access to its use.

The interhousehold organization of access to resources for agriculture is based on, but not exclusively defined by, land groups structured around a core of agnatically related men. Where agnatic ties are not primary, as in the case of neighbors who took their land together, the decisive tie seems almost always to have been between male household heads. Indeed, the only exception to this that I can identify involved a strong female household head in a uxorilocal marriage.

The specific characteristics of informal cooperation in unnamed land groups in Huaili are surely connected with local specifics, including capital requirements for irrigation, the multisurname context of the village (compare Harrell 1982), and the conditions of its decollectivization. This emergent pattern of cooperation is an informal, practical working-out of structures that are unlikely to be created in exactly the same form in other rural communities. Certainly, recent research (see Cohen 1990) indicates considerable flexibility in the organizational forms and networking patterns of rural north China. I would predict that further attention to informal practices in rural political economy will reveal similar processes in a variety of forms.

There is reason to believe that such forms are already pervasive in decollectivized rural China, that they are recognized as such within China, and that they share some common features with Huaili. A major government report (Fazhan Yanjiusuo 1987) recently identified spontaneous organization based on ties of kinship, neighborhood, and connections as "pervasive in the countryside" (*jihu biandi dou you*) and as problematic from an official point of view. The official view prefers formal, approved organizational forms, such as Huaili's formal agricultural groups but not its land groups, and favors an expansion of the scope of formal organization at the expense of informal organization. Some informal organizational structures might persist in newly formalized and approved form, but the informality would be dissolved if this official path were to be followed. Informal organization eludes official control.

Emphasis on the formal structures of the post-decollectivization rural economy, and especially on the resurgent role of the household, may have obscured the importance of these informal practical structures. The implications of these emergent structures for the recreation of gender and power relations in the Chinese countryside requires that much closer attention be given to this dimension of social organization. In the present context, the extent to which these structures are efficacious in the rural political economy, in competition with official structures, is a major concern. However, the potential of informal structures for representing and realizing popular values contrary to official policy should not obscure the androcentry evident in forms such as Huaili's land groups.

Working the Land

The official household register for Huaili records an occupational category for each resident of the village: those who are of working age and who do not hold some other specific status are recorded as "grain peasants" (*liangnong*) if male, and as "cotton peasants" (*miannong*) if female. However, this register was last compiled in the early 1980s, before the land was divided in Huaili; the only changes made to it since then record transfers to nonagricultural residence status. The association between men and grain and between women and cotton is one that is expressed in Huaili as a traditional pattern of division of labor. It is not clear how far back this may be traced in local history, but it is in any event clear that women are well-established elements of the agricultural labor force in this area.[12]

The division between men working on grain fields and women working on cotton fields may actually best represent the situation during the collective era, when agricultural work groups were single-sex and the scale of work facilitated organization in this fashion. Whatever the arrangement then (I did not seek to reconstruct past patterns of division of labor), only partial and residual signs of this difference remain. Women are described by villagers as better suited for the close care of cotton plants and for picking cotton; men are viewed as especially valuable for the planting and harvesting of grain. Nevertheless, the actual pattern of agricultural work has become much more complex, as the practical demands of performing a multitude of agricultural tasks with a limited number of available hands has generated new approaches—approaches that are characterized both by more versatility and flexibility on the part of the workers and by a more subtle patterning of gender differences in agricultural work.

The following discussion is based on detailed data on all economically active members in a sample of 40 households in Huaili in 1989, 61 men and 67 women in all.[13] At that time the village claimed 486 males, of whom 232 were defined as labor power units (between the ages of 18 and 55), and 489 females, of whom 220 were defined as labor power units (between the ages of 18 and 50). My sample is not a subset of the officially defined labor force, although there is substantial overlap. I included all persons who were economically active (including domestic labor) regardless of age, so my sample includes a few persons under 18 and many over 50 or 55. I made detailed inquiries about each person's economic activities, including the specific types of agricultural work performed by each and estimates of time spent in agricultural work. In some cases it was possible to obtain reasonably precise figures for time spent in particular agricultural activities, although in other cases only more general estimates could be elicited. Some households were able to provide detailed and reliable information about specific aspects of agriculture (such as seasonal labor requirements for different crops, factors in crop choice, agricultural costs and prices, and the economics of raising domestic livestock) that marked out general possibilities and constraints for Huaili's agriculture in 1989.

A major issue in the study of contemporary rural China is that of the "feminization of agriculture." The key point here is the movement of rural men into preferred nonagricultural occupations, often in towns and cities at some distance from their rural homes, leaving the least preferred work of all—agriculture—to rural women. A purpose of this chapter is to examine this process in relation to the specific situation of Huaili, and to raise questions that will broaden the concept and range of discussion as to what may constitute "feminization of agriculture."[14]

The first important issue to note is the gender distribution of the portion of the labor force in this sample who are removed from agriculture either because they hold nonagricultural registration (implying no land allocation) or because they are employed on a full-time basis outside the village. Although avenues for employment outside the village, and for obtaining nonagricultural registration, exist for both women and men, Huaili conforms to the commonly observed pattern in which men's external opportunities are greater. Huaili's situation in this respect is not extreme, but this factor promoting the feminization of the agricultural labor force is present. Of the 67 women, 10 are effectively removed from agriculture through work or registration elsewhere; of the 61 men, 16 are removed from agriculture in the same ways. The result is a distinct imbalance in the gender distribution of those who remain available for agricultural work: 57 women and 45 men. Nineteen of these women, or 28.4 percent of the working women in the sample, reported that their main work was agricultural. If one excludes from the total the 14 women primarily engaged in domestic labor and childcare[15] and then calculates the percentage of the female extradomestic labor force whose main work is in agriculture, the figure rises to 44.2 percent. Fifteen men, or 24.6 percent of the total working men in the sample, reported that their main work was agricultural. If one excludes from the total the one man primarily engaged in childcare, the percentage of the male extradomestic labor force whose main work is in agriculture is 25 percent. The combination of extravillage opportunities and domestic demands results in a disproportionate concentration of village women who find their main extradomestic work in agriculture.

At the same time, it is worth observing that most of the extravillage employment provides for employees to have time off work at the two agricultural peak seasons, the spring harvest of winter wheat and the fall harvest of maize. (Perhaps this is so because the closest large center is only a county seat.) All but two of the fifteen villagers working outside the village report that they do some agricultural work, and the two exceptions are both young female members of landless households. The seasonal return of outside workers eases peak labor pressures with respect to the grain harvests, although it does not help with the more constant demands of tending vegetables or cotton. Men and women who are not regularly part of the agricultural labor force at least do contribute occasional agricultural work where they are able to do so. This is even more true of villagers whose primary work is not agricultural but who are normally resident in the village.

On the basis of informants' descriptions of the work they did and the time the work required, I classed both men and women in terms of quantity of agricultural work and types of crop on which they worked. I also asked each informant to identify, in his or her own view, which type of work (agricultural and several other varieties) was his or her main work. For the most part, self-classification of main work was straightforward, but a few problems did arise with women. Nine of the nineteen women who said that agriculture was their main work spontaneously made it clear that it was *not* their *only* main work, and that there was no way to give clear priority to agriculture compared with some other demand (usually domestic labor) that was also essential and time-consuming. This view coincided well with the work they reported doing, and several other women who reported their main work as simply being agriculture showed a similar "double burden," to a total of thirteen.

Although the work reported by men, especially in the poorer households, was often heavy and almost year-round, men rarely contributed to domestic labor, and many found the idea that they might do so laughable. The male contribution to a household's economy was usually very significant and, in the absence of more attractive employment, would include varying amounts of agricultural labor. Land was not always sufficient to absorb all such available labor, and some men were underemployed. But except in the rare case of a very elderly man in a household that lacked anyone else to tend small children, men's extra time would not be taken up with domestic labor.

The pattern for women is very different, and here the gender difference is complicated by generation and wealth differences, both of which are structured differently for women in comparison with men. Women begin working as soon as they leave school (many leave early in order to start work sooner), and young women in rural China, provided they are not in poor regions of generally high unemployment, experience something very close to full employment—their labor is in demand by agriculture, rural industry, household-based enterprises, and contract employment in towns and cities. Young village women, unless they work in factories, will likely do some domestic labor from this time through to the end of their physical capacity to do so: grandmothers are a mainstay of childcare and of many other forms of domestic labor in rural China. Some form of domestic labor is a constant in their lives, although it may be reduced in later years, or come to consist largely of (usually) daytime care of young grandchildren.

Participation in other forms of work for women is more variable, especially after marriage. A married woman will have a much lighter load if she has a mother-in-law to help with domestic labor and childcare, or a mother to help with childcare (a common alternative). Otherwise, she may well carry an extraordinarily heavy burden—rural households in Huaili can rarely manage an adequate standard of living without sizable income-generating contributions from at least two members of the household. Consequently, wives tend to find themselves heavily involved in agriculture while having to ensure that the domestic labor of the household is completed.

Respite from this double burden is possible under two alternative sets of conditions. First, the household may be exceptionally prosperous and able to dispense with income-generating work on the part of the wife. A very small number of women enjoy this possibility. Second, the mature wife may be able to retire from income-generating work (with the possible exception of caring for domestic livestock) when a daughter or daughter-in-law becomes available to replace her. She may then have the lighter load of managing only the domestic labor of the household, but this alternative also depends on the household being sufficiently prosperous to forgo the additional income she would otherwise be contributing. In short, factors of generation, stage in the domestic cycle, and, above all, wealth are major determinants of women's work. An analysis based solely on gender difference would be a misleading simplification.

This is not to suggest that gender can be omitted from the analysis. Men's lives are shaped by parallel differences in generation, domestic cycle, and wealth, but not in the same way that their wives' and sisters' lives are. Young men often experience lighter demands on their labor than do their sisters, and live out their lives almost completely free of domestic labor. The intensity of men's work outside the home is affected by the availability of other household members to share the work and by the types of income-generating work to which they have access. While beginning entrepreneurs may work long hours, the longest hours and hardest work among rural men fall to those at the poorest end of the economic scale. These men cannot expect any reduction in their work load as long as their capacity for physical labor remains. They are also unlikely to be able to offer their wives any relief from their double burdens of agricultural and domestic work. The differences in question here are ones of comparatively small quantities of money, but of enormous qualitative import—differences that can be readily deciphered in the bodies of mature Chinese villagers, whether haggard and worn or soft and comfortably round.

The type of agricultural work performed by both women and men is determined by some customary and persisting actual gender differences in whether women or men perform a specific agricultural task, together with considerable flexibility. Of the nineteen women who reported agriculture as their main work, nine reported that they worked growing all three types of crop (grain, cotton, vegetables), three that they worked on two of the three, five that they worked solely on cotton, and two reported only the general quantity of agricultural work that they did. Of the fifteen men who reported their main work as agriculture, eight said that they worked on all three major crop categories, six said they worked on at least two of these three, and one simply indicated that he did a great deal of agricultural work. This confirms the overall sharing of agricultural work within small household productive units, and indicates some tendency for women to concentrate on cotton cultivation.

Although it was not always possible to pin down exact amounts of time spent at specific tasks, some informants were very detailed, and their comments shed light on finer divisions of labor within these broad categories. It should be kept in mind that part of the gender overlap with regard to crop is directly related to patterns of crop choice and crop rotation: a few households concentrate almost entirely on cotton because their land is better suited for this crop than for grain, so the entire household's agricultural work revolves around cotton. Other households variously choose a mix of cotton and grain each year, or a rotation between the two in different years. All households grow vegetables each year, but with varying intensity of cultivation and some variation in area.

Mature women tend to report that they take responsibility for "managing" (*guanli*) the cotton crop, and women are the preferred tenders and pickers of cotton. This work is dispersed through the several months of the summer growing season and does not require cooperation on a scale comparable to that of either grain harvest (i.e., the spring harvest of winter wheat and the fall harvest of maize). Several women identified the application of insecticide—an unpleasant and probably hazardous aspect of the cotton-growing cycle—as normally part of their own work but as actually done by someone else. Men who do not necessarily take on any other part of the care of the cotton crop may apply insecticide. This and any other cooperation involved in cotton production is carried on within the household.

Vegetables are tended by both women and men, whether on the separate vegetable plots, in courtyards, or interplanted with or in place of cotton or grain on other household land. There is some sharing of a type of water pump for irrigating the vegetable plots, which takes place among larger groups of households (commonly more than ten) and involves less close cooperation than the shared irrigation equipment and work on the basic land allotments.

There is very rarely any other interhousehold cooperation regarding vegetables.[16] Cooperation between households tends to occur, and is expressed as occurring, only when necessary. Choice of vegetables and choice of intensity of cultivation can obviate the need for such cooperation. Further, the importance of vegetables to each household's cash income discourages involvement with other households. The vegetables are marketed by any adult in the household—female or male, and of any age—provided this is done at the nearest rural market and involves only the household's own produce. Young unmarried women very often do this marketing. If the quantity of vegetables is sufficient to require more marketing time and more distant markets, or if it is a matter of buying vegetables from other households and selling them at markets in some quantity, this work is done by men. I was told that a large proportion of the men in the village do at least some business of this nature in vegetables, although they rarely distinguished it in their own accounts of their work. The profit margin is very slender (or households would market all their own vegetables) but can provide some extra income.

The most elaborate cooperative relations in agriculture involve grain. The typical grain-growing pattern in Huaili is that of two harvests, one of winter wheat, for household food consumption and for tax payments, and a second of maize, for direct use as fodder or for sale as fodder. In 1989, pig raising was viewed as one of the more profitable activities in which a household could engage, provided that inexpensive fodder could be obtained—its supply and price was then a subject of some concern, and the latter was noticeably on the rise. Maize was therefore an attractive crop. The chief alternative was a summer cotton crop, which required that the household either purchase grain for both food and tax purposes or use extra grain accumulated from a previous year. A summer cotton crop would have to replace both the grain crops in value. The economic complications here are complex and unpredictable, involving not only predictions of weather and yields but also of government and private-market price levels and any available government incentives for sale of particular crops to the state.

Villagers concurred that one cotton crop, at that time, worked out to about the same as the two grain crops in a year. This verbal assessment is confirmed by the economic figures the villagers reported and by their practices, which most commonly involved a mix of all three major crop types every year, and, in almost all cases, such a mix within any two consecutive years.[17] There were also isolated cases of other crops being chosen; for example, one household replaced the wheat crop with a barley crop in 1989, for purely economic reasons, and many households planted beans and a range of other plants that could be planted late in the season, following hail damage to some fields of young cotton plants in 1989. In short, the villagers strove to ensure their own supply of food grain, fodder, and vegetables while maintaining a cash income through other crops, primarily but not only cotton and vegetables. Grain could also be sold and bought on the open market, but this was subsidiary to its importance for guaranteeing the household's basic food supply.

Grain-growing involved significant cooperative relations (and limits to those) of both a practical and a symbolic nature. I have already discussed the fundamental matter of organizing the allocation of land to form (agnatically based) land groups, thus facilitating the sharing of investment in pumps for irrigation purposes, and of course this equipment could also be used for cotton grown on the same fields. The other distinguishing element of grain cultivation in terms of cooperation consists of the peak labor demands during the two harvests each year—especially the heavy and important demands during the June harvest, when the household's food supply may be at risk from poor weather (as was the case in 1989), and when the wheat harvest must be concluded quickly to make time for the maize season. All household members who live in the village and who can possibly help with the harvest do so, while members working outside the village seek to return for the harvest period. Married-out daughters, sometimes accompanied by their husbands, may also appear to help their natal families. The work is heavy, usually done in very hot weather, and must be completed as quickly as possible to avoid spoilage in event of rain.

However, the small amounts of land and the surplus of labor in Huaili mean that much of this help is not actually needed. Everyone who expects to eat in the harvesting household will want to make a contribution to the spring grain harvest, and assistance with harvesting staple food is a culturally significant statement of social ties. More help is given than is strictly necessary, but not to give it would be unacceptable in the absence of a recognized reason (such as no time off being granted from a factory job, or greater need for her labor in a woman's marital family).

The harvest also marks a point where cooperation finds its limits. Households that may work their land together or cooperate in manifold ways throughout the year, and even in the work of the harvest itself, will carefully separate the products of each household's respectively allotted land. Each household takes a lot to determine its place in line to use its agricultural group's threshing machine. Each machine is in steady use for several days, and a household's placement in the order may determine whether or not cut grain becomes ruined by rain during the intervening days. There is no mechanism to even out the effects of such an eventuality—each household takes its chances and deals with the consequences independently. (Available alternatives are nonmechanized threshing and the use of local traffic on the nearby highway to separate the grain.)

In summary, there are some indications that Huaili shares in the general trend in contemporary rural China toward the *feminization of agricultural work*. This tendency should be seen within a context in which both men and women, and especially men, have alternative income-generating opportunities, but in which these possibilities rarely require long-term absence at a great distance. The situation is neither that of the poorest regions of China, where unemployment and underemployment are extremely severe, nor that of suburban or heavily migrant areas, where large portions of the labor force are absent. But it is essential to observe that the agricultural work that men and women do, although flexible and overlapping within households, shows a pattern of gender difference that has social implications extending beyond agricultural work. Men's work—or, more precisely, the work identified as men's work—creates interhousehold cooperative ties usually formed around a core of agnatically related men. Women's work in agriculture is at least as important in terms of time and product but does not form the basis of interhousehold cooperation. (The cooperation women report with each other is not agricultural.)

If agricultural *work* has been to some extent feminized, neither access to agricultural resources nor important structures for interhousehold cooperation have been feminized in the slightest. The concept of feminization of agriculture must be put in question and reformulated within the wider field of relations of gender and power in rural China.

Agriculture, Gender, and Kinship

The usual formulation of questions regarding gender and agriculture in China are ones that have treated women as the marked gender, the gender about which questions must particularly be raised. This has obscured aspects of the role of men as *gendered* actors in Chinese agriculture, and has contributed to the partial view of Chinese agriculture as feminized. A more complete view of Chinese agriculture requires detailed examination of the relations between women and men, which permeate all aspects of agriculture in China. Some aspects of this have been raised above, especially gendered differences in allocation of land, in work, and in relations of agricultural cooperation. The patterns through which men share resources and cooperate on an interhousehold basis—patterns that also significantly (but indirectly, through related men) structure aspects of the lives and work of their daughters and wives—show elements apparently suggestive of patriliny, and even of a landed corporate basis to this patriliny.

It is, however, questionable whether concepts of patriliny provide an adequate framework for understanding the relations discernible here. Patriliny in China has recently been the subject of renewed debate (see Ebrey and Watson 1986); the discussion that follows will be informed by this debate, although not primarily oriented toward it. The starting point of the present analysis is a set of questions regarding gender and power. Kinship relations, such as those of patriliny, are an unavoidable part of any such analysis. In empirical terms, virtually all social relations in rural China are expressed in the idiom of kinship and are incomprehensible without reference to kinship, even when complicated by additional influential elements, such as access to state power or commercial resources, which are only sometimes and partially kin-based. In theoretical terms, gender and kinship are most fruitfully examined together (see Yanagisako and Collier 1987).

Rural communities in China are significantly structured by continuing norms of exogamy and virilocal postmarital residence, which create territorial groupings of men who are lineally related and women who are usually either married in or preparing to marry out. These territorial groupings have been bounded, since the 1950s, by de facto collective ownership of resources and politico-administrative measures structuring access to wider political power and even, since the early 1960s, legitimate residence. Part of the continuing basis of patriliny (as it may provisionally be termed) in China still rests with formal political-administrative organs of power based on territorial units, as analyzed by Parish and Whyte (1978) and by Croll (1981) for the collective era.

This pattern is most strongly marked in communities such as Qianrulin or Zhangjiachedao, where there is a material basis in village-owned industrial enterprises and where the villages are essentially single-surname communities. The situation in Huaili is more complex—the village lacks a corresponding large-scale material base and is a multilineage village. The patriliny of Huaili is a compound of selected tradition (from precollective and collective eras) and emergent relations created during decollectivization and on its material basis.

The relations involved are *not* amenable to description in the conventional genealogical terms of patrilineal kinship. This is so despite the pervasive use of kinship terms for both address and reference in the village, and despite the less consistent but also evident description by the villagers of their relations with one another in terms of agnatic relations between men, or (for women) mediated by agnatic relations between men. Expression of kinship in Huaili represents not only kinship but a range of other significant social ties and barriers, such as differential access to state and market resources and means for maintaining interhousehold boundaries.

It is commonplace to note that Chinese patriliny has mechanisms for simultaneously preserving genealogical principles and evading them.

The questions here are not whether either of these mechanisms can be found, but how they operate in present conditions and how these operations can be conceptualized. The critical issues are not the formal structures of descent groups but the informal workings of a multiplicity of social processes.

Patriliny

Huaili traces its origins to founders surnamed Kang, who moved to the area from Yutian County in Hebei Province during the Ming dynasty (1368–1644), when Shandong Province was being officially and forcibly resettled. This is a common Shandong history, and one roughly shared with the central Shandong communities of Qianrulin and Zhangjiachedao, which also trace their founding to Ming-dynasty settlers from Hebei. In contrast to the other two, Huaili has long been a multisurname village: Kang remain in the majority, but Wang, Hu, and Meng are well-established and there are at least six other surnames represented in the village household register, although some are recently settled individual households and none of the others comprises more than a few closely related households.

Even "single-lineage" villages often have a few households of other surnames—it is the other established and comparatively numerous surnames that define Huaili as a multisurname one. At the time of fieldwork, both the village leadership (with the exception of the head of the village women's organization) and the Party leadership were entirely male and predominantly surnamed Kang. A few positions during this period, including (until 1988) the prime position of Party branch secretary, were held by Hu. A Meng had recently served as village head, and a Ma had held the post around the time of Liberation. Village leadership was not exclusively in the hands of any one surname.[18]

Holders of each surname in Huaili, together with their wives, viewed themselves as distinct from holders of other surnames, but the degree of closeness expressed varied with the size of the surname group. The smaller surname groupings considered themselves to be definable, separate, and inclusive groupings. The Hu, who claimed 60 to 70 people in the village, also presented themselves as united. Both the Wang and the Kang, however, had explicit internal divisions. The common term in use in the village for contemporary internal groupings was yuan. A yuan is a genealogically based patrilineal grouping of flexible scope. According to the man in the village who appears to be the most knowledgeable regarding Kang lineage affairs, there is no fixed criterion for the limits of a yuan. These depend on its size—when it grows too large for convenience in the ritual observations at New Year's, the members will agree to divide. Other considerations may be taken into account, including wealth, but the familiar one of corporate property is not relevant, nor is genealogical reckoning. The emphasis on size may well imply recognition of the fact that a yuan's chief resource is its people.[19]

The Kang possess a written genealogy (*Kangshi zupu* 1965) in four stenciled volumes. I was first shown a set by a man who, as the senior male in his yuan, had held it since the 1960s. He had it wrapped and stored but accessible; it was in complete and undamaged condition. He said he did not look at it because he could not read it (this copy may never have been read until I looked at it, together with one of the men— the senior male of another yuan—who had produced it in 1964–65), and viewed its prime use as providing a list of characters for the male naming cycle. Indeed, the need to provide this written ordering of names was cited as the reason for producing the 1960s edition of the genealogy. Yet the four thick volumes contain much more information, including genealogical information proper, a history of the Kang, and a map of the burial grounds of the Kang ancestors. The genealogy contains much information not readily available to memory. The man holding this copy, for example, had a precise sense of his agnates within his own yuan but not beyond it; in fact, he said that Huaili had "at least four yuan," in tones of uncertainty.

According to the written genealogy and its interpretation by the elder who had joined in producing it, the Kang had one brief moment of ascendancy in the Wanli era (1573–1620), when a member of the seventh generation, as recorded in this genealogy, rose to a senior official position (*jiancha yushi*). His grandsons commissioned the genealogy in his honor, and his grave (still visible as a mound comparable to nearby Han-dynasty graves) is the apex of the oldest Kang graveyard. The genealogy identifies this man's ancestors back to the (first) generation that moved to this area of Shandong, but it is inclusive only of this man's line of descendants.

The Kang split symmetrically in the ninth generation to form thirteen branches (*zhi*), each derived from one of the official's grandsons. The village of Huaili was founded by at least the thirteenth generation (the eighteenth to twenty-fourth are extant), and contains descendants of four of these branches. The branches are not ordinarily mentioned, and the significant distinction is that between each of the nine Kang yuan that now exist in the village. In comparison, the Wang comprise two yuan that are not closely related but represent distinct migrations into the village. The other surnames in the village are not divided into yuan.

Both men and women have a complete knowledge of membership in their own yuan, and this knowledge is expressed and activated in a variety of ways, both ritual (for weddings and funerals) and economic (as an optional basis for land groups and other forms of cooperation or mutual help). It is difficult to be entirely certain of the strength of the ties in these units—although patrilineal ties are not officially approved, they are legitimate and respected within the village, and nonspecific assertions of close ties within a yuan may, in some cases, be as much statements of an ideal as descriptions of actual social relations.

Such expressions of closeness within a yuan were moderated by another norm, which strongly held that it was desirable to be on good terms with everyone and not on especially good terms with anyone in particular. Closer ties between parents and children or between brothers in different households were readily acceptable, but other signs of special closeness were avoided as likely to alienate larger numbers of people in the small community of the village. The yuan, if mentioned, would be spoken about in uniformly positive terms, but the emphasis was on maintaining a much wider range of neighborly relations, rather than on yuan distinctiveness or separation.

Indications of actual patterns of close economic and social ties in the level above the household but below the village show a positive value on ties through agnatically related men, but no strict adherence to genealogical principles. There are cases in the village, as already described, where efforts were made to establish land groups on the genealogical base of a yuan. The cases of which I am aware either broke into smaller groups or incorporated smaller and more intense cooperative groupings within a larger, loose framework. The yuan has been tried as a land-based corporate agnatic form but has not won acceptance in Huaili. Where agnatic ties are found in close economic association, as in the land groups, they are much more restricted or clearly selective (on nongenealogical criteria) in inclusion.

Cooperation in agriculture outside the structure of land groups bears no relationship to the yuan or to larger-scale lineal units. Such cooperation occurs commonly on a small scale, and often very flexibly, between persons or households that have either close agnatic ties between their household heads or ties of neighborhood (of residential or agricultural land) or friendship within the village. Cooperation may also occur, although less commonly in agriculture than in non-land-based enterprises, on the basis of other ties within and beyond the village, including ties through women or connections built through men's work as local cadres. Agnatic ties are only one possible resource for personal and household networks of cooperation.

Large-scale cooperation is also present within the village, for the most part involving the use of some remaining collectively owned resources, such as threshing machines, but also including a level of village-regulated ritual activity. Weddings and funerals in the village are subject to common village norms, and since 1987, in response to official instructions from above, Huaili has had a village-level body (*hongbai lishihui*) responsible for the practical arrangements for weddings and funerals there. This body—which in 1990 consisted of the village Party branch secretary, village head, village accountant, and the three agricultural group heads (of whom one would be involved in any particular instance)—provides one man (all current and recorded members of this body are male) who is responsible for making practical arrangements, such as those for transportation and music; one to keep accounts; and one to preside as master of ceremonies at each village wedding and funeral.

Members of the groom's (father's) yuan are called upon for greater assistance with a wedding, but it is significant that a portion of the arrangements are actually out of the hands even of the surname. A prominent village wedding among the Hu that I attended in 1988 was presided over by the village master of ceremonies, who was a Kang. The current organization includes five Kang and one Hu. The decisive factor in the acceptance of the shift from the former yuan management of weddings and funerals to the current management by village government appears to be control of resources, especially use of village-owned vehicles.

Generation is also an important element in structuring social relations. It bears some connection with patriliny, in that the markers and points of reference are found in male names in each surname, and both men and women are aware of and sensitive to relative seniority in generation. Beyond the bounds of one's *yuan*, this is the most salient marker.

Daughters may be, although usually are not, given the same generation markers as their brothers. In any event, as adults they will derive their generational status from their husbands: indeed, in Huaili women were very generally *referred* to simply by their husband's name, without even the addition of the phrase meaning "wife of"—that is, their persons could be collapsed into their husbands' when they were referred to, even by other women, in their absence. (Women were, of course, *addressed* by appropriate kinship terms, derived from male agnatic relations but recognizing the person of the woman, such as *saozi*, "older brother's wife.")

Ideally, women marry within the same generation—different surnames in the area have matched generations that allow relative generation to be calculated beyond lineal limits. It is nevertheless possible for a woman to marry out of the appropriate generation, although this is not advantageous—one woman in Huaili who had married a man of a generation below her own was assimilated to her husband's generation when addressed in her marital village, but retained her premarital generational status when addressed in her natal village. She described this as complicated and troublesome, and was evidently sensitive to the loss of generational seniority in her marriage.

Such an arrangement is possible between villages and surnames but would not be acceptable in the case of an intravillage, intrasurname match: in that case only marriages within the same generation are permissible, and this was identified as a factor that restricts intravillage marriage by limiting the number of possible matches. The generational element, often presented in kinship discussions as a facet of lineality, extends beyond it to structure affinal relations, and is most fully understood when also seen in the context of gender.

Corporate Patriliny or Landed Androcentry?

It is possible to see elements of the complex commonly associated with patriliny in China in the material presented above. Additional support can be found beyond the realm of land-focused relations, especially in political and ritual aspects of rural social life. Yet an emphasis on patriliny would be misleading and would imply a methodological lapse of the nature critiqued by Bourdieu (1977)—namely, a conflation of indigenous "official models" with "anthropological models." Patriliny is prominent in the discourse of both rural Chinese and professional anthropologists and, perhaps in both cases, is especially evident in the discourse of the men. However, the microlevel dynamics of social relations often escape the bounds of this discourse, a phenomenon that is pervasively evidenced in the margins of anthropological writings on China, and one that is at times prominently and influentially at its center, as in the work of Margery Wolf (1972). A more appropriate view of the role of patriliny in rural China is expressed succinctly by Myron Cohen (1990: 513): "A fixed genealogical orientation . . . provides one set of referents for the assertion and negotiation of social relationships in a context where every family is strongly motivated to look after its welfare by participating in a network of relationships that involves many kinds of social ties."

Land was, in the collective era, a resource that could, with the support of the political and economic structure of the commune system, provide a corporate basis for a renewed form of patriliny. Something of this nature may indeed have occurred in single-lineage communities whose boundaries coincided with those of a production team or brigade. It is significant, however, that the most detailed anthropological account of kinship in relation to the commune structure emphasizes the collective reinforcement of primary groups in general, rather than lineal units in particular (Croll 1981).

Decollectivization has enabled land to be held by a wider range of social units or levels. The household by itself is not a wholly adequate unit for agriculture in contemporary China, yet the levels of the former team or brigade have lost political legitimacy as units of agricultural control[20] and production, and are generally viewed as too large in scale. Units based on lineality have not emerged as corporate landholding groups in the level between household and village, although, as described above, some experiments along these lines were tried in Huaili. Agnatic ties have, rather, been drawn upon in much more flexible ways, as part of a wider repertoire of cooperative possibilities. Agnatic ties retain some symbolic power, but this power is constrained by other forms of available symbolic power, such as those based on community, political, or matrilateral ties, and by the attractions of commoditized alternatives, which are now politically and practically acceptable.

Land and agriculture are enmeshed in a highly commercialized rural and national economy, and many of the social ties involved in making a living from the land are either a matter of commercial exchange or can be made so. Huaili is a community that presently shows an effective but unstable mix of cooperation based on noncommercial ties of kinship or community, purchase on the market of goods and services needed for agriculture, and active involvement in commerce and production for the market. The imperative of astute juggling of numerous possibilities in a context of considerable economic risk may well favor a form of socioeconomic organization that allows agnatic ties to be available as a resource, but not to be the only possibility.[21]

But an explanation in economic terms of the relationships described above is, however strong the argument, not wholly adequate. Alternative economic arrangements are unquestionably possible, and are amply demonstrated in modern Chinese history. Patriliny *could* presumably serve as a structuring principle for land-based relations in a more significant way than it does, but there is no reason to suppose that this should occur.

A new look at rural social relations is possible if the genealogical element is moved to the margins of the discourse and treated as merely one of many available symbolic resources upon which villagers may legitimately draw at their convenience. Certain of the phenomena otherwise subsumed under patriliny can then be examined in a new light. This chapter has been structured to facilitate such a process, by presenting the concrete arrangements of land allocation, division of labor, and agricultural cooperation prior to a discussion of patriliny. The arrangements described here are in no obvious contradiction with presentations that depart from assumptions of patriliny, but neither do they require those assumptions.

It is preferable to leave those assumptions aside and to proceed inductively. There is a significant and helpful precedent in analysis of a closely related issue in the work of Norma Diamond (1975), which emphasizes the implications of patrilocal postmarital residence norms for creating localized communities of related men, and for dividing women from their natal communities and from equivalent networks of kin in the communities in which they normally spend their adult lives. The phenomena presented here rest on precisely the same feature of Chinese social life—the residentially structured predominance of agnatically related men in territorially based communities. Patriliny can, of course, be derived from this, as well as from other cultural sources, but it is *residence centered on related males* that is the decisive element in the gendered politics of everyday rural life.

Communities previously existing on this territorial, residential basis were further consolidated from the 1950s by rendering them fundamental political and economic units, as well as social ones, during the collective era. Governmental restrictions on migration and the official household-registration system further consolidated these territorial units and sharpened their boundaries. Decollectivization, and the reform program of which it was part, reopened the question of a landed basis for these communities, and opened also the boundaries of rural communities. Subsequent social changes have been varied, more so than during the collective era. The reform program's various other implications for gender and power in rural China will be discussed in the chapters that follow with reference to all three communities studied, but Huaili itself points to some of the interesting possibilities for a land-oriented community.

The critical step here is a deceptively obvious one: that of analyzing men, as well as women, as gendered persons. It is readily apparent that the preferential pattern of land allocation to men is more accurately described as androcentric than patrilineal, and that the differences in division of labor and organization of labor in agriculture are also better viewed in terms of gender difference than of lineality. The specific organization of land groups is open to interpretation in qualified agnatic terms but may also be viewed primarily as androcentric, where it is understood that this androcentry is enabled by gender differences in postmarital residence. In short, androcentry, gender differences in residence, and the central importance of localized, bounded communities in rural life are sufficient and appropriate to explicate the social patterns based on land found in Huaili, with no more than marginal reference to the cultural resources of patriliny.

CHAPTER 3

Village Enterprise(s)

The countryside is commonly thought of as a space devoted to agriculture, and this may be accurate in the strictly literal sense of the use of land area. Agriculture—specifically the production of grain and other basic necessities—has been a keystone of rural economic policy throughout the history of the People's Republic. But whatever the value of this policy in providing security of subsistence, prosperity in the countryside has long depended on other avenues: cash crops, handicrafts, commerce, or labor migration. In recent decades the importance of handicrafts, stressed earlier by Fei Xiaotong (1968), has been recognized and transformed by the promotion of rural industry. This transformation began in earlier years and grew significantly in the 1970s, but its growth during the period of market-oriented rural economic reform in the 1980s was especially rapid.

Much of the increase in prosperity in rural China during that decade was directly connected with rural industry. Its growth provided employment, stimulated the production of industrial crops, contributed to capital formation, and generated tax revenues. In the early years of the economic reform, from 1978 to 1986, employment in agriculture grew at an average annual rate of less than 1 percent, whereas employment in rural industry grew at an average annual rate of almost 20 percent (Taylor 1988: 756). Even following the economic reverses of the end of the decade, rural "enterprises" (qiye) remained one of the most important components of the rural economy. The closure of about

three million rural enterprises in 1989 still left 18.7 million in opera-
tion. These employed 94 million people, or an estimated one-half of
the rural surplus labor force ("Quarterly Chronicle" 1990: 768; also see
Aubert 1990, Luo Xiaopeng 1989, Watson 1989). Moreover, at least in
Shandong Province, 45 percent of enterprise personnel are women
(Yang Yanyin 1989: 8).

At the same time, the rural political economy was being formally
and informally restructured through the dissolution of the commune
and the progressive dismantling of the collective system in the countryside. For the previous two decades the countryside had been characterized by a three-tier structure of collective economic organization:
"production teams" (*shengchan dui*), which were the locus of land management and agricultural work; "brigades" (*dadui*), which increasingly
became a focus for rural "sidelines" (*fuye*), including rural industry; and
"people's communes" (*renmin gongshe*), which also organized sidelines
and were distinctive in fusing the highest level of rural collective economy with the lowest level of formal government and state services.

In this chapter I explore the restructuring of rural political economy and gender relations through examination of the changes occurring at the nexus of emergent village (*cun*) organization[1] and village-
level rural industry. In the course of doing so, I will also touch upon
altered modes of state-building now discernible in the countryside.

Some aspects of the reform program appear, on the surface, to
constitute a diminishing penetration of rural society by the state. This
especially appears so where the state is primarily understood as consisting of the formal arms of the government. Certainly the replacement of the commune with a more conventional administrative township (*xiang*) and the general process of decollectivization have removed or restructured the most obvious vehicles of formal state power
in the countryside. The township, village, and other levels of administration that have been officially introduced in their place have more
limited scope and powers, at least formally. The rural economy has been
very significantly opened to market forces, which are only partially
controlled or regulated by various levels and organs of government.
Restrictions on migration have been loosened, although the household registration system remains in effect. As will be demonstrated below, these changes have altered the structures and practices of state
power, but it is highly doubtful that they have reduced the power of
the state in the countryside (Shue 1988).

Contemporary processes of state-building are redefining the formal structures of the state, and rely on those structures much less than in the immediately preceding period. Policies of decentralization have somewhat loosened the control of higher levels of the various bureaucratic systems and have opened a window of opportunity for pervasive restructuring of state power in rural China. The increased role of market forces has reinforced the flux in power relations. There is no rigid separation between state and market, and the reworking of this relation is a dynamic aspect of processes of state-building at work in present-day China.

The state, as it is conceptualized here, does not simply refer to government. Instead, it refers to the entire complex of institutionalized and hierarchical power relations that are found most explicitly in the linked formal organizations of government, Party, army, and "mass organizations" (*qunzhong tuanti*), but that are also found in more diffuse relations and conceptions of power. This is neither a new perspective on the Chinese state (see A. Wolf 1978) nor a radically new feature of the Chinese state. Nevertheless, the concrete specifics of the emergent Chinese state of the late twentieth century do demonstrate particular features. A microanalysis of state processes at the village level contributes to understanding these particularities.

I have chosen the village as my focus for this part of the present study because it loomed so large in each of the three fieldwork communities. The village was not a predetermined focus of my study, which began as one centered on households, but it moved toward the forefront because of its evidently critical role in each community. Perhaps this should be seen in the light of the possibly pivotal role of the village in rural north China (see P. Huang 1985, Duara 1988).[2] It could also be argued that there are demonstrable continuities with very recent history—namely, in the hardening of local boundaries that accompanied the collective system in the countryside, and in the mechanisms of tight control over population movement implemented during the same period. Decollectivization and the rural economic reforms generated widespread shifts in the balance of local state power. These varied in their direction and specificities, but it is probably true that there was a widespread loss of power at the level of the team. At least in the three fieldwork villages, there was also a distinct strengthening of the former brigade, which was in each case formally transformed into an administrative village. Each of these villages continued to be referred to by the villagers as "the brigade," even years after the formal change.

I have selected the issue of village-level enterprises (*qiye*) as the focus of this chapter. Many of these fall within the category of rural industry, which was the fastest growing and most vital component of the rural economy throughout the 1980s (Byrd and Lin 1990, Perkins and Yusuf 1984, Song Linfei 1984, Tu Nan 1986, Wong 1988). Even where village enterprises are of a different character, as in the case of orchards or construction teams, they contribute critically to the local economy (see Taylor 1988). All these enterprises, with varying but overall impressive success, generate employment income for rural residents, and many are significant vehicles for capital formation in the countryside.

Here I focus specifically on enterprises run at the village level. These were prominent in the economies of two of the three villages examined, and significant in the third. Exploration of the relation between emergent forms of the state at the village level and production for newly invigorated marketplaces opens an avenue for study of the restructuring of the Chinese state in a market-oriented context. As will be seen, these processes are internally and fundamentally connected with the structuring of the enterprise labor force along lines of gender and age.

The enterprise of rebuilding the state at the village level and the development of village enterprises can be collapsed in English in a manner not possible in Chinese, although the concept and the process are inductively derived from the concrete histories of Qianrulin, Zhangjiachedao, and Huaili.

Decollectivization

The most surprising of the villages studied is Qianrulin. As of December 1987, it had still not decollectivized and had no plans to do so. I was told at that time that this was the case for about 5 percent of previously existing collectives. The major thrust of decollectivization occurred earlier, and even collectives reluctant to decollectivize had commonly done so by the mid-1980s (see, for example, Huang Shumin 1989). The sense in which Qianrulin is collective is not a static one, and although most of the formal features of the collective era were still to be seen in Qianrulin in 1987, there were also signs of accommodation to the surrounding market economy. Indeed, the village was thriving in exactly this context, more than it ever had in the past.

Qianrulin is a land-poor, single-lineage village that takes pride in its lineage history and established customs but that makes no claims to historical eminence. The village has always been one of poor peasants and artisans, and many who sought to improve their lot in life migrated to the Northeast (a common choice in Shandong) and never returned to Qianrulin. Among the older men in the village there is a noticeable body of experience in commerce, which has brought some of them into sales and procurement work for their village's enterprises. As far as I am aware, none of the previous commerce was on a large scale, and the village's very recent success in rural industry may well be the apex of its economic success.

Qianrulin's history of collectivization is not especially distinctive, although it is illustrative of the constant fluctuations in collective organization in China and underlines the need to see the present arrangements as part of a highly fluid process. According to several of the senior men in the village, most of the mutual aid groups formed in the early 1950s had a basis in formal genealogical reckoning, and comprised groups of agnates within the "five mourning grades" (wufu). Only a minority of the village's residents joined mutual aid groups at this time, although by 1955, when about half the village was organized in lower-level agricultural producers' cooperatives, most of the remaining residents were in mutual aid groups. As the pace of collectivization quickened nationally, 90 percent of the people of Qianrulin joined higher-level agricultural producers' cooperatives in 1956, and everyone joined the leap into communes in 1958. By that time it was no longer possible to remain outside the collective political economy.

The production teams into which collective Qianrulin was divided were constructed on changing residential lines. Initially the entire village constituted one production team, formed in August 1958, but with two "divisions" (pai) within it. In 1960 this large team was split, and the two divisions formed two separate teams in the village—north and south. These were again split to form four teams—north, south, east, and west—when collectives were further decreased in size throughout the country. In the case of the small village of Qianrulin, this resulted in teams of about 30 households each. These teams were not connected with the pre-commune-era agricultural producers' cooperatives. Further adjustment reduced the number of teams to the present three, but the most important organizational change was the shift of the level of "accounting unit" (*hesuan danwei*) from the team to the brigade level in 1976.

This shift is a particularly interesting one, especially but not only because of the date of the change. Early in 1975, a major theoretical initiative was launched under the names of Zhang Chunqiao and Yao Wenyuan, who were later to become notorious as members of the "Gang of Four." One of its significant practical elements was advocacy of a concrete plan to reduce rural inequities by building rural industry at the brigade level and using the income generated at this level to enable the raising of the level of accounting unit from the team to the brigade. This was a step with enormous direct economic implications for rural residents. The accounting unit was the level that exercised direct control and management of local resources, primarily land and labor power, except as restricted or regulated by higher-level state policy.

The usual situation following the retreat from large-scale collectives in the wake of the Great Leap Forward was for small teams to form accounting units. These varied considerably in their resources: even teams bordering directly on each other could have significant differences in their ratios of persons to land, the quality of their land, or their access to water. Additional differences in quality of management or initial resources could contribute to very large disparities between teams, even within brigades. The value of a rural person's workday was tied to his or her team's economic situation. The result was that the same work in different, even if adjacent, teams produced widely different levels of remuneration. Leveling the difference by administrative decision would have been resisted by the relatively better-off teams.

The 1975 policy proposed the generation of sufficient collective income at the brigade level to enable moving the level of accounting unit up to the brigade level without imposing unacceptable disadvantage on the wealthier teams in a brigade in the process of aiding the poorer ones. Following extensive press attention in 1975, some mostly quiet moves were organized in this direction, especially in 1976.[3]

The experiment was formally cut short by the fall of the Gang of Four in the fall of 1976. Occasional mention of the policy since that time has rejected it as, in effect, "ultra-left," but any policy associated with the Gang of Four is a prescribed object of denunciation in post-Cultural Revolution China. Political contingencies aside, the promotion of rural industry began before 1975 and has been absolutely essential to the rapid economic growth of the 1980s. As earlier researchers have noted (Perkins and Yusuf 1984, Song Linfei 1984), much of the basis of the growth of rural industry in the 1980s was established in the 1970s. It has been essential to rural economic policy in the 1980s to insist that it is the antithesis of earlier policies, but continuities of lasting significance can be found, especially in the area of rural industry.

Qianrulin had collective nonagricultural enterprises from the early years of collectivization. The first factory made felt hats and was in existence as far back as 1956. Although it was described to me, in interviews in the factory that succeeded it, as having been a brigade-level enterprise even then, this was an anachronism. A more precise and detailed account nevertheless confirms the existence of this and two other small factories (carpentry and dyeing local cloth) by 1964 at the brigade level, and identifies all Qianrulin's substantial development in rural industry as being at the brigade level, but in two important cases involving links beyond the village.

It may be useful to observe here that enterprises categorized as rural industry may be rudimentary and consist of little more than a space in which some very simple processing is done by a small work force using labor-intensive methods and very basic equipment. Even in 1987, this was true of some of Qianrulin's factories, such as the one recycling plastic bags. The factories that contributed to Qianrulin's earliest diversification were of this nature. Qianrulin's first move into larger-scale enterprise was in 1973, with the establishment of a chicken factory. This factory benefited from official promotion of large-scale chicken-raising on the part of higher state authorities in the area, and was the village's best economic performer until 1976, when funds generated by the chicken factory provided the initial capital for transforming the felt factory into a commercial felt-mat factory.

The mat factory quickly expanded and became the center of the village economy. It is highly profitable and employs a large number of workers from Qianrulin and neighboring villages, but the processing is rudimentary and the work unpleasant. Funds generated by this factory are now being used to establish a technologically more complex factory producing packaging for chemical products (from 1984) and a local branch of an urban factory producing aluminum furnishings for homes and shops (from 1986). Both these factories are providing more attractive employment than the earlier factories could, as well as diversifying and strengthening the village's economy. By 1987, virtually the

TABLE 3.1
Collective Income for the Village of Qianrulin, 1978–87

Year	Nonagricultural gross income (% of total)	Nonagricultural net income (% of total)	Net income (RMB per capita)	Distribution to villagers (RMB per capita)
1978	74.5	73	289	230
1982	86	75	670	560
1983	87	76	616	605
1984	88	83	700	729
1985	88	82	1,006	784
1986	89	84	1,230	1,004
1987	96	90	2,030	1,200

SOURCE: Official Qianrulin records, 1987.

entire village income was derived from nonagricultural enterprises (see Table 3.1), although the village continued to provide its own basic food supply from its meagre 550 mu of agricultural land.

Qianrulin's economic organization remains essentially and formally collective, but the collective has made significant adjustments to the rural economic reform program. Qianrulin describes itself as implementing a "collective contract" (*jiti chengbao*) system, in which the village is divided into three "agricultural contract teams" (*nongye chengbao dui*) and seven enterprises, for a total of ten contract units. The accounting system is a hybrid of the former collective and newer market-oriented systems. Workpoints still exist and provide a unified framework for the village economy and for its remuneration practices. Staff in each unit are credited with workdays calculated according to the former workpoint criteria (combinations of time, skill, piecework, and customary distinctions according to age and gender). The value of output of the ten units varies widely: the agricultural teams are calculated to produce a value of RMB 6.5 per day, while the enterprises each generate higher amounts, ranging from RMB 8 to RMB 15 per day.

Crediting staff with workpoints, rather than paying wages on a more market-oriented basis, serves to reduce income differences resulting from different work assignments. This is a method of subsidizing agricultural work with income from rural industry that was characteristic of policy during the collective era. In the case of Qianrulin in the late 1980s, however, some departures from previous collective practices and accommodations to the market context are apparent. The one that directly affects the largest number of people is the provision that, for each extra RMB 10 of value a person is calculated to have produced, (s)he receives credit for one extra workday at the village standard of RMB 6.5.

The system of remuneration for cadres (management) also includes explicit but controlled incentives. For example, in each agricultural team the average of the highest five incomes of ordinary agricultural workers is first calculated. Each cadre receives that average figure plus a specified additional percentage: 20 percent for the team head, 14 percent for the deputy head, 18 percent for the accountant, and 16 percent for the storeman. Each enterprise has similar arrangements for its managerial staff.

As far as economic activity is concerned, the ten contract units are parallel units at the level just below that of the village itself. In other respects, there is a fundamental difference between the three agricultural teams and the remaining seven contract units, because the agricultural teams retain many of the nonagricultural functions of the previous production teams. Each person in the village is officially born or married into a team, and it is the team which holds that person's official household registration. This distinction is observed to the point that an intravillage marriage between members of different teams necessitates a change in registration.

The actual practical significance of registration at the team level is that distribution of both grain and cash income is done through the teams, and allocation of labor is also done largely through the teams, although the village (brigade) oversees labor allocation. When young people complete their formal schooling, or when they move their registration into a team through marriage, the team head is responsible for assigning them work. This may be agricultural work within the team, although only 58 of the village's 326 labor power units are in agriculture, or it may be work in a village enterprise. The enterprises obtain their labor force by requesting it from the agricultural teams or by hiring outside workers.

There is no shortage of employment opportunities in Qianrulin, although there are more and less desirable positions. Teams allocate their labor—people do not, or at least do not openly, look for jobs within Qianrulin—but they do so within some constraints. Some of these derive from overall brigade management of the village labor force and the specific demands of various enterprises. Others are matters of local policy or custom, such as normally having a maximum of one person per household assigned to agricultural work, and usually assigning all nonagricultural staff in a household to the same enterprise.

In short, Qianrulin is formally still in the collective system and does preserve significant elements of that system, while flexibly accommodating and flourishing in the wider market-oriented context of the 1980s. Village leaders in Qianrulin make no criticism of decollectivization; instead, they point to the village's severe land shortage and its reliance on rural industry to thrive. The shortage of land (less than 1 mu per person) does make dividing land among households and simply relying on agriculture a strategy that would condemn the village to poverty, especially given its lack of close proximity to large urban markets. As the case of Huaili indicates, however, a shortage of land does not lead in one direction only.

The argument on the basis of rural industry has a certain persuasive value, especially because Qianrulin has demonstrated a high level of competence in managing sustained and diversified growth in this field since 1973. But as the case of Zhangjiachedao indicates, village enterprises can operate successfully without the formal trappings of the collective system.[4] Qianrulin leaders also point to the fact that it is a single-lineage village, and assert that if the village were a multilineage one, it would not have been able to stay collective. This presumably is also a relevant factor, although numerous single-lineage villages have decollectivized.[5] A search for deterministic causes of the differences among these villages in the era of decollectivization would be elusive. Rather, it is the variation and range of choices that are potentially illuminating.

Zhangjiachedao is the other village in this study that is heavily involved in rural industry. In contrast to Qianrulin, it is formally decollectivized and there was no trace whatever of the village's former three teams at the time of my research in 1986. I do not have a precise date for Zhangjiachedao's decollectivization, but it was the earliest of these three villages to embark on the rural reform program. The village's own account of its recent history emphasizes 1978 as a turning point. This is in large measure simply an ideologically correct reference to the Third Plenum of the Eleventh Central Committee of the Communist Party of China, which met at the end of that year and endorsed the rural reform program. But there is also some degree of substance in referring to this date, because it does appear to mark the beginning of initiatives to transform Zhangjiachedao's political economy. In this respect Zhangjiachedao exemplifies both long-standing features of rural administration and specific features of the rural reform program.

In 1978, the Zhangjiachedao brigade was the third poorest of the 70 brigades in its commune. Units in exceptional poverty are routinely identified for assistance by levels above them, although this does not necessarily involve direct relief. Indeed, a change of leadership is often the prescription, perhaps combined with some officially provided economic opportunities. This matches Zhangjiachedao's history very closely, and it is worth noting that the economic reform program was targeted initially at the poorest collectives—those which had had the least success in the collective era, as evidenced by continuing poverty.

Zhangjiachedao's Party branch secretary in 1986—and, from its beginning in 1979, also the head of its main factory—was a native son of the village who had acquired some experience in leadership in the army. Acceptance into the army is often a sign of a promising future for young rural men, especially if they are kept in the army and promoted, as was this man. On leaving the army, he became an official in his home county until 1974, when he returned to Zhangjiachedao to lead its transformation. Discussions with him and with others about his role invariably focused on him personally or on the village's development plans, but it is nevertheless clear that he was able to access resources beyond the village (machinery to begin a weaving and dyeing factory ahead of other villages in the area, and a loan to develop the same factory), and that these external resources created favorable conditions for the subsequent turnaround in Zhangjiachedao's economic fortunes.

As with all the villages in this study, Zhangjiachedao suffers from a shortage of land (about 1.4 mu per person), which in its case is aggravated by the land's poor quality. The village had previously had negligible development of rural industry. In trying to trace possible roots for the success of the weaving and dyeing factory, I explored the village's history in this field and found that there had been handloom weaving on a putting-out system earlier in the century, which continued on a private (*geti*) basis until 1956. During the 1960s and early 1970s, there was a small brigade factory that did some silk processing for a large factory in nearby Liutan. This brigade factory employed fewer than 20 people and was closed in 1976, when the Liutan factory ceased its silk production. But there appears to be no direct connection, beyond taking over four old looms, between this earlier enterprise and the later one, which has been the key to Zhangjiachedao's economic success. There is also no indication that the village embarked on its economic program with any basis in brigade-level enterprises. All the current village enterprises were set up during the 1980s, within the context of the economic reform.

The first step in developing Zhangjiachedao's economy was the allocation of 300 of its 1,000 mu of land to form an orchard. This was probably an astute economic decision—the orchard has successfully generated funds for the village and continued to thrive in 1986. The decisive step for the village was the beginning of a weaving and dyeing factory in 1979. Even at the outset, it was much larger than the previous village weaving factory, with 20 looms and about 50 staff. This factory grew rapidly in terms of equipment, employment, and income generation. The initial loan was paid off; moreover, funds from the factory allowed for the establishment of some other small enterprises, the provision of an unusually good benefits package for all residents of the village, and, most importantly, continued investment and growth for this factory, which in 1986 was still the mainstay of the village economy. From 1983, the village was a conspicuous economic success. Larger-scale diversification was nevertheless seen as necessary: a shop and hotel building was under construction by the village in 1986, and there were plans to build a fruit canning factory.

Zhangjiachedao's management of agriculture, and agriculture's place in the village political economy, have been very different than in Qianrulin. No effort was made in Zhangjiachedao to preserve agriculturally oriented teams, nor teams in any other sense, including the administrative. Following a brief period of cultivation along "production-responsibility" (*lianchan chengbaozhi*) lines, Zhangjiachedao experimented with two other approaches to the problem of meeting its official agricultural obligations in the face of much lower returns to agriculture than to rural industry.

The first experiment ran from 1983 to 1985, at the beginning of the period when Zhangjiachedao was able to absorb a large portion of the village work force in the weaving and dyeing factory. During those two years it implemented a scheme of specialized households in agriculture, whereby twelve village households each contracted 50 mu of land and concentrated on agricultural production, while the rest of the village left agriculture. This experiment was abandoned for several reasons (see "Tongfen" 1986). Among the most important of these were the economic disadvantage of specializing in agriculture, the low yields produced by poorly motivated agricultural households, and an unwillingness to see economic disparities grow within the village along the agriculture-industry divide.

Beginning in 1985, Zhangjiachedao moved toward combining agriculture and industry in every household. Working hours in the weaving factory were changed from two twelve-hour shifts daily to three eight-hour shifts, and an equal land allotment was made to each village resident. An agricultural machinery unit, composed of 17 men and machinery purchased with funds derived from village industry, was set up to help with the heavier demands of agriculture, such as plowing, and the commonplace adjustment of factory workhours at peak agricultural seasons was reaffirmed. The goal of the Zhangjiachedao leadership was to make every working person in the village both a worker and a peasant, and in 1986 the village leadership continued to affirm this goal and to claim that it had been achieved.

My survey of 84 of the 170 households in Zhangjiachedao showed that village policy had very effectively combined agriculture and industry in village households. The allocation of labor among household members was, however, a result of decisions made within households and did not necessarily accord with village policy. Some individuals did primarily do agricultural work, and these were more likely to be mature women.[6]

Aside from this unintended gender imbalance, which was commented on by some women but not officially recognized, Zhangjiachedao had by 1986 achieved a remarkable degree of economic growth combined with equity, and was appearing as a model (see Diamond 1983b) of "shared prosperity" (*gongtong fuyu*), which higher levels of the state had decided by that time to promote, in place of the earlier emphasis on allowing "some to get rich first."

This brings the discussion back to the familiar point of the critical importance of developing economically strong brigades through the wealth generated by rural industry. Zhangjiachedao's marked prosperity—it claimed a per capita income of RMB 1,000 in 1985, exclusive of substantial funds for village benefits and investment—exceeded what could be achieved by most impoverished villages during a short time; moreover, when Zhangjiachedao was being proposed as a model, the exceptional burst of economic opportunity in the countryside during the early 1980s had already passed. Zhangjiachedao's success was closely related to timing—almost all the other villages in the same township had set up weaving factories during the early 1980s (after Zhangjiachedao) and were much less successful in a marketplace that was, by that time, glutted with the products of similar rural enterprises. These contingencies should not, however, obscure the essential points: rural industry was the key to Zhangjiachedao's economic transformation, and this transformation was effected through the village level of state organization.

Zhangjiachedao and its leadership showed marked enthusiasm for the reform program that had benefited the village so greatly, and several aspects of the reform were in evidence: a strong orientation toward the marketplace and an ability to flourish in what was, even by 1986, a complex and difficult-to-manage marketplace; the institution of the contract system for all village enterprises; an openness toward villagers themselves choosing to operate as entrepreneurs, although this was the choice of only a few; and a remuneration system consisting of wages and bonuses, with no trace of the previous workpoints.

At the same time, and this is the point of special interest, Zhangjiachedao accomplished this turn toward the market while continuing many of the ideals of the collective system, and, in fact, realizing some of them (such as village benefits) at a higher level than had previously been possible. This could only be done because of the increased prosperity brought by rural industry, but the wealth need not have been used in this direction.

Zhangjiachedao developed a political economy during the reform era that resulted in a dual emphasis on the household and the village. The household emphasis has received much more attention in policy, rhetoric, and research than has the village, which is the focus of attention here. Zhangjiachedao's village political leaders are also its economic leaders and are committed to economic reform and to strong economic incentives. The same leaders who are making the village collectively strong are sharply critical of earlier egalitarian policies associated with the collective era, commonly described as "eating from one big pot" (*chi daguo fan*). Zhangjiachedao's village-level economic growth, its strong package of benefits for village residents, and the de facto village allocation of labor among households represent a commitment to the village reminiscent of the collective era, but the wage system, based largely on piecework, combats the problems of poor motivation and dependency, which are the chief weaknesses of the collective system in the eyes of Zhangjiachedao's new leaders.

Compared with the still collective Qianrulin, Zhangjiachedao at first appears to be at the opposite pole of economic organization in the reform era. This appearance is deceptive. Zhangjiachedao is a noticeably more open community than is Qianrulin, but both show a strong orientation to the village—an orientation that has become grounded in rural industrialization at the village level. The capacity of the village level to organize rural industry successfully is related to the prior institution of the brigade, which, ironically, while disappearing in a formal sense, has become more significant than before through the institution of village-level administrative structures and through the direct economic power generated by village enterprises once these are established.

Contrasting this with the village of Huaili, where rural industry has appeared but has not been emphasized, may add a sharper outline to this argument. Much of Huaili's decollectivization process has been presented in Chapter 2; here I will only add a discussion of Huaili's village-level enterprises.

Huaili was not previously a village that concentrated on handicrafts or rural industry, nor has it concentrated on those areas in its recent economic development. Huaili was long a successful agricultural village, at least relatively speaking, in a region of Shandong that is less prosperous than some others. Huaili was officially classified as an "advanced" (*xianjin*) village from 1967 through to the end of the collective era. Its relative prosperity during those years was partly related to an emphasis on vegetable-growing. Although Huaili is not a suburban village, or one close enough to any population center to be primarily a market vegetable producer, it nevertheless did find this avenue to enhance local income during the collective era.

Huaili was, perhaps, less motivated to turn to nonagricultural enterprise than were villages where cultivation had been less successful. In any event, there was no brigade-level rural industry to disband or transform when decollectivization finally took place in Huaili in 1984. From 1984, the village leadership and residents did seek nonagricultural avenues, both because the rural economic reform had opened up many opportunities much more lucrative than agriculture and because the loss of 250 mu of land for a water control project in 1986 had had a serious adverse effect on the village's ratio of persons to land. The avenue primarily chosen within the village, with the encouragement of village policy, was household-based, small-scale commerce and commodity production. These activities were for the most part undertaken on a self-employed basis; thus they provided (uneven) opportunities for skilled or entrepreneurial villagers, and only a few employment opportunities for the remainder.

Unlike Qianrulin or Zhangjiachedao, which achieve full employment for their own residents and employ many workers from nearby villages, Huaili illustrates the much more common situation of significant rural surplus labor power and the difficulty of absorbing it productively and profitably. Most of Huaili's ventures into village-level enterprise are aimed directly at the problem of generating incomes for people in the village who would otherwise be at risk of un- or underemployment. The one partial exception is a small grain mill built early in the reform period, which operates quite successfully and provides a service to residents of Huaili and nearby villages but does not create very many jobs.

Huaili has organized two main vehicles for generating employment within the village, one targeted primarily at young women and men,[7] and the other at men of all ages. The first of these is a small weaving factory with 20 looms that first went into operation early in 1988. This is a joint enterprise with the township "supply and marketing society" (*gongxiaoshe*). The village provides the buildings and the workers, while the township supplies the machinery and the liquid capital. Initially, the village had a role in the management of the factory and a claim on 20 percent of the profits. However, this factory was set up in the declining economic context of the late 1980s, and well after many similar factories had been established in the countryside. The factory has had trouble obtaining raw materials and has had difficulties in management. It closed its doors a few months after opening and was reopened later, under altered terms.

To persuade the township to keep operating the factory (at a loss in 1990), the village has given up its role in management and any claim on the (nonexistent) profits. The size of the factory has also been decreased. By the summer of 1990, its staff had been reduced from 34 to only 14: four male managers and technicians from the township, and ten young unmarried women workers from the village. This was almost certainly an unstable arrangement, but does indicate the village's willingness to resort to rural industrial development to generate employment, although all agreed that these jobs, in common with rural factory jobs elsewhere, were far from ideal. Nevertheless, unemployment was a serious issue for young people in this area, and the factory made at least a small contribution to solving the problem. In this case, the village itself did not have the resources to establish such an enterprise on its own, but was able to use its limited resources and official connections to bring in a small township-level factory.

The second village-level employment project is an all-male transportation team. The core of the team consists of ten members, although others are added when there is sufficient work. Most or all of the regular members are mature men whose only other source of income is work on their household's land allotment, which is insufficient to occupy them for the full year or to provide an adequate income. The village has organized this team since 1981 in an effort to provide employment. The village does not keep the team on salary but helps it in finding work in and beyond the village.

This work is not of the preferred, skilled, and remunerative nature of truck- or tractor-driving, but is unskilled manual labor. The skilled and better capitalized workers in transport, such as former tractor drivers in the collectives, are now operating as independent entrepreneurs in this village (although similar work is done on a village-enterprise level in Qianrulin and Zhangjiachedao). In much the same way as with the village's weaving factory, Huaili does not provide resources nor does it benefit directly from organizing this endeavor, but the village does make it possible, and the employment generated helps some of those in the village most in need of employment assistance. In the increasingly difficult economic climate of the late 1980s and early 1990s, this was not sufficient to create full employment in the village, but it did make a difference.

Unlike Qianrulin, Huaili did not embark on decollectivization with any significant basis in village industry or with significant resources at the village level. Prior to decollectivization, the brigade of Huaili had been an economically empty level of the local collective system. The process of decollectivization involved some transfer of resources from the former teams to the brigade, but these were not substantial—one two-story building was constructed, parts of which are contracted out to village households as shops and a hotel, and three vehicles were purchased for village use.

Thus there were not sufficient funds available for large-scale development, and the brigade Party branch secretary said that he was unwilling to acquire debt for the village. Instead, the village has pursued an indirect economic policy of (1) facilitating numerous small-scale household enterprises through some subsidies and the absence of village-level business taxes, which is possible because the village has no debt or major investment plans; and (2) seeking low-overhead means of creating employment. Huaili has taken a quite different route to village economic growth compared with the other two villages, especially Qianrulin, but even in Huaili, the village plays a pivotal role.

The Village

The village emerges from all three cases as central to the operation of the state at the microlevel of political dynamics in the Chinese countryside. The program of reform relies much more on informal than formal mechanisms of state power, but it is nevertheless a program dedicated to modern processes of state-building. Indeed, the shift toward somewhat greater use of informal and market mechanisms may well signal a deeper permeation of rural culture than did the comparatively uniform promotion of formal structures during the collective era. A synthesis of formal and informal mechanisms of state power is a familiar element in Chinese political institutions and culture, which may further facilitate this penetration. The fluidity of the processes of change and the conflict inherent within them do not prevent them from being efficacious. The very capacity of these processes to accommodate flexibly to changing historical and varying regional conditions, and to encompass multiple lines of conflict, enhances the efficacy of the contemporary state-building process.

The formal withdrawal of state power in the countryside, in certain specific senses, is associated with the increased importance of the village. The general dismantling of production teams, which had previously been of critical economic significance in the lives of rural Chinese, together with some restrictions on the roles of other formal state structures, such as the commune (transformed into the township), which have had their formal functions sharply curtailed, have made the brigade (transformed into the village) the chief formal vehicle for state activity in the countryside.

The administrative village usually, as in these three cases, inherits a basis derived from a preceding brigade. In many cases, the administrative village also coincides with a previous natural village in residential terms. Even where that is not so, or where the contiguity of settlement is such that one cannot visually discern village boundaries, the previous clearly defined boundaries between brigades have, over time, generated communities of interest and organization that coincide with the present village units. They are, therefore, real social units as well as administrative units, and this means that they stand at the intersection of the abstraction between state and society. The everyday world of village (community) life is the equally everyday world of village (state) affairs.

The boundaries between villages are historically and currently real in a multiplicity of senses. The fundamental factor here is the activity of higher levels of state organization and national policy, which carve the entire countryside into discrete units for administrative purposes. The lowest level for this administrative marking of boundaries is now the village, which currently has formal administrative status as a level of government required to establish village-level bodies known as "village committees" (*cunmin weiyuanhui*). These are partnered by parallel "Party branches" (*dang zhibu*),[8] which substantially or wholly overlap with the village committees. I found no indication that the separation between Party and government advocated in China in the early 1980s had become effective in any of these villages.

The most straightforward situation was found in Zhangjiachedao, where there was a village committee of five and a Party branch of five, and these were exactly the same men. The usual arrangement is that the Party branch secretary has overall responsibility for all matters, while each other person in the leadership has specific areas of responsibility. This was generally so in Zhangjiachedao, except that the Party branch secretary also held the role of head of the village's large weaving and dyeing factory. Perhaps because of this dual role, the five leaders were generally described as dividing their labor such that there were two men responsible for industry (including the secretary), one for agriculture, one for the orchard, and one for administration and leadership. This was only a rough division of labor: some held additional duties, and some responsibilities were carried out by persons outside this five-man group. For example, the man responsible for the orchard is also the vice-head of the village and the village "mediator" (*tiaojieyuan*); the woman responsible for woman-work in the village is not in either body and is not (or not yet) a Party member.

It is membership in these leading bodies, or the holding of some other leadership post, such as head of an enterprise, which marks a person as playing a leadership role in the village. Ordinary Party membership does not do this, although entering the Party may be a mark of leadership potential. It is possible to be a virtually inactive Party member without leaving the Party, and this is perhaps more common in Zhangjiachedao than in the other villages examined. Zhangjiachedao was the site of a small underground Party school in the 1940s, and recruiting was done in the area. About 60 percent of Zhangjiachedao's 44 Party members in 1986 had joined the Party during the years 1940–47, and many of these are now retired from public life. Several are women, including one who served as village head briefly in the late 1940s, but none currently plays a role in Zhangjiachedao's public life. A few women do have minor responsibilities in Zhangjiachedao, and the village is comparatively supportive of women's interests, as shown concretely in its employment and education practices, but public leadership remains in male hands.

Qianrulin has a somewhat more complicated formal leadership structure, perhaps because it is a village resisting decollectivization and thus wishes to show adherence to other policies of restructuring. Qianrulin is the one village of the three that had, at the time of fieldwork, incorporated its women's head into its village committee, a step being advocated by higher levels of the state, including the Women's Federations. The Party branch in Qianrulin consists of five men: the Party secretary, who is in charge of all matters in the village; a vice-secretary, who shares responsibility for industry; a vice-secretary in charge of political study; a "member responsible for organization" (*zuzhiyuan*) and Party life; and a member responsible for the Young Communist League, culture, education, and health. The village committee consists of six men and one woman: the village head is formally responsible for all village affairs (he is also the vice-secretary in charge of political study); a vice-head is responsible for agriculture; another vice-head is responsible for industry (he is also the fifth member of the Party branch); a third vice-head is responsible for financial affairs (he is also the Party branch member in charge of organization); a younger member of the committee is in charge of public safety; another man is in charge of construction; and the one woman is in charge of woman-work and education. All members of the village committee are Party members, who total 33 in the village, of whom three are women.

This formal structure shows considerable overlap and concentration of leadership roles, but this is still only part of a denser pattern of informal connections among the leading members of the community. The leadership of Qianrulin is also closely knit through agnatic ties. Village leaders not only share a common surname—or, in one exceptional case, have a mother of the shared surname—but are also almost entirely clustered within a limited portion of their common genealogy. Holders of this surname within Qianrulin are divided among three segments that branched in the twelfth generation (the senior living adult men are members of the twentieth generation). The first segment has only two Party members: one reached his position of leadership through education and responsibilities as an accountant; the other is a retired cadre holding urban registration. The second segment has no Party members and no persons in leadership positions. The leadership of the village is clustered in specific lines of descent traceable from the fifteenth generation within a much larger third segment, and can be defined with even greater precision from the sixteenth generation. The three women Party members in the village are married into this cluster.

Huaili was passing through a period of transition in leadership during the time of my fieldwork in that community. The man who had long served as Party branch secretary left his position due to illness shortly before he had intended to retire, and the vice-secretary was in the same situation. For a time, both continued to hold their positions formally, while interim and longer-term arrangements were made for succession by younger, healthier men. By 1990, the arrangement was structurally identical to the leadership of the preceding few years, except that all posts were filled by the men actually performing the duties of each position. The Party branch consisted of five men: a secretary, responsible for all work; a vice-secretary and mediator; an organization member; a "propaganda member" (*xuanchuanyuan*); and an education member (a younger man being prepared as a future secretary).

The village committee was explicitly described as operating under the leadership of the Party branch and was quite minimal in structure, perhaps for this reason—perhaps also because teams did still exist and because Huaili did not have extensive village enterprises. The village committee consisted of five men: a village head (he was also the vice-secretary, while the current secretary was the former village head); the village accountant (he was not a Party member but had served as the village's accountant for more than fifteen years); and the heads of each of the three agricultural teams in the village.

Each team currently has a head and an accountant. The village also has a "storeman" (*baoguanyuan*) and a women's head who are not included in either the village committee or the Party branch. The one female Party member in the village (out of a total of 34) is comparatively young but not in good health. She does not play a prominent role in village affairs and has never served as women's head. In the summer of 1990, the post of women's head was temporarily vacant because the previous incumbent had recently left the village. There was no indication that her successor would become a member of the village committee, unless this were to become a formal and obligatory requirement in the countryside.

Even where there were some differences in membership of the village committee and the Party branch, it was unambiguously clear in each case that the village Party branch secretary was the ranking village-level official. The overlap between the two formal structures and the recognized practice of Party precedence require that the two be analyzed as operating in tandem. The Party branch secretary and the branch operate both through the branch itself and through the village committee, with the occasional addition of individuals who have positions in the village committee but not in the village Party branch. There is no divide between the local government and Party structures—they both terminate at the same level and work closely together. (Whatever conflicts exist—and they do—are between persons in these posts, rather than between government and Party at this level.) The chief lines of state authority therefore coincide closely at the village level: the territorial boundaries are the same, the populations affected are the same (non-Party members are less affected by the Party than are members, but are not outside its scope of authority), and the leadership personnel are substantially the same.

With the demise of the production teams and their control over land resources, the degree of control over resources that the state devolves upon local communities now rests at the village level. Access to land allocation for housing plots, for cultivation, or for any other purpose, such as setting up a shop, depends on access to village-controlled land resources. In those cases where villages have additional economic resources, especially in the case of village-run factories, the control exercised over the village economy is still greater.

Population is also controlled at the village level. This is so in the formal sense in which the village is the holder of each rural resident's official household registration, which grants rights to reside in a village, to receive access to its resources, and to be eligible for its bene-fits.[9] Official residence also makes the village the body that must ap-prove and facilitate significant life changes for each individual, includ-ing marriage, household division, and change of residence status.

In nongovernmental senses, the village may also control each per-son's work situation. In the case of remaining collectives (such as Qianrulin) or near-collectives (such as Zhangjiachedao), village resi-dents are more or less directly allocated to any work that involves use of village resources. In Zhangjiachedao, but not Qianrulin, the oppor-tunity also exists for individual entrepreneurship, but even this is de-pendent on village willingness—as shown, for example, in allowing villagers to act as self-employed sellers of the products of a village fac-tory, or in refraining from establishing a village-run shop in competi-tion with an existing independent one. In Huaili, residents can more freely seek employment or self-employment on their own, but access to commercial land sites, village subsidies to business, and employ-ment through village-facilitated channels within or beyond the village remain economically very significant elements even of this market-oriented village.

The extent of village economic control is variable. There is no doubt that villages possess an officially legitimated degree of control over land and population. This is no longer restricted by competing claims from teams below, and official policy in the 1980s discouraged levels above the village from direct appropriation of village resources in most in-stances. Whether the village operates as a highly vigorous and effica-cious arm of the state depends on such factors as its resource base, its residents' access to non-village-controlled economic resources and ac-tivities (especially commerce and labor migration), and the quality of village leadership. The range of variation is presumably wide, but the structural factors that favor authority residing in this level are weighty.

The villages examined here are in important ways vital communi-ties in dimensions that sometimes overlap or encapsulate state struc-tures, but that also have bases of authority which lie at least partially outside the state. The role of lineality is perhaps the most obvious of these. Two of the three villages are single-lineage communities, and the other is a multilineage community with one predominant lineage. This is not unusual in the Chinese countryside, and even if this dimension of social relations is viewed in informal, flexible, and questioning terms, the existence of a core of related males with long-term legitimate relations of co-residence and associated rights to resources is significant in providing social depth to a community beyond that generated by state mechanisms.

In each of the three villages, formal village leaders have assumed certain community leadership roles formerly performed, at least ideally, by informal community authorities or village elders. Each village committee has a designated senior member responsible for mediation, that is, for presiding over household division and mediating disputes. This is part of the formal village structure. On a less formal but clearly common and expected basis, village leaders—commonly, but not only, Party branch secretaries—play a prominent role in making hard-to-arrange marital matches. This may involve searching for a spouse for a person disadvantaged in the marriage market or for a person choosing an atypical match (such as an uxorilocal or intravillage marriage); it may also involve legitimating a match that might otherwise face some disapproval (such as remarriage for women). Village leaderships also assist in handling domestic disputes, for example, by providing village-owned housing space as temporary accommodation for one side in a domestic dispute intense enough to drive part of a household out of its home.

Involvement in domestic matters is, at least officially, viewed as a proper concern of local arms of the state. Where this contributes to solving problems for people, as in matchmaking, it may contribute to a sense of harmony in the community and in community-state relations as well. But the state is also, of course, prepared to use the village level of its structure to intervene in community and household affairs to a greater extent than rural residents welcome. This is most evidently the case with respect to the birth limitation campaigns officially implemented throughout the 1980s, with varying degrees of strictness. These were almost certainly the policies that placed the most stress on the village organization's capacity to combine service to the hierarchical structures of the state with service to the communities of which they are part.

The village is currently the structural focus of state-building attempts to reconstruct rural social organization. To the very considerable extent that rural society is not left to market forces and spontaneous forms of social organization, the village is the vehicle through which the state permeates and attempts to shape rural life. This extends far beyond mechanisms for control of resources and population.

It is especially evident in policies regarding the critical rituals of weddings and funerals. During the collective era, national policy defined norms for marriage—both formal, legal ones, in the *Marriage Law* of 1950 and that of 1981, and less obligatory ones, such as late marriage and the promotion of uxorilocal marriage during the Cultural Revolution. With respect to funerals and associated arrangements, state policy included such demands as simplicity and limited expense (as was also the case with weddings); it also discouraged the use of cultivable land for burial plots. The three levels of the collective structure acted both as a conduit for these policies and as a buffer protecting communities that wished to maintain customary practices disapproved of by the state. The balance of this synthesis shifted constantly.

Changes in policy and adjustments in their negotiation continue. The point to note here is that the dissolution of the collective system has not deprived higher levels of the state of means to attempt to regulate rural social life. Zhangjiachedao, for example, had implemented the collective wedding policy optionally advocated by the state in 1986. This was a policy designed to reduce the draining expense of rural weddings, which had escalated nationwide in the early 1980s, a period of lessened restrictions. The institution of collective weddings scheduled together at the peak wedding season, prior to spring festival, was intended to establish a modest norm of expense that would not be pushed upward by interhousehold competition. Zhangjiachedao added the incentive that the village provide some of the resources and a commemorative wedding gift to each couple, which further reduced the cost of the wedding. In 1986, the village had two fixed dates for these weddings, near spring festival (the one actually used) and May 1 (a date that was also available).

I expect that the reason Zhangjiachedao implemented this policy, whereas most other villages did not, is that it is a prosperous village into which families are pleased to marry their daughters, who then have future prospects of attractive employment in Zhangjiachedao's weaving and dyeing factory. Zhangjiachedao is noticeably wealthier than neighboring villages; thus its households need not fear loss of face in failing to provide more elaborate weddings, and can even claim the symbolic capital of leading in the implementation of a new wedding ritual in the area. These factors enabled Zhangjiachedao to implement this policy without coercion; households can still add private banquets or other extras to the extent that they choose, but they can also choose not to do so.

In Huaili, there is now a village-level "wedding and funeral committee" (*hongbai lishihui*) that is responsible for arranging weddings and funerals for the entire village, regardless of lineage. This committee consists of four men: the village Party branch secretary presides; the village Party branch vice-secretary, who is also the village head, is responsible for making arrangements for the ritual event; the village accountant manages the accounts; and the head of the appropriate agricultural team completes the committee. This village organization for ritual events reduces expense and lessens competition, as does the institution of collective weddings.

The assumption of these responsibilities by the village, in its dual character of representing community and state, constitutes a further penetration of rural communities by the larger hierarchical structures of the state. The importance placed on wedding and funeral rituals has deep popular roots, and increased attention to them in the countryside was one of the more obvious spontaneous changes when state control was loosened there in the 1980s. Household responsibilities for these rituals, and the ties between households that are created and reaffirmed through them, are among the most serious life concerns of rural residents. The introduction of practices such as collective weddings and village wedding-and-funeral committees was a higher-level policy decision that inserted the reconstructed basic level of state organization into the center of rural social life.

Village Industry

Official Chinese statistics on rural industry in Shandong Province at the beginning of the period studied here show the decisive importance of rural industry in rural economic development. For 1986, Shandong's rural total product was estimated to have increased by 18.2 percent over the previous year, but the increase in output value of rural industry, building, transport, and commerce increased 34.8 percent, and these sectors grew to account for 47.7 percent of the rural economy, compared with 41.8 percent only a year before.

If the growth of rural industry is compared with the growth of the rest of the province's industry, the results are also striking. In 1986,

Shandong's total industrial output value rose 16.4 percent over the previous year, but the same figure for industrial units at or below the village level was 63.8 percent, compared with 7.6 percent for state-owned enterprises and 37 percent for township-run industrial enterprises ("Shandong's Economy in 1986" 1987; also see "Shandong's Performance in 1987" 1988, "Shandong's Economy in 1988" 1989, and "Shandong's Economic Performance in 1989" 1990). Thus rural industry in the mid-1980s was a major factor in Shandong's economic prosperity at the level of rural localities; it was also an important factor in the province's industrial growth. In this respect Shandong has been in line with general trends in China, although each province has, of course, its own special features. Shandong is neither at the forefront of contemporary China's economic development nor is it trailing behind (see Walker 1989).

The importance of rural industry to economic growth requires little argument. Here I will attempt to add to the existing body of economically oriented material by addressing the intersection of the growth and restructuring of rural industry with the concurrent restructuring of the gender division of labor in the countryside.

One significant dimension of this is the continuing almost total exclusion of women from leadership roles. This is not a new finding for the Chinese countryside, and the material on the gender composition of village leadership for Qianrulin, Zhangjiachedao, and Huaili is not exceptional in any respect. It does require mention, however, because of the structural importance of social stratification defined in terms of access to political and leadership roles in societies of "actually existing socialism," which have made some progress in reducing stratification along other lines (see Bahro 1978). It is also important because this is one of the prime concerns voiced by Chinese women doing rural woman-work, as well as by other women in the Women's Federations.

Women have actually become less well represented in the highest levels of leadership during the reform era, and this highly visible shift is interpreted within China as setting a pattern at the top of the national hierarchy that has influential repercussions at all lower levels. The one countervailing measure at the village level—the inclusion of the village woman's head in the village committee—is now recommended but not required. And it is, of course, a limited measure. It is also not the priority for the Women's Federations, which in any event do not

TABLE 3.2
Resident Labor Force of the Village of Qianrulin, 1978–87

Year	Population	Resident agricultural labor force	Resident nonagricultural labor force	Resident nonagricultural labor force (% of total resident labor force)
1978	639	115	103	47
1982	665	75	149	67
1983	673	75	188	71
1984	675	76	232	75
1985	680	56	262	82
1986	686	58	268	82
1987	690	58	268	82

SOURCE: Official Qianrulin records, 1987.
NOTE: "Resident" refers only to those whose household registration is recorded as Qianrulin.

directly reach down to this level and have little impact on it. Their focus, instead, is on devising means for women to enter the political hierarchy at much higher levels.[10]

This wider political context has local repercussions, but the everyday world of rural gender and politics is more directly determined by processes of social structuration in the immediate milieux. Questions of gender and power at this level are also more complex than the issue of access to formal public leadership.

The growth of village industry represents an expanding and vital sector of rural political economy. The gender division of labor realized in these enterprises is significant in the immediate daily life of large numbers of women and men, and hence has far-reaching implications for the transformation of rural society.

Qianrulin provides a convenient starting point. Tables 3.1 and 3.2 present a few key indicators from Qianrulin's official economic figures. In the case of Qianrulin, nonagricultural work and income derive almost wholly from village industry. The labor-force figures should also be seen in the context of a sizable portion of Qianrulin's industrial labor force consisting of workers from outside the village who do not appear in the figures in Table 3.2. Table 3.3 provides a summary of employment in Qianrulin in 1987, including employees hired from outside the village. Note that Qianrulin's own labor force is still subject to formal labor allocation. This, combined with the village leadership's control over the employment of workers hired from outside the vil-

TABLE 3.3
Employment and Gender in the Village of Qianrulin, 1987

Enterprise	Managers		Staff		Total		Migrants[a] (in total)	
	F	M	F	M	F	M	F	M
Felt mats	0	18[b]	99	83	99	101	60	19
Furnishings	0	3	5	38	5	41	0	16
Chemical packaging	0	3	5	28	5	31	0	2
Plastic recycling	0	3	6	7	6	10	0	0
Clothing	1	1	6	1	7	2	0	0
Agricultural machinery	0	3	0	9	0	12	0	0
Chickens[c]	0	3	22	4	22	7	22	4
Agriculture[d]	0	12	26	20	26	32	0	0

SOURCE: Official figures provided by the Qianrulin village accountant, supplemented by figures provided by selected enterprises, accurate as of the end of 1987.
[a]"Migrants" refers to those persons employed in Qianrulin's enterprises whose household registration is recorded as other than Qianrulin.
[b]Includes managers down to the workshop level, a level comparable to the smaller enterprises in the village. Lower levels of designated responsibility also exist but are not wholly supervisory.
[c]This enterprise is seasonal and operates only in the warmer months of the year.
[d]Includes all three agricultural teams.

lage, allows Qianrulin's leadership comprehensive economic control over its labor force.

It is immediately apparent from Table 3.3 that the founding of rural enterprises has opened up numerous opportunities for entry into management, and that these opportunities are being provided to men within the village. Although one migrant—a male engineer in the chemical packaging factory—holds the post of factory vice-head because of his expertise, migrants to Qianrulin are either unskilled workers or quite highly skilled and well remunerated ones who nevertheless do not enter into the direct management of the village's enterprises.

Village women are for the most part also excluded from management. The one woman who formally holds the post of vice-head of a factory does so in a very small enterprise in which women's labor in sewing is the main activity (see Table 3.3). The two men in her enterprise occupy the posts of factory head (a younger son of the village Party branch secretary) and sales representative. Two other notably able and well-connected women in the village occupy more minor positions of economic responsibility. One young married woman (a daughter-in-law of the village Party branch secretary, a daughter of her natal village's long-serving Party branch secretary, and herself a Party member) leads three other women in sewing and one male carpenter in a unit producing sofas from waste material in the felt mat factory. Another young married woman (the wife of the factory head) heads one of the workshops in the chemical packaging factory. These are the only women whom I could identify as holding any posts of economic responsibility in any of the village's enterprises, and two out of the three are not formally recognized or sufficiently responsible to be considered managers.

Women are still more completely excluded from the critical economic activity of sales and procurement. This is not a pattern over which the village has any effective control—the work requires travel and contact with buyers and suppliers elsewhere, and it is a strong norm in China that this travel and work be done only by men. (Long-distance travel alone, individual social contact with unrelated men, and the drinking involved in doing business all work to keep women out of this dimension. Women are more likely to be found in production management within enterprises.) Procurement of raw materials can be difficult, and sale of the products of the mushrooming number of rural enterprises is competitive and absolutely essential to the success of the enterprises.

Sales is therefore a valued and demanding economic task that occupies a considerable number of the men in the village. For some enterprises, the issue of sales either does not arise or is a relatively minor matter—namely, in the agricultural teams, the agricultural machinery team, the chicken factory (linked with higher state levels), and the plastic recycling factory. In the other factories there are full-time sales and procurement personnel who work on a commission basis. In addition to some of each factory's top management being involved in sales, the felt mat factory has eight sales personnnel, the chemical packaging factory has five, the clothing factory has one, and the furnishings factory has an undetermined number. All these are mature, capable men who are removed from direct involvement in production and who operate with a degree of independence. These numbers should be taken into account when viewing the gender imbalance between management and other staff in Table 3.3.

Another factor that might be considered, although it will emerge as being important in an unexpected way, is the gender disproportion in skilled and unskilled labor.[11] Data on women and men in these categories were provided to me by the village leadership, but I found these impossible to use because the criteria for distinguishing between the categories was problematic. For example, none of the people involved in agricultural production was classed as skilled, neither those engaged in cultivation nor those with specialized tasks in livestock raising; of the nonmanagerial staff in the clothing factory, only the sales representative was classed as skilled; and all the members of the agricultural machinery team were classed as skilled except the accountant. These categorizations may reveal something about the local valuations put on types of work or on particular workers, or they may be quite arbitrary. Later in this chapter I will approach the question of differences in skill levels from a more definitely employment-related basis and in relation to large magnitudes of difference.

An additional factor that frames this pattern of gender difference in employment concerns the different worklife patterns of women and men in Qianrulin. Men of all ages are present in Qianrulin enterprises: younger men in less skilled positions or in ones that promise futures in leadership, middle-aged men very often in more responsible positions, and older men in less physically demanding but still remunerative positions (such as watchman).

Women face quite different employment patterns. Young unmarried women are commonly employed as unskilled workers in one of the village enterprises, although a few are to be found in agricultural work. Young married women are typically assigned to agricultural work, on the grounds that this allows for flexible hours convenient for the mothers of young children. In my sample of 33 of the 140 households in this village, I found ten women working in agriculture, of whom five were married and five were unmarried young women.[12] This pattern appears to result from a slight concentration of women in nonmanagerial agricultural work and from the workings of the village quota of one person per household (in some but not all households) engaging in agricultural labor. Somewhat older married women who had spent their working lives in agriculture were at this time retiring at or shortly after the age of 40, provided that a younger woman was available in the household to replace the retiring woman in agriculture.

More generally, young unmarried women formed the core of the female work force in the village's enterprises. Married women below the age of 40 were to be found either in agriculture or in better factory work than that available to the younger, unmarried women. Only a few women over 40 were employed, and these were all to be found in work groups of their own in the felt mat factory. They appeared to be the women in the village in greatest economic need—indeed, this group included one woman over 70 years of age.

This description of the gender and age distribution of work assignments in Qianrulin is not the result of an analysis of employment patterns in a free market for labor. The description of gender and age patterns in employment can be precise because each job is effectively defined as a job for a person of a certain gender and age.[13] Labor allocation is still a centralized matter handled by the village leadership. Fixed gender and age categories follow widespread cultural patterns of the gender division of labor (men should do "heavy" work, women should do "detailed" work) as well as norms of preference for older men in positions of authority. The only (partial) deviation from this is the comparatively wide range in age possible for men in managerial roles—younger men often have substantial authority, although placing them in positions directly above older men who also hold posts of some authority is avoided.[14] This description of the exact lines of division of labor by gender and age in Qianrulin is derived from detailed inquiries in a selection of Qianrulin enterprises (the felt mat factory, the chemical packaging factory, and one of the agricultural teams) as well as from official village data. The description is confirmed by employment data from my sample of 33 households.

At the center of Qianrulin's largest enterprise (the felt mat factory), the following pattern is apparent, in addition to what is evident from Table 3.3. The workshop that prepares raw material is divided into women over the age of 40, who cut up large pieces of material by hand, and men in their early twenties, who use machines to shred smaller pieces of material. Their products go to the next workshop, where men between the ages of 18 and 35 feed the material into machines and tend the machines, while the youngest women in the factory (all under 20, except for one who is just 20 years old) remove the pressed material from the machines and deliver it to the next workshop. In the factory's main workshop, twelve groups, each consisting of three women and one man, soak and press the mats. The three young unmarried women in each group work together soaking and rolling the mats, while the one young man takes the finished mats outside and hangs them up. In the packing workshop, two men bring the mats in and eight others cut them into shape. All are young men between 18 and 25. Eight women, mostly between 30 and 35 years of age, sew the cut mats into bundles. One unmarried 25-year-old woman weighs the bundles.

Workers from outside the village also have their clearly defined places in Qianrulin's work force. All the women workers from outside Qianrulin are unmarried young women from nearby villages. There are no skill or educational requirements for these women, and their positions offer them no employment future or movable skills. The only hiring criteria mentioned by the village leadership were good health, hard work, and obedience. Many of the men fall into the same category; the only distinction is that they are not required to be unmarried. These unskilled men are nevertheless likely to be young and comparatively short-term workers because they, too, have no future in Qianrulin, which will prefer its own men for advancement wherever possible. All the workers from outside the village in the felt mat factory and in the chicken factory fall into this category. In the case of the chicken factory, Qianrulin provides the site and all the management for the factory, but the less desirable, seasonal work (coinciding with, rather than offsetting, the agricultural season) is done by outside workers.

The wages earned by unskilled workers from outside Qianrulin are significantly lower than wages for the same work done by Qianrulin residents. In the felt mat factory, the main employer of outside workers, Qianrulin residents are calculated to earn RMB 6.5 per basic workday, whereas outside workers earn RMB 4.0. This is explained by the factory leadership as a reasonable differential, on the grounds that the investment for the factory was provided by Qianrulin. The factory leadership does not make the observation that the funds generated by the outside workers and accumulated within the factory provide for investment and benefits in Qianrulin that the outside workers do not enjoy.

The wage differential should also be seen within the context of widespread rural un- and underemployment and the operation of the market in labor power. These factors facilitate the flow of labor from less-well-off rural communities to those able to provide employment to more than their own residents. Those most likely to avail themselves of such opportunities are young entrants to the labor force, especially young women. Men will prefer employment that promises more of a future, when they can find it; they are also better positioned in the labor market in terms of wages. Young unmarried women constitute a pool of healthy, hardworking laborers who are seeking (or whose families are seeking) only the best income they can generate for a few years before marriage, after which their futures will become tied to their marital homes and marital communities. From the employer's point of view, women will accept lower wages than men, do not compete with residents of the employing community, are mobile and comparatively free of domestic demands, and place no long-term demands on their employers. The availability of abundant labor power in this category is one of the conditions of rapid growth in labor-intensive rural industry.

The remaining employees from outside the village provide a sharp contrast. Three are retired engineers providing essential expertise to the newer and more sophisticated village enterprises, and fifteen are highly skilled workers[15] who are similarly essential to the same enterprises. The technicians are all mature men; the engineers are older men who have retired from urban positions.[16]

The engineer in the chemical packaging factory is a 64-year-old retired engineer from Shenyang who maintains his urban registration and can leave at any time. While he is in Qianrulin he serves as vice-head of this factory, which was founded only in 1984 and was still in the early stages of development in 1987. He is paid the high wage of RMB 300 per month and provided with numerous extras, including free housing for himself and his wife, basic food supplies, and two visits to Shenyang each year. The two engineers in the furnishings factory are also retired and from Shenyang, but they have moved to Qianrulin on a permanent basis, together with their families. They have given up their urban registration, although their children have not.[17] These two engineers each receive RMB 500 per month.

The chemical packaging factory has one technician hired from a village only 6 kilometers from Qianrulin. He maintains his registration in his own village. Except for the engineer, he is the most skilled person in the factory and has been the technical teacher of the Qianrulin residents who now head the factory's three workshops. He lives in his own village and comes to Qianrulin only twice a week now that his trainees are able to work without his constant presence. He has received RMB 200 per month since beginning work for this factory and is, in effect, continuing to be paid for expertise that he has already transferred.

Fourteen highly skilled workers classed as technicians work in the furnishings factory under an agreement with this branch factory's parent factory in Shenyang. The actual workers change, but the complement is stable at fourteen. Each receives a basic wage of RMB 250 per month, a supplement of RMB 75 per month, a bonus of RMB 500 per year, and one week at home in Shenyang every month. These personnel, and the tie with the parent factory, are essential to this factory's production. The arrangement for the technicians may have been temporary, since the factory was established only in 1986 and was still partly under construction at the end of 1987, but no indication was given that the arrangement was expected to be very short term.

The migrant labor entering Qianrulin reinforces and heightens stratification within the work force, including stratification along the lines of gender. Young unskilled women from outside the village are a substantial component of the basic manual labor force and receive reduced wages, no job security, and no prospects for advancement. The men who are recruited into the village from outside include some young workers in a similar position to these women, but also a significant category of mature and older men who provide expertise that Qianrulin requires for its enterprise development but cannot provide itself. The latter are paid well, are respected, and occupy important positions in village enterprises. However, they are displaced from the operations of the village political economy: the engineers are retired outsiders and may enjoy high levels of remuneration, but they have no entry into the political affairs of the village; the technicians are not fully resident, and most are not long-term employees in the village.

The positions in which women and men of various ages enter the Qianrulin work force are consistent with the village politics of gender and age, and are distinguished from those politics only in adding to the extent of differentiation within the Qianrulin labor force. The entry of all these categories of workers is controlled and structured in such a manner as to have no destabilizing effect on the established village hierarchy.[18] The very presence of the outside workers is dependent on hiring or negotiating by the leading men within the village.

Zhangjiachedao represents a slightly different road toward the development of flourishing village industry. It was a later entrant to village industry than Qianrulin, and some of the differences, especially in degree of diversification, are related to Zhangjiachedao's later start. Both villages had significant assistance from higher levels of the state in the early stages, in the chicken enterprise in Qianrulin and in the beginning of the weaving factory in Zhangjiachedao. Qianrulin utilized knowledge and contacts from the village's earlier out-migrants to diversify and expand its village enterprises. The faltering felt hat factory[19] was replaced by an industrial felt-mat factory as the consequence of information and contacts provided by a worker in the factory who had apprenticed in Weifang before Liberation, and whose fellow-apprentices told him of the closure of their urban felt-mat factory. They also facilitated the transfer of the closing factory's equipment to Qianrulin. Qianrulin's newer factories draw heavily upon contacts made by the village's out-migrants to the Northeast, especially one village cadre who worked in the Northeast until the economic reversals of the early 1960s sent him back to Qianrulin.[20]

Zhangjiachedao, in contrast, relied on more local sources, in the form of assistance from a local weaving factory. Its own history of migration is less concentrated on the Northeast, although that is a common destination for Shandong migrants and some Zhangjiachedao people have moved there. The most concentrated exodus from Zhangjiachedao within living memory occurred in the late 1940s, when many villagers in this area of Communist political activity moved south with the advancing People's Liberation Army. Many men who left at this time remained in the south of China as cadres and never returned. While the poverty of their village contributed an economic reason for their departure, they were essentially political migrants and did not constitute a direct economic resource for the community.[21]

Zhangjiachedao's development plans remained heavily focused on the expansion of its weaving and dyeing factory. The factory began in 1979, with an initial debt of RMB 100,000 and an output value from its 20 machines and 50 workers of only RMB 300,000. By 1983, the factory had paid off its debt and was beginning to produce high profits. In 1984, its approximate output value of RMB 3,500,000 produced a profit of RMB 1,000,000. This high profit rate was partly the result of tax relief from higher state levels. In 1985, when this tax relief had terminated, the value of output rose to RMB 4,500,000 but the profit fell to RMB 980,000. The tax relief may well have been a valuable aid to the factory's initial development,[22] but a successful rural enterprise can generate such high rates of profit that it is not essential in the long term. On the contrary, rural industry then becomes a major mechanism for local capital accumulation. Both Qianrulin and Zhangjiachedao exemplify villages that have turned modest industrial ventures into the motors of highly successful village economic development.

In the case of Zhangjiachedao, this development remains focused on growth of a single factory that dominates the village's economy. This one enterprise generated 70 percent of all village income in Zhangjia-chedao in 1985. It is also the main employer in the village and a significant employer for the surrounding area. In 1986, the Zhangjiachedao weaving and dyeing factory had a staff of 244 in a village with only 280 working people ("labor power units," *laodongli*). This was feasible because 99 of the staff were recruited from outside the village. Nevertheless, the preponderance of this factory in terms of personnel is nearly as marked as its preponderance in economic terms.

Aside from the weaving and dyeing factory, there are few other village enterprises or avenues for employment, and none of these is expanding or intended to form the basis for further village economic development. The orchard, which was established prior to the weaving and dyeing factory, continues to be a viable economic endeavor but is restricted in size by Zhangjiachedao's limited amount of land. It has a total staff of 40, of whom one is a male skilled worker (technician) from outside the village. The management of the orchard is entirely male, but 14 women who work there include both ordinary workers and more skilled ones classed as technicians. Several other village enterprises are wholly or almost wholly male: a construction team (20 village men, 10 skilled men from outside the village, and women only as casual laborers), a concrete factory (8 village men and 1 skilled man from outside), a wooden tool factory (10 village men), and an agricultural machinery and transport group (10 to 20 village men).

These enterprises provide employment and generate some funds for the village, but they are not areas of growth. Zhangjiachedao does not send construction or other work teams elsewhere in the country, and its work in construction and related fields, such as concrete production, is directed toward its own local market. Most of this involves building new homes for the entire village, a standard early step when a community begins to prosper. By 1986, the majority of Zhangjiachedao residents had moved into new row houses built according to village specifications regarding the size of lot but with some individual variations. The style of house was reminiscent of those described by Martin Yang (1945) decades earlier as the residences of wealthier peasants. The demand for improved homes, which by 1986 extended to building the first two-story houses in the village, together with the construction of factory, office, and shop facilities, keeps these small enterprises busy. The agricultural machinery and transport group supports the household-based agriculture in the village and uses the ma-

TABLE 3.4

Gender Division of Labor Among the Staff of the
Weaving and Dyeing Factory in the Village of Zhangjiachedao, 1986

Category of work	Female	Male	Total
Weaving workshop	95	18	113
Management	0	4	4
Machine maintenance	0	14	14
Apprentices	13	0	13
Loom operators	82	0	82
Preparation workshop	76	17	93
Management	0	4	4
Shipping	2	3	5
Machine maintenance	0	9	9
Technician from outside	0	1	1
Other workers	74	0	74
Dyeing	6	9	15
Management	3	6	9
Workers	3	3	6
Finance	1	10	11
(including factory management)			
Other	4	13	17
(repair, electrical and carpentry work, driving, boiler work, dining hall, security, reception)			

chinery at other times for transport, a profitable pursuit in the country-side throughout the decade.

The one enterprise that bears some connection to the village's expansion is a small clothing factory set up to make use of odd pieces of material from the weaving and dyeing factory. All its thirteen staff are women, with the exception of a male factory head (the vice-head is a woman) and a retired male tailor from Qingdao who is in the village on a one-year contract to train the factory staff. A few women and men in the village are independently employed—the men as small-scale merchants (selling some of the village cloth) or artisans, the women doing some home-based industry, making rope or string or producing net bags.

It is the weaving and dyeing factory that dominates the employment pattern of the village and that has given shape to some shifts in employment-related gender relations within Zhangjiachedao. Table 3.4 provides a summary of the gender division of labor in the various categories of work in the factory. The division of labor represented in Table 3.4 is similar to that already described for Qianrulin. With the exception of one woman soon to marry out of the village, who is one of the accountants, all the managerial positions in the factory are filled by men. One other possible exception is the woman who heads the factory dining hall. She is the wife of the factory head, and in some sense this is an extension of her domestic duties. She also plays a role as an informal leader in the community, and although this is derived from and enabled by her husband's role as Party branch secretary, she does this more than other women I have observed in similar positions. Men are also concentrated in positions involving the use of machines other than looms, and this is a similarly common pattern.

In the gender division of labor in both management and use of machinery, general cultural patterns of work appropriate to women and men are in evidence. Neither Qianrulin nor Zhangjiachedao has made any significant move toward placing women in managerial roles, which would be against the grain of local cultural expectations. Zhangjiachedao does, however, offer noticeably better employment opportunities for women workers. Again, this is partly a matter of cultural expectations, because tending looms is a comparatively skilled form of labor that only women are expected to do.

Some of Zhangjiachedao's policies serve both to promote maintenance of a skilled female labor force and to favor the status of women in the community. In contrast with Qianrulin, where the work done by young women in the felt mat factory is unskilled and many of the workers appear to have cut short their schooling to enter the labor force for a few years prior to marriage,[23] Zhangjiachedao requires that all people hired to work in its weaving and dyeing factory have at least lower middle school education. In the countryside this represents more education than many young women are currently receiving. Zhangjiachedao is well aware of this—it has found that it has little trouble with the educational minimum when hiring its own villagers, because education is comparatively valued in Zhangjiachedao and employment in this preferred factory is virtually guaranteed to healthy young women, but that women in surrounding villages often do not have this minimum. Zhangjiachedao's educational requirements for factory work ensure a skilled labor force, remove the economic incentive that might otherwise exist for withdrawing teenage women from school, and provide a positive incentive for women to continue in school.

Another policy that favors women in Zhangjiachedao, compared with Qianrulin, is the employment of married women in the weaving and dyeing factory. Young daughters-in-law are not relegated to agricultural work but work together with the village's daughters in the weaving workshops. Indeed, some of these women were formerly workers from outside the village who married into Zhangjiachedao and have continued their previous work. Even when they were not employed by the factory prior to marriage, they are likely to become employed there after they marry into the village. Younger married women almost invariably work in this factory, provided they are able to make adequate childcare arrangements, which in most cases requires having a mother-in-law available. The village does have an underutilized kindergarten, but it operates only during the day, whereas work in the factory is continuous, with three daily shifts (on weekly rotation) and no days off. A few slightly older women work in quality control or other day jobs, or in the clothing factory.

In my sample of 84 households in Zhangjiachedao, I found 58 women working in village enterprises: 1 born in the 1920s, 3 in the 1930s, 11 in the 1940s, 12 in the 1950s, 26 in the 1960s, 4 in the 1970s, and 1 of uncertain age. Some married women, especially those who have no mother-in-law, are unable to make suitable arrangements and may do some home-based craft work or concentrate on agriculture and domestic labor. Women who are already mothers-in-law themselves tend to combine childcare, domestic work, and agriculture while younger women in the household bring in wages from the factory. This pattern of difference in work according to age for women is not prescribed or enforced by factory hiring policies or village labor-allocation mechanisms, but arises from the combination of a time-managed workplace and childcare placing demands on women that a young mother cannot manage without the assistance of another woman.[24] With the exception of the occasional grandfather, men do not do sufficient childcare—and cannot, given their own work demands—to provide a conjugal solution to the problem. Men's work situation in Zhangjiachedao is not influenced by age or marital status, except insofar as mature men are more likely to be found in managerial positions.

The availability of skilled work that pays well for women in Zhangjiachedao—and not only briefly, before marriage, but after marriage as well—has contributed to improvements in the status of women there. Although it is difficult to demonstrate a direct relation, the official birth-limitation program is having more success in this village than in many others, and the village women's head (who is also the paramedic—former "barefoot doctor"—responsible for women's health) said that she found it much easier to promote this policy in Zhangjiachedao than in her nearby natal village, where she had had the same responsibilities.

In Zhangjiachedao, this is probably also related to official approval and active encouragement of intravillage matches designed to provide for the care of the elderly who have daughters but not sons. The village leaders, especially the Party branch secretary, have been energetic in seeking to care for the elderly through arranging intravillage marriages, which had in any event already occurred in Zhangjiachedao spontaneously. Several young village women expressed a wish to marry within Zhangjiachedao in order to keep their factory employment after marriage.[25] They also observed that young village men had no such incentive toward intravillage matches, so that this would not be easily arranged. Although intravillage marriage may not change rapidly in frequency here, the factory does seem to have generated a sense of women being a valuable source of wage income—and not only temporarily, before marriage—which makes daughters also a source of economic security for their parents' futures. To the extent that this is so, it is a product of both the economic basis provided by the textile factory and the pursuit of policies that moderately favor women's interests.[26]

Labor is not formally allocated in Zhangjiachedao, nor is it as tightly controlled as in Qianrulin, but there are policies at the village level that determine the outline of employment in the village. These are easily effected by the overlap in leadership of the village government and Party branch with that of the village enterprises. There is a strong sense in which the village has formally decollectivized but remains an effectively cohesive political and economic unit reminiscent of many features of collective social organization. The village leadership made a policy decision in 1985 that ended the specialization of some households in agricultural work and instead divided agricultural responsibilities among all households, with a corresponding adjustment of enterprise working hours. The village implements policies of striving to provide employment that pays well to all employable members of the community, equitably distributing the less preferred work of agriculture, and protecting its young people's access to education. Where some village people are not suitable for employment in one of the enterprises, whether because of domestic demands or poor health, or where a resident of the village prefers to be self-employed, the village permits independent work (unlike Qianrulin), although it does not promote this as the preferred choice (and so differs from Huaili). All these are dimensions in which village-level policy substantially determines the income and work of village residents, and subtly shapes gender patterns.

As with Qianrulin, Zhangjiachedao is sufficiently successful that it cannot meet its labor needs with only its own people. The weaving and dyeing factory employs 75 young unmarried women and 24 men from outside the village. The women are ordinary workers in the factory, as are most of the men. The weaving and dyeing factory did formerly have more outside skilled workers, but it is now capable of providing for its own technical needs, and only one outside technician remains. The gender imbalance in migratory labor apparent in Qianrulin is therefore also to be found in Zhangjiachedao, although in less exaggerated form. The women outside workers are expected to meet the same educational and skill demands as are workers resident in the village, and they do acquire some skills on the job. The men from outside are in some cases at the same level as the women, although a few—one in the factory, one in the orchard, one in carpentry, one in the clothing factory, and about ten in construction—add significantly to the village's complement of skilled workers. None except the tailor is currently critical to any of the village's enterprises, although a comprehensive historical view would show that such workers were critical earlier in the development of the weaving and dyeing factory. If the planned canning factory is established, there may again be a need for specialized skilled labor beyond what the village itself can provide.

Zhangjiachedao benefits as an entire community from the work performed primarily by women in its weaving and dyeing factory. Seventy-five of the 172 women working in the factory in 1986[27] were from outside the village. They were paid on the same piecework basis as workers from within the village, and differed in remuneration only in not enjoying the benefits available to village residents. Village policymakers considered any other differences to be undesirable, partly on grounds of equitability and partly on grounds of worker motivation. High levels of production of good quality material are extremely important for the success of the factory in a market that by 1986 was already glutted with the products of rural weaving factories. There is some reference still to be found in Zhangjiachedao to "March 8 Flagbearers" (*sanba hongqishou*), a commendation used in earlier years for women, especially young women, who make strong economic contributions through labor. The conditions for earning this commendation include political correctness, harmonious family relations, and dedication to public economic interests (rather than only individual ones). Values such as these were widely promoted in the years when China was forging its own path to socialism, and although much less in evidence in the reform era, there is evidently a utility in promoting these values among the work force in a market economy as well.

The automatic exclusion of women outside workers from benefits immediately available to women workers within the village should be placed in context. Much of the benefit derived from the factory is of a long-term nature, providing future investment for the village of Zhangjiachedao. Many of the women from within the village would, after marriage, also lose access to these benefits. Despite Zhangjiachedao's favorable policies, the structure of rural society works to separate women workers from much of the product of their labor. *Women not only produce value at a high rate in rural industry, they are separable from that value to the advantage of capital accumulation on the part of villages structured as co-residential communities of agnatically related men.*

Huaili represents both an alternative path to rural economic development and an indication of the view of work in rural industry held in villages that export labor to rural industry elsewhere. Huaili embarked on decollectivization with no prior basis in rural industry, and consequently with no reserves available for investment. The village leadership, principally the Party branch secretary of the time, decided against taking a loan for industrial investment. Despite the success of Qianrulin and Zhangjiachedao, it should be remembered that not all rural industry has been so successful, and that late starters entered an already crowded field in which credit, raw materials, and sales could all pose difficult problems. Huaili had also been successful in agriculture in the past, so it could not expect special state assistance. Huaili's decision to concentrate instead on small-scale commodity production and commerce set the course of the village economy for the reform era. It was a decision made in light of Huaili's economic conditions—and a decision made at the village level by the village leadership.

One consequence of this is a relative economic weakness on the part of Huaili compared with the other two villages. The village level retains a significant degree of power through its political-administrative role, and through its discretionary use of the limited resources that it does hold. Huaili is nevertheless a noticeably less centralized village than the other two, which may partly be attributed to this economic difference. It is also a result of the policy decisions made by the village leadership not to concentrate on development at the village level, but rather to facilitate the growth of household enterprises as widely as possible. Accordingly, the village makes no attempt to levy a tax on household enterprises, but meets its modest expenses through contracted rents on the few village-owned commercial premises. This also has the benefit of relieving the village of the problems of tax collection and tax evasion, at least insofar as its own finances are concerned.[28]

The contrast between the work force of Huaili's two main village enterprises, the weaving factory and the transport team, and villagers involved in household-based enterprises is instructive. The village-run enterprises in Huaili generate no profit for the village but do provide employment for those villagers (unskilled youth entering the labor force and unskilled men) least able to flourish independently. Those villagers who can set up their own small enterprises on the basis of some skill, initiative, or capital available within the household prefer to do so. This has proven remunerative in the relatively open economic world of the Chinese countryside in the 1980s. Household-based enterprises faced some setbacks as the economic climate deteriorated in the late 1980s, but that was also true for rural industry. Huaili's ventures in commodity production are discussed in Chapter 4. Here it is only necessary to note some of the reasons the people of Huaili prefer household-based enterprises to rural industry.

One of the major disadvantages of rural industry in the eyes of the people of Huaili is that it is not sufficiently remunerative. Young people in Huaili do seek employment in rural industry in order to have some cash income, but it is not a preferred alternative. The economic value of successful rural enterprises is only partly to be found in job creation and wages. A very large part of the value is in the profit made by these enterprises. There are substantial advantages in developing a factory in one's community that will generate profit for the community, but much less benefit in being one of the workers in an enterprise where the profits go elsewhere.

In addition, not all rural industry is on a firm financial footing, and the problems this creates can be passed onto the workers. This most obviously takes the form of insecure employment, but, at least by the time of the economic downturn at the end of the decade, workers also could not count on having their wages paid and might even have to "purchase" their jobs by working free for an initial period of time or by making a substantial cash contribution to the factory. These latter arrangements were a means factories were adopting to solve funding problems in a tight credit market and generally difficult economic climate. The shortage of employment among young people in the countryside meant that this was feasible. Even the reasonably well-off village of Huaili had a number of unemployed young people at the end of the decade, and in 1989, the county openly recognized three to four thousand "young people waiting for employment" (*daiye qingnian*).

To the extent that factory employment might be positively attractive to young people in the countryside, this was for noneconomic reasons. Temporary employment in a town or urban enterprise might open the door for a change to urban registration, although the chances of this occurring were acknowledged to be slim. Rural industry cannot offer this nonmonetary compensation.

Household-based enterprises can be a highly attractive alternative for those who are able to take advantage of it. All the products of the self-employed workers are returned to their own household, and this is a significant financial advantage. The members of the household can also work autonomously, and this aspect of working conditions is valued. The younger members of the household may be working under the supervision of their parents, and in the case of daughters may not personally enjoy the product of their labor—which may be destined for the expense of their brothers' weddings and new marital homes—but they are no worse off in this respect in the household than they would be in rural industry. There is also some structural potential here for self-exploitation, as has been observed in Taiwan. The enterprises I observed in Huaili did not appear to have been extreme in this respect; the most overworked people I met in the village were people who were struggling economically to make ends meet without a household enterprise, by working longer hours in agriculture and in manual transport work. Household enterprises could be very demanding, but also offered some respite from hard labor when they were flourishing.[29]

Household-based enterprises seem especially favorable for the interests of mature women. Some of the reasons for this will become more apparent in Chapter 4. The material presented here strongly indicates that the majority of mature women have few attractive alternatives in rural industry. The opportunities for mature women to control their own conditions of work and to enjoy the product of their own labor are greater in the smaller units of the household than in the larger units of rural factories. Arguments that have previously seen rural Chinese women at a special disadvantage in the patriarchal household have failed to take adequate notice of the concentrated patriarchy they face outside the home. I found no indication that rural Chinese women experienced extradomestic work as liberating either during or after the collective era (also see M. Wolf 1985). Women doing rural work in economic development targeted toward women argued that suprahousehold rural enterprises employing primarily women would certainly be managed by men, and that this was not in women's best interests. Women are better off working for themselves, and can come closest to this in their own household enterprises.

Gender and Accumulation

In conclusion, rural industry is one of the main vehicles of economic growth and capital accumulation in the countryside. This accumulation should be seen as substantially consisting of the appropriation of the product of women's labor, and especially young women's labor. Similar appropriation of young women's labor has been reported for nearby Taiwan (Diamond 1979) and Hong Kong (Salaff 1981).

At a slightly greater remove of time and space, it is also similar to processes observed for Europe, in which socioeconomic changes in capitalist modernization were facilitated through a reliance on young women's labor. Their relative powerlessness enabled their labor to fuel capitalist economic growth and to reconcile it to a domestic economy that, at least on the surface, was at odds with the principles of the capitalist economy (Fox-Genovese and Genovese 1983). The encapsulation of domestic economy within capitalist economy stabilized the latter and opened the domestic economy to processes of transformation obscured by representations of it as separate and antithetical to the market. In Europe, this involved an ideology of womanhood and domestic economy. In China, parallel mechanisms, in which working women are identified by the male leadership (but not by themselves) as "housewives," as in Qianrulin, simultaneously deny their role in the extradomestic economy and allow it to continue to the benefit of local industry.

Even more obviously, the work of young unmarried women can be defined as temporary and as posing no challenge to either household or suprahousehold forms of social organization that appropriate the product of their labor. An extreme form of this process has been analyzed from a cross-cultural perspective by Mies (1986), much of whose argument is readily applicable to the material analyzed here.

The appropriation of women's labor, together with cultural representations that mystify this appropriation, should not be a surprising finding. Nor should there be any surprise at finding processes of demystification at work, especially in communities such as Huaili, which benefit only marginally from rural industry, and especially (but not automatically) in women's organizations.

The agents appropriating women's labor in rural industry in China vary, but most are directly tied to the state, and all operate under state regulation and with the legitimacy conferred by state policies promoting rural industry. The exact relationships here depend both on the level at which the state is involved (for the most part, either the village or the township level) and on the degree of directness and formality of the ties. The particular focus here has been on village enterprises, and some of the relationships involved may be particular to that level. However, the intersection of rural industry with local levels of the state, and the permeation of both by the mechanisms of patriarchy, are not restricted to the village level. Rural industry is almost wholly managed by men, roles involving business or technical knowledge are almost wholly reserved for men, and the capital accumulated is under the management of public bodies controlled by men.

The immediate division of labor through which rural industry operates is only part of its political economy. Another, critically important part is the role of the patriarchal state in penetrating this growing area of the rural economy. The male predominance in state structures blocks women's advancement in structural terms, even in a market-oriented rural economy. And, to the extent that the state is able, it confers a degree of legitimacy as well as force to this structure. In the 1980s, the state's prestige has been low in formal terms, and here the village level is especially important.

At the village level, the structure and mechanisms of the state substantially coincide with living human communities. Villages vary in the extent to which this is true, and are themselves crosscut by numerous divisions and conflicts. These include the conflict of emergent class difference, which is especially pronounced among men (it is only a minority of the men who control the accumulation of capital or the operations of the local state) and which is also increasing among women (to the extent that a very few gain positions not available to the rest). Nevertheless, the village itself is a social entity that must be given particular attention. Some villages have a prior sense of community based on lineality and co-residence; virtually all have a history of being distinct and discretely bounded units during the collective era. The local histories of villages forged during that era have also generated communities on the basis of the village's dual position in both the formal and the informal structures of state power.

The replacement of the collective structure with administrative units, such as the village and township, has partially transformed the relationships involved but has widely confirmed their boundaries. This has allowed contemporary processes of state-building to draw on informal dimensions of rural community life. One of the areas of intersection has been the interlocking of patriarchal relations based in local co-residential groupings of agnatically related men with state structures and mechanisms of patriarchy.

CHAPTER 4

Socialist Commodity Production

Recent steps in commodity production in China do not indicate an entirely new departure. Commodity production, broadly conceived, has extremely deep roots in rural Chinese life; at the same time, the forms of political economy, and of official discourse regarding it, mark the 1980s as an era of transformation. If this transformation is understood as "the undermining of reproduction, and the recombination of some of the old elements of production into new relations" (Friedmann 1980: 162), then attention must be given to the reworking of preexisting elements of rural commodity production into the emergent contemporary form of "socialist commodity production."

Background

The transformation to a new form of commodity economy is complicated in China by the nonunilinear history of China's political economy over the past half century. The analysis of contemporary China must allow for a deep but uneven permeation of commercial relations throughout rural society, together with alternative and opposing ideals and practices. One set of these resides in personalistic, often kinbased ties linking the members of rural households. Another resides in supracommunal demands on the part of the state and of cultural authorities associated with it, especially the imperial scholar-gentry. Some of the strands of Chinese tradition include a weaving together of kin-like solidarity and supracommunal demands, very notably in long-standing and powerful traditions of peasant rebellion. In the twentieth century, these traditions have been continued and superseded by the series of revolutionary movements led by the Communist Party, and subsequently by the policies of the governments it has led.

These policies have varied, but in general have continued imperial distrust of commerce and aimed at restriction and control, and, in some crucial areas, at monopoly of certain factors of production or sectors of economic activity. The People's Republic has a record of greater success in restricting independent commerce than previous Chinese governments. It has accomplished this with real economic growth, as expressed in somewhat improved per capita incomes despite a doubling of the population during its first thirty years, and high rates of state-imposed accumulation. Yet increases in living standards did not keep pace with popular expectations or official plans, and blocks in the path of commercial development were officially identified by the late 1970s as one of the major causes of lower-than-desired rates of economic growth. The economic reform program instituted step by step through the 1980s was partly aimed at fueling economic growth through a revitalized market-oriented system.

In the most immediate and concrete sense, this meant removal of prohibitions on free markets in both rural areas and cities, although regulation and taxation of the revived free markets are standard. Upward revision of prices for agricultural products and reduced rates of surplus extraction from the countryside have left more income in the hands of villagers. This has then moved through the market system, as villagers improve their living standards and invest in productive inputs. The vitality of rural markets has opened income-generating opportunities for many villagers in commerce, including independent purchase and resale of agricultural produce, small-scale peddling of durable consumer goods, local retail and wholesale shops, and long-distance trade in scarce goods.

Except where the level of commercial activity was directly limited by regional poverty, the rural scene in China in the 1980s became one characterized by an expanding market sector, as levels of market activity increased and as the range of acceptable and legal commodities widened. This included leases on land contracted from collectives, sale and purchase on the free market of grain and other essential foodstuffs (previously marketable only through state agencies), and the emergence of a market for labor power.

The re-commoditization of land, basic foodstuffs, and labor power are critical markers of the profound transformation in the rural political economy underway through the 1980s. During the decades of the socialist collective system, treating any of these as commodities was strictly prohibited. Occasional sale of foodstuffs presumably did occur, and one might question the nature of wage labor within the socialist economy, but the means of production and the fundamental means of sustaining life could not be openly bought and sold on the market. These prohibitions have been progressively abandoned through the 1980s.

There are substantial and significant debates regarding how best to characterize the present Chinese economy, but the terms officially adopted by the end of the decade—"socialist commodity economy" or "socialist commodity production"—do express the critical elements of the present situation. This is marked by popular orientations toward the market; official willingness to use market mechanisms for promoting and organizing economic activity; official commitment to a continued and strong role for the state in the economy, despite disputes and policy shifts regarding the precise features of that role; and a continued commitment to the identification of current policy as "socialist," whatever the shifting content of that term might be. The policy changes of 1989 marked a turn toward a stronger state role in economic and political matters than in the earlier 1980s, along with increased stridency regarding "socialism," but did not imply an abandonment of the market.

Socialist commodity production is evidently in a state of crisis as these words are being written in 1990. The exceptional rates of economic growth in the early 1980s slowed in mid-decade, and serious economic problems were in general evidence by 1988. As always, there were regional differences and rural-urban differences, but the overall economic trends were clear, and rural residents in all but the poorest regions were too tightly enmeshed in large-scale commercial networks to be sheltered from national economic setbacks. The political crisis in the redefinition of the Chinese political economy gravely exacerbated what was in any event proving to be a difficult economic transformation.

The state is presently committed to a greater economic role than in the immediately preceding years, but has a significantly weakened ability to play such a role. Its financial resources are severely limited and its popular legitimacy is lower than at any point since the founding of the People's Republic. The immediate future of the Chinese political economy is one of a market orientation under the direction of the state, of market instability and political uncertainty, and of both overt and silent questioning regarding the character of a socialist commodity economy.

Concepts in Flux

In everyday speech, as well as in formal discussion of the economy and of public affairs in general, people in China often speak of "commodity production" (*shangpin shengchan*), only adding the qualifier "socialist" if the context is an overtly politicized one and if the speaker is attuned to nuances of political policy. The following discussion commonly adopts the same shortened usage, although the problem of the relationship of China's emergent commodity-production system to socialism—or, more accurately, to socialisms (classical, ideal, historical, and rhetorical)—is always an implicit element in that discussion.

The direction of change in China's political economy connects with fundamental questions regarding the nature of what can be understood as socialism in many late-twentieth-century societies. The divergences of each particular and actual socialism from "socialism" have produced a plethora of new terminologies, with attendant related but different analyses of the relation between the actual and the ideal. The discussion here is informed by analyses of "actually existing socialism" (Bahro 1978), "social capitalism" (White 1987), and "postsocialism" (Dirlik 1989), as well as by debates on the same subjects internal to China, issuing both from official and from unofficial sources (such as Chen Erjin 1984). The focus throughout, however, is on the everyday world of socialism and of commodity production as lived by villagers in present-day Shandong.

In the countryside, the elements of socialism that are being most directly reconstructed by the emergent commodity-production system are those of the former system of collective control of material resources, collective allocation of labor resources, and mixed collective and state control of distribution. Elements of socialist ownership of the means of production do persist in the countryside, both in formal legal and in explicit ideological terms, as well as in much more limited practical ones. Ultimately, the state claims ownership of all land and can, as in Huaili, expropriate a significant portion of collective land for the larger public interest without compensation or negotiation. The collective level of the two-level (state and collective) socialist system of ownership continues to hold some ownership rights, as manifested in its authority to allocate land and to manage or to contract out local productive and commercial enterprises, such as village-level factories or stores.

These collective ownership rights are now formally vested in local government (at the lowest level, either village or township governments), but the contrast with the previous system can easily be overestimated. In Zhangjiachedao, Qianrulin, and Huaili, villages (replacing brigades) embody complex continuations and transformations of socialist collectives. The terminology of the "production responsibility system" (*shengchan zerenzhi*), "contracts" (*chengbao*), and "commodity production" itself are all revealing in their ambiguity. The market has been given vastly increased scope in China's economy, but it coexists with at least some aspects of the socialist system as the latter was variously constituted in China from 1956. In terms of the system of ownership, this now implies multiple layers and meanings of ownership, which allow national state, local state, and private interests to simultaneously enjoy differing qualities of "ownership" in relation to identical resources. Similar but ideologically less complex systems of interlocking claims apply to distribution systems, where multiple streams of distribution and regulation coexist and compete in the marketplace.

Collective control over labor allocation has been very much weakened during the course of the rural reforms. A few villages, such as the collective Qianrulin, do still exercise almost total control over labor allocation within their own boundaries. Less direct control may be more common, as exemplified by Zhangjiachedao, where the allocation of land and of employment opportunities in the major village enterprises approximates the former collective control of labor allocation. A village with strong leadership and with some control over village-level economic resources can indirectly exercise control over labor, although in a less administrative form than that implied by the term "labor allocation."

There is greatest loss of this control where the market for labor power is most open and competitive. Private hiring of wage labor became acceptable and legal in gradual steps through the 1980s, and was without effective constraint by the end of the decade. The substantial pool of surplus labor in the countryside does, of course, put employers in positions of strength. A major alternative is self-employment within a household-based economy, making use of allocated or otherwise contracted agricultural land, or of other resources available within the household. The household is the basic socioeconomic unit in the countryside, and considerations of labor power revolve around households, as do many considerations of production and distribution.

The place of the household economy is consequently pivotal in discussions of the shape of China's rural commodity economy. A variable but significant degree of autonomy has devolved upon households, and this, together with the reinvigorated market and the reduced scope of state planning, has resulted in increased activity in the rural economy and increased diversification in production and commerce. Households, as well as larger economic units, have expanded former domestic sidelines, small- and medium-scale rural industry, and commerce.

All this growth (as well as its subsequent decline toward the end of the decade) has been driven by state policies that Conroy (1984) has described as "laissez-faire socialism." These policies have encouraged economic growth without any particular emphasis, in contrast with previous policies, on equitability of either opportunity or distribution. Indeed, the policies are well known for their advocacy of the "trickle down effect"—that is, for their confidence that allowing some "to get rich first" will contribute more effectively to the socioeconomic betterment of the whole society, and even of its poorer members, than will more egalitarian policies. A trend toward economic "polarization" (*liangji fenhua*) is openly recognized as implicit in even moderate promotion of the reform program, and should be seen as being as much a consequence of official policy as of the operation of market forces.

Economic differentiation has the potential for creating differences within communities that may form incipient socioeconomic classes with opposed interests, and that may, on that or other bases, generate explosive social tensions. It has also been a source of serious concern in its regional dimension, as the coastal and more industrial provinces prosper while others stagnate in severe poverty. The potential for exacerbated gender inequalities has also drawn comment, although primarily from outside China.

Gender equality issues, in common with other social justice issues, have been given low priority within the framework of a reform program oriented overwhelmingly toward economic growth. The reform program was formulated without consideration of its impact on any aspect of gender relations in the countryside, although the official network of Women's Federations did increasingly, if also unevenly, attend to these issues as the decade progressed. A substantial portion of feminist commentary outside China has emphasized the predominance of the rural household and its internal patriarchy as profoundly threatening to women's distinct interests (see, especially, Davin 1988). Some others have observed women's significant role within extracollective spheres, such as sideline production, as giving them the potential basis for an expanded role in a market economy, while also noting the weakness of an organized women's movement in China (see M. Wolf 1985).

There are substantial uncertainties regarding the impact of the reform program and the commodity production system on gender difference and gender relations in rural China. Both continuing patterns and values regarding gender division of labor and gender-specific roles, as well as preexisting socioeconomic structures fundamentally structured by gender, suggest that gender relations are unavoidably being affected and reconstructed in the course of the transformation to an altered commodity economy.[1]

Following a brief summary of some pertinent theoretical work on commodity production, in this chapter I approach an analysis of some aspects of the transformation to socialist commodity production in contemporary rural China, from the perspective of villagers' practices and strategies as they confront the reform policies and new market conditions and strive to create a viable political economy within their own everyday worlds. Attention is given both to the modes of involvement in commodity production available to the best-placed villagers and to those available more diffusely in the countryside of Shandong, a comparatively commercialized province. Specific attention is given to gender and to its intersection both with other lines of differentiation and with the potential for incipient class re-formation.

Petty Commodity Production

Commodity production in the contemporary Chinese countryside is rooted in a household-based rural economy but is simultaneously enmeshed in wider networks of relationship. These wider networks are those of the state's mechanisms of surplus extraction and politico-economic administration and those of increasingly important large-scale regional, national, and international markets. If one sees socialism in China as a distinctly statist version of socialism that owes as much to indigenous Chinese political institutions as to Marxist-Leninist imports, there is a sense in which the concept of a socialist commodity economy succinctly represents the linkage between the larger state and the market milieux in which the small-scale economic activities of rural Chinese find their place.

The history of the Chinese political economy may be left in the background of the present study, although analysis of small-scale rural household enterprises requires the use of models that see those enterprises as internally related to and significantly determined by those larger processes. The concepts of petty commodity production are an appropriate starting place for this analysis.

Petty commodity production is a conceptualization of a subordinate form of production that operates within an encompassing commodity system. It was originally devised by Marx to address the question of economic relations in an early, transitional state of capitalism, and has since been used primarily with reference to dependent capitalist economies. Petty commodity production is a partial system of commodity production in which labor and the means of production are not separated in the production processes under examination, but in which commodity relations necessarily intrude in the cycle of reproduction. The typical example of this situation is an artisan or peasant who owns or controls his or her means of production and works directly on them without hiring wage labor, but who must purchase productive inputs (such as wood or fertilizer) and also some necessities for consumption, and who must sell a portion of his or her products on the market to enable the cycle of production to repeat itself. This contrasts on the one hand with subsistence production, in which market relations are no more necessary for reproduction than for production itself, and on the other with petty capitalist production, in which the production process itself has also been commoditized by the use of hired labor within the production process (see Babb 1984, Cook and Binford 1986, and Friedmann 1978, 1980).

If the question of the socialist elements of commodity production in present-day China are for the time being left to one side, the utility

of the concept of petty commodity production is immediately apparent. Pure subsistence production is hardly to be found in China; the
closest approximations are in the most remote and desperately poor
regions. Some such areas are to be found in the interior mountainous
regions of Shandong, but they are not part of this study, which is instead focused on communities indicative of possibilities within an increasingly commoditized rural economy. Within these communities,
increasing commoditization in the forms of both petty commodity production and petty capitalist production are emerging.

Commoditization is pervasive in the entire Chinese economy, although it sometimes occurs in a mixed form, together with either kinship or administrative-political modes of relationship.[2] It is readily apparent in the villages under examination in both these mixed modes,
but the specific point of emphasis here is commoditization in the
household-based economy.

The rural household is the basic unit of economic production and
reproduction in the countryside. Throughout the 1980s, it was the focus of policy directives aimed at revitalizing popular economic initiative and at harnessing that initiative to structures, both institutional and
ideological, that are under substantial state control. The household in
China is extraordinarily well suited to perform the dual mobilizing role
of stimulating and controlling devolved popular initiative in the interests of state policies for transforming the political economy. The official
promotion of commodity production in China as socialist has been aided by its being presented in terms that evade the more perilous language of (bourgeois) individualism or (private) business, and that instead conflate the supra-individual context of the household with the
civil quality of the family. Household-based enterprises *practically* resolve contradictions in socialist commodity production that are apparently irreconcilable in rigorous theoretical terms.

The utility of domestic forms of social organization for promoting
systems of commodity production has been persuasively argued by Fox-
Genovese and Genovese (1983) in their studies of the relation between
the "domestic economy" and merchant capital during the growth of
capitalism in France, England, and the United States. They found the
ideology of the domestic economy to work strongly, albeit indirectly,
to infuse money and commercial relations into domestic relations in a
manner firmly based on bourgeois individualism, while simultaneously denying any such penetration. The domestic economy was a sphere

in which income earned outside the domestic unit, in a more commercial milieu, was managed for the household on a putatively separate basis that also presumed and consolidated a separation of female and male spheres. The household economies examined here do not so strictly relegate commoditized relations, including commoditized relations of production, to the extradomestic world, *but there are striking points of similarity between the historical formation of these Western "domestic economies" and the household economy taking form in China during its transformation to a socialist commodity production system.*

Fox-Genovese and Genovese (1983: 306) note that, in the formation of the domestic economies they studied, it was significant whether the metaphorical emphasis was on the family or on the household. If the former, kinship relations tended to dominate; if the latter, the unit of economic production and reproduction tended to dominate. This pattern may be found to hold in China, where the emphasis is definitely on the household and its economic role. The emotive power of the family, and of kinship relations more broadly considered, is implicitly drawn upon as well, but current policy and the commoditization process have less need of family and kinship (and actively discourage its very strong pronatalist tendencies) than of the economic household. This argument is, of course, conditioned by the politico-administrative determination of the household in China, which makes it a different entity from the households discussed by Fox-Genovese and Genovese, but an entity equally or better suited to a centrally driven commoditization process.

Although a domestic economy, as in these Western cases, may apparently operate on the basis of noncommoditized relations, it effectively buttresses the transformation to a commodity production system by adding an element of domestic stability as a counterweight to the profound changes underway in the society as a whole, as well as by ideologically obscuring those changes. The refuge provided by the domestic group facilitates the very upheavals which render that refuge essential.

The domestic economy is structured by differences of gender that can be elaborated, as in the West, into ideologies of womanhood, which once again support commoditization by embodying values purportedly opposed to it. Gender appears also as an element in current Chinese discourse on the household. Yet because a significant amount of production takes place within Chinese households—and because women play an essential role in the household production of commodities for the market, as well as in the production of use-values for their households—women in China are not ideologized as antithetical to emergent economic values as women of at least some socioeconomic classes have been in the West.

Still, the role of women is crucial in China, too, in the course of this transformation. Chinese women may also be seen as agents in creating domestic compromises between their aspirations for themselves and their commitments to their households and classes. It is instructive that the first full modern work on domestic economy was written by a committed feminist of the French bourgeoisie who, despite her optimism regarding the path she was advocating, showed some ambivalence about it. Certainly, the efficacy with which preexisting dominant ideologies and practices of gender differentiation permeated the social changes accompanying the rise of merchant capital, even in (post-)revolutionary France, is pertinent here (Fox-Genovese and Genovese 1983: 334–36).

"Commodity Production"

In 1988, a "peasant entrepreneur" (*nongmin qiyejia*) in a Shandong village not far from one of the villages studied here told me that it was necessary to go beyond the fear of being called "capitalist." He said that the difference between socialism and capitalism lies in the ownership system, and that apart from that there is no real difference in doing business. In both systems, what is at issue is using modern management methods in order to make money.

This point of view is by no means unique—it is, indeed, a major strand within the national move toward a market economy. It is evident in officially approved publications in economics and management, and China assiduously acquired expertise in Western business-management techniques throughout the 1980s. It is perhaps more worthy of comment that this view should be so clearly expressed by someone described as a "peasant." There are several elements in both the context and the text of these words that reward closer examination, and that aid in mapping out both areas of openness and of ambiguity regarding commodity production.

The emphasis on ownership is common in contemporary Chinese discourse that tries to distinguish current Chinese economic-policy directions from capitalist ones, despite the substantial resemblances. The Chinese political economy can be declared to be socialist on the grounds that significant portions (not all) of the economy are state- or collective-owned, even if they are contracted out, and even if effective economic control is in many cases private, ambiguous, or in contention. There are sufficient levels of ownership and mechanisms of public regulation or control to argue for effective restrictions on the private market, but this is also a characteristic of mature capitalist societies.

Although the issue of ownership is considered to be decisive by some Chinese involved in current debates regarding changes in the Chinese political economy, it appears to the outsider—and, I suspect, to many Chinese—to be a formalistic and possibly empty issue. What might perhaps make the Chinese commodity economy "socialist" is better indicated by the context of the "peasant entrepreneur's" comments: he was speaking as village head (*cunzhang*) and local Communist Party branch secretary, and as the key person in devising economic growth plans for his community that could continue to make it prosper. This politicized and statist form of controlled growth in commodity production, even at the lowest rural level, is what practically implies a form of commodity production that is not immediately or simply describable as capitalist. Where some socialist element does exist, it is not in abstract considerations of ownership but in the actual embeddedness of commodity production in effective structures of communal political organization that operate on a nonmarket basis.

Nevertheless, people in contemporary China directly active in commodity production and in the reform toward a commodity economy remain uneasy about the political implications of this economic activity. The old, explicit vocabulary of socialism versus capitalism has been virtually abandoned in everyday speech (although not in official discourse and pronouncements) and seems widely viewed as vacuous or embarrassing. Certain real issues do surface but are expressed in somewhat more concrete terms. These issues include methods of management, making money, and fear of being criticized as capitalist.

The resulting political context in which commodity production in China is taking shape is one in which there is continuing official reference to "socialism" but a disjuncture between this reference and the everyday practices through which the political economy is being transformed, regardless of whether specific changes seem closer or farther from received conceptions of socialism. The terms of the formal discourse have lost their capacity to describe and to prescribe the character of the Chinese political economy, but more adequate theoretical or systematic terms have not appeared. The changes are being worked out in a still politicized but largely silent or ambiguous mode, at least as far as verbal representations are concerned. Some of the actual decisions and practices are less ambiguous, although it could be argued that there is a degree of indeterminateness about some of these as well.

Foremost among these indeterminate elements is the issue of economic growth. Economic growth is an agreed goal of both the reformers and their critics. It is essential to all relevant capitalist or socialist models for contemporary China,[3] both in terms of the internal dynamics of either type of economic system and in terms of winning a popular mandate. What is at issue, then, is the means by which economic growth is to be accomplished and the types of accommodation that will be made. How much reliance can be placed on market mechanisms? How much reliance can be placed on the mechanisms of state planning? How much increase in inequality is acceptable in the interests of overall economic growth? To what extent are restrictions on prosperity acceptable in the interests of limiting inequality?[4] As soon as these questions are raised—and even more when they are placed in the context of very concrete decisions about what types of rural economic activity to encourage, permit, or prohibit (and in each case how to do so)—it is apparent that the current rural economy is an unstable mixed economy in which most choices have, at least temporarily, an ambiguous and indeterminate quality.

Throughout the 1980s, the balance on these questions shifted toward a willingness to further develop a commodity economy and to tolerate perceptible increases in economic differentiation in the interests of higher rates of economic growth, a general (but not uniform) increase in living standards, and the prospect of prosperity in the future. This direction has not been pursued to the exclusion of other considerations: those profiting from the economic reforms are well aware of the possibility of future political reversal (of which there have been indications since the summer of 1989), and of both present and future envy on the part of the less prosperous and those less committed to the reforms. While political leaders and even comparatively low-level cadres may find it difficult to avoid committing themselves to one or another policy direction, most ordinary rural people are under less ideological pressure. All will normally find it in their best interests to ride with current policy and, if conspicuous either on grounds of political position or economic prosperity, to take steps to obtain a degree of insurance in the event of changes in either political or economic conditions.

The recent history of China has been so volatile that everyone is attuned to the temporary quality of every policy. The rapid rates of economic growth in the early 1980s were followed by a distinct slowing in the mid-1980s and a deepening economic crisis toward the end of the decade. Official assurances of a stable political and economic climate in which to pursue goals of economic prosperity were always received with reservations. Reiterated pronouncements of an overall stable policy were accompanied by concrete changes in economic policy through the 1980s, and a concerted retrenchment from 1989. Both because of prior decades of instability and because of clear indications that this pattern of instability has yet to end, the Chinese have adjusted their practical activities to this configuration of time.

As Bourdieu (1977) noted in a slightly different theoretical context, timing is critical in the enactment of practical strategies. This is so for microeconomic and micropolitical initiatives in the straightforward sense of knowing the best moment for a given action. In the present context, timing is also critical for the effective meshing of strategies that have differing time durations. If Harrell (1985) is accurate in viewing the Chinese entrepreneurial ethic as a long term one aimed at the enhancement of either a patrilineal estate or a uterine family, this is nevertheless not an ethic that can be effectively pursued with attention directed solely toward long-term goals.

Harrell's argument becomes stronger—in reference to the contemporary People's Republic—if the long-term entrepreneurial ethic is conceptualized as operating in two temporal directions. The first may be conceived of as the long-term enhancement of the well-being of one's descendants, agnatic or uterine. This is, at present, only partly a question of building an estate: it is also, importantly, a question of establishing a political background and connections that will be beneficial to one's descendants. Pursuing this goal definitely requires a long-term strategy of adapting to changing political and economic conditions. Several alternative strategies are possible, most of which involve minimizing risk-taking.[5]

However, the pursuit of long-term strategies does not obviate the utility of complementary short-term strategies. Indeed, the short duration of any particular policy favors those who are able to take quick advantage of a new policy without undue risk to their long-term positioning. An inability to pursue short-term strategies is, in the case of China, tantamount to an inability to benefit from any policy, because they are all short-lived. The ideal is effective movement from short-term to long-term advantage. This is obtainable at present, for example, by obtaining nonagricultural registration status for one's children or, to cite a more generally achievable method in rural China, by acquiring enough wealth to build one or more fine new houses, a form of tangible affluence that is durable and unlikely to be lost.

Rural Chinese certainly do have a repertoire of strategies for economic mobility (Harrell 1983: 219) as part of their practical knowledge of everyday living, and even if it is not astute to express this openly, it is nevertheless substantially conscious and shared knowledge. This cultural context is important in interpreting the enthusiasm with which rural Chinese have embraced many aspects of the reform program, while also actively retaining elements of the preexisting collective system and socialist ideology.

During the 1980s, the market has been seen by many in China, with more than a little encouragement from official policymakers, as a fast solution to China's long-term and difficult economic problems (see Hsu 1985). It is important to remember that the popular legitimacy of earlier policies—not only those of the early 1950s, but also those extending through the Cultural Revolution—was firmly based on the aims and on the claims of these policies to promote prosperity and to improve the people's livelihood. The economic reform movement drew upon widespread frustrated hopes by making claims that much more would have been accomplished during those decades with different economic policies, policies that the reform program was about to provide.

Some of the faith in the economic reform program is not new; rather, it is a transferral of earlier hopes for prosperity through socialism to hopes for prosperity through the market. To the extent that those pursuing these policies are doing so in the interests of social entities that transcend themselves, especially in initiating and managing large-scale rural enterprises, these people can justifiably claim to be pursuing goals that differ little from the goals of comparable collective-run enterprises. The value placed on the "socialist entrepreneur" in the 1980s is less internally contradictory than might initially be supposed.[6]

However, regardless of the immediate milieus and motivations of

China's new entrepreneurs and more ordinary citizens caught up in the everyday workings of an increasingly ubiquitous market, the structure and dynamics of the larger commodity economy are indirectly but effectively transforming the economic basis of the society. It is for this reason that the models of petty commodity production and petty capitalist production are being used in this analysis. The determining forces of the transformation now in process in China are centered at an enormous social distance from the peasants whose lives are the subject of this study. They must construct their lives within the framework of the possibilities allowed by this transformation. It would be entirely misleading to present or to perceive that transformation as being driven by peasant entrepreneurial behavior, although it is true that rural entrepreneurs are a force within this altered social field and that they are active agents in the transformation.

The rural entrepreneurs themselves partake of several different qualities, and some more closely approximate the official ideal of the "socialist entrepreneur" than do others. There are signs of a restructuring of class in the countryside, and of incipient class conflict. As the rewards for the entrepreneur become open and avowedly legitimate, and as the unit in whose interests the entrepreneur works becomes more restricted, a divergence from the socialist model is more apparent. Where the unit is simply a small household-based enterprise, as most are, the situation closely resembles that of a traditional peasant endeavor to establish or maintain a familial estate; moreover, in the more commoditized economic context of the past decade, such a situation approaches (bourgeois) individual entrepreneurship to a problematic degree. The very emphasis on defining entrepreneurs and entrepreneurial units on something other than an individual basis, even if that is only a household basis, as in state-recognized "specialized households" (*zhuanye hu*), serves to underline this political difficulty and to highlight the ideologized quality of the household as an economic unit.

There are also factors that act to restrict the market. There is a sense in which people's goals transcend individual interests, although often extending only to household and descendants. There is also a sense in which people are wary of the political repercussions of present economic success that might follow future policy changes. These changes are unpredictable in detail and timing but are widely, perhaps universally, viewed as inevitable. These factors act to restrict the scope of the market and to encourage caution and secrecy in market activities, but they have by no means prevented widespread and intense market activity.

Indeed, I would argue that the temporary quality of the market-oriented prosperity of the 1980s acted less as a retardant than as a spur to intense market activity. The perception and the actuality that the opportunities provided would be very brief encouraged maximum involvement and a willingness to take quick profits. Indeed, the political economy strongly favored precisely short-term economic activity, including officially disapproved forms of commerce.[7] The profits from these could be converted to safer economic or noneconomic "investments" and thereby protected, or so those engaged in such business could reasonably hope.

For these reasons—together with the more obvious ones presented by enhanced prosperity for a rural population that has for decades (or, more accurately, for centuries) known little comfort or security—the onward rush to "become rich," and to "become rich first," is no surprise. Wealth is a long-standing value in Chinese society, despite Confucian denials, and people are once again free to cultivate it. They are doing so with great assiduity. They seek whatever economic avenues they can find, work formidably long hours, build "connections" and make commercial deals where they can, and glorify their success, or even their hopes, with elegant flourishes on new homes built in a style formerly exclusive to the richest of peasants. The character for prosperity (*fu*) or a picture portraying it on the wall (*bimen*) inside the entry to a domestic courtyard has become a common feature of new rural houses in Shandong.

In the expanding commodity economy, money is highly valued and significantly contested.[8] Behind a common, but also commonly breached, reluctance to speak of money openly, everyone agrees that everyone takes money prominently into consideration in all manner of interactions. It is, perhaps, a more complex subject in directly commercial contexts than in some other cultures, because commercial norms are not well established and there are significant areas of uncertainty (and lack of trust) in business dealings. In rural life, the commercial and noncommercial dimensions of life are impossible to separate strictly, and the sphere of the commercial has increased.

Money, and shifting norms and practices regarding it, are a significant part of everyday life in rural China, and one about which feelings are very strong. The intensity of concern about money is marked by pervasive small talk in which the price of goods figures as a constant topic of conversation. The concern is still more strongly marked by a reluctance to talk about money in contexts where it might be a potential source of dispute. The importance of acquiring and having money, and the fact that one person having more of it may be directly related to someone else having less, lie behind excessive talk about the small matters of money (the price of tomatoes in various markets) and reluctance even to raise the issue of money in highly important contexts (wage or salary levels).[9]

Money symbolically represents, and often enables, the realization of more than strictly economic aspirations. One need not underestimate the importance of the economic to observe that the strong attraction of many or most rural Chinese toward the commodity production system and the market has other very important sources. The reform program's implications in terms of devolution of power are complex and in the process of being worked out in practice. It appears highly unlikely that the reforms will significantly weaken state power as a whole, but they are restructuring state power in some far-reaching ways. To the extent that the move toward a market has weakened the arbitrary power of administrative organs of the government, and of some levels of officialdom, ordinary peasants experience the change as a highly desirable increase in their own personal autonomy. This is a material change grounded in immediate political and economic realities, but it is of a somewhat different quality than the income-oriented advantages already discussed. The advocates of reform have emphasized this dimension of the reform program, and it is one that has met with popular welcome. At the same time, the reform program's market orientation has created attractive opportunities for many cadres and former cadres, so their interests are not necessarily threatened by it and they do not always oppose it.

The extent to which ordinary rural residents are acquiring more autonomy in their lives remains an open question. The autonomy gained may be much less than hoped, but the hope itself and the changes in this direction that have come with the reform movement are powerful forces in this cultural field. In the economic sphere, peasants in household-based enterprises may work very hard but be more willing to do so, both for themselves and in hopes of future benefits for their households, than under alternative, larger-scale forms of economic organization.[10] Their willingness may amount to a form of extreme self-exploitation, but the force of this willingness to work in a milieu perceived as more autonomous contributes to the popular basis of the reform movement in the countryside. This quest for freedom has been openly admitted and encouraged. It has not been rejected as bourgeois, despite historical and possible future connections between ideologies of freedom and the rise of bourgeoisies. Instead, it has been possible to define this quest politically as a popular resistance to "feudal" statist and bureaucratic practices, and therefore as a trend that supports "socialism."

For a multiplicity of reasons, a commodity economy offers much to Chinese peasants that resonates with values long and deeply held. Questions about the role of a commodity economy within socialism, even "socialism in its initial stage," as it has recently been termed in China, remain problematic. These issues involve national and international levels of economic organization, and the determining factors lie, for the most part, well beyond the scope of this rural study.[11]

The types of commodity production discussed here are continuations or alterations of handicrafts, artisanal production, putting-out systems,[12] cash-crop production, courtyard production of vegetables and domestic animals, and relatively small-scale commerce. These are all activities that could be found long ago in Chinese villages as essential components in a variegated repertoire of strategies for making a living. Fei Xiaotong (1983) pointed early to the importance of nonagricultural sources of livelihood for the peasantry. Even during the collective era, some of these activities—especially courtyard production of vegetables and domestic animals—were encouraged, but within limits and within the context of denying that the products were commodities (Croll 1982). Certainly, a large portion of these products was consumed within the household; ideally, the remainder was produced within the plan and marketed through controlled channels.

Household-based production on the margins of the collective economy was an especially significant part of women's economic contribution during the collective era (M. Wolf 1985). This prompts questions regarding the reform program's implications for rural patterns of division of labor by gender and for the relative economic positions of women and men (see Andors 1981, Croll 1982, 1987b, Davin 1988). At the same time, the reform program also raises questions about and has provoked changes in the dynamics of class.

Household-based Commodity Production

Commodity production in Chinese households is now standard rather than exceptional. Most households are also engaged in some subsistence production and in production designed to meet state tax demands, but households must involve themselves in commodity production and exchange if they are to meet the full range of their needs, and especially if they are to achieve a degree of material comfort or prosperity. Active involvement in the commodity economy was one of the more widely available and actively sought means of achieving economic mobility in the Chinese countryside during the 1980s.[13]

Access to the commodity economy is regionally variable. Although it is true that people in less favored parts of China, principally the interior provinces, are more free than before the reform program to migrate in search of opportunities elsewhere, such migration is usually temporary, restricted to certain sectors of the population (primarily male), and often less attractive than opportunities in a more prosperous home area. Most of Shandong is well situated for the development of a commodity economy. Aside from ripple effects from coastal and urban areas, even ordinary rural communities (exclusive of the mountainous regions) enjoy comparatively favorable conditions of access to goods and markets.

The data base for this chapter is primarily the three villages of Zhangjiachedao, Qianrulin, and Huaili, although data from briefer visits to three other villages in Dezhou Prefecture are also used. All these villages are located toward the middle of a continuum that reaches from relatively isolated, poor communities that are less involved in the commodity economy, at one extreme, to highly prosperous villages in the developing coastal regions or in the suburbs of major cities, at the other. All these villages are somewhat more prosperous than the average, and all have a weak agricultural land basis that makes them particularly reliant on the growth of nonagricultural production.

Each of the three villages more intensively studied has its own history of involvement in commodity production reaching back before 1949. In Zhangjiachedao this most notably consisted of household-based silk weaving on a putting-out basis. Qianrulin had a number of men involved in small-scale commerce or working as artisans. Huaili had artisans and a history of market vegetable production. Each village also had variations on the usual mix of rural nonagricultural occupations (see M. Yang 1945) and scattered household sidelines, such as raising domestic animals within courtyards.[14]

Prior involvement in commodity production has fed into the recent history of each of the three villages, but in distinctly different ways. Qianrulin has remained collective and strongly discourages business activities outside the scope of the collective while encouraging village-level business operations. Although the village shop has been contracted out to the village's longtime storekeeper, all the other village enterprises are directly owned and operated collectively at the village level, or by the village in association with extravillage entities. The established commercial skills of several of the older men in the village have been put to work for the collective by making them commissioned sales and procurement personnel for the village's larger enterprises.

Zhangjiachedao has less of a history in commerce and appears not to have inherited a body of experienced salesmen. The village has a few men who independently engage in commerce, some selling the products of the village's main factory, and some who work as artisans or shopkeepers. Some of the women produce net bags and various types of twine and rope on a putting-out basis. The village leadership is untroubled by the presence of independent productive and commercial activities in the village, and simply allows them to be overwhelmed by the successful village-level enterprises. The one man in the village with an extensive personal history in the weaving business before 1949 was incorporated into early efforts to develop weaving in the village, but he is now elderly and has not been involved in the village's economic growth during the 1980s.

Huaili entered the era of decollectivization with a more scattered and small-scale experience in the market and with little in the way of collective assets. A combination of several factors—pressure to decollectivize, a limited village-level nonagricultural economic basis, considerable surplus labor, and a favorable commercial site[15]—have allowed it to develop an economy emphasizing small-scale household-based enterprises. Huaili's household-based commodity economy will be the basis of this segment of the discussion, although the small household enterprises of the other Shandong villages studied are similar and pertinent.

Households in Huaili can be involved in the commodity economy at several levels. The simplest and most pervasive level consists of very small-scale raising of animals and growing of vegetables for the market and is similar to the domestic sidelines of the collective era. This level of activity is typical of ordinary "rural households" (*nonghu*), which will be referred to here as *nonspecialized households* to facilitate comparison. At the next level, a person or household has a substantial income-generating enterprise, but one that does not remove all members of the household from agricultural work and that can typically be carried on with only the household's own labor. This category consists of *self-defined specialized households*, which are a prime subject of interest when considering the growth of petty commodity production in rural China. At a still higher level, all members of a household are removed from agricultural work and there is probably some hired labor involved in the enterprise. These are the *state-recognized specialized households*, which are of interest when considering both petty commodity production and a transition to petty capitalist production.[16]

All three of these forms of economic enterprise are referred to in China as "commodity production" (*shangpin shengchan*), although the smallest-scale activities in the first category are often more simply described by the older term, "domestic sideline" (*jiating fuye*). All three are part of an increasingly commoditized economic system, but the change is greatest for those of larger scale and those which involve economic activity that would have been difficult or impossible to pursue on a household basis before the reforms. Emphasis on promoting commodity production is dependent on the further development of the latter two categories but is expressed more broadly in terms of expanding the quantity of goods produced for the market. This represents a shift from emphasizing increased production in itself—and, by implication, associated use-values—to emphasizing the sale of goods, and therefore their exchange value.

To a considerable extent, what is referred to as commodity production is less a matter of *production* than it is of *commerce*. Many of the most successful household enterprises are specifically involved in marketing, and this is where much of the greatest profit is to be made. Nevertheless, the norms of orthodox political discourse in China require that the expressed emphasis be on production. This requirement is enhanced by the fact that, although ordinary commerce is legitimate, there are many areas of commerce that are of dubious legality but very lucrative. The conflation of production and commerce is also possible because many of the economic activities involved combine the two. These include common forms of activity (raising pigs for the market) as well as less widespread ones characteristic of households in which commodity production assumes a greater role, such as the processing and sale of food items (dehydrated noodles, sesame oil). It is these households involved in commodity production on a larger scale—those which by differing criteria can be categorized as specialized households—that are the central subject in this chapter.

Virtually every household in Huaili, with the exception of the handful of state-recognized specialized households, is actively involved in some form of domestic sideline that marginally involves it in the commodity production economy. This most commonly takes the form of raising a few animals in the household courtyard. This is a nearly universal pattern in the Chinese countryside wherever conditions permit. Pigs are raised in most households in Huaili to the limit of affordable fodder supplies, and this, too, is a common constraint. Qianrulin and Zhangjiachedao also raise pigs, but Zhangjiachedao has a large shortfall in fodder; most households in Zhangjiachedao find it more advantageous to raise chickens, primarily for eggs to be either eaten or sold in local periodic markets. Pigs and chickens are the most widely raised animals in these villages, but other animals are occasionally selected, especially goats, sheep, geese, and, near Hui areas, beef cattle.

Pig-raising in Huaili in 1989 may serve as an example. Some households that had recently raised goats, sheep, or chickens switched to raising pigs in response to rising demand and prices for pigs.[17] There was widespread agreement in the village that raising pigs was a good source of income. The exact amount to be made depends on some predictable factors, such as seasonal price changes, and some less predictable ones, such as market fluctuations in the price of piglets, fodder, and pigs. In the spring of 1988, small piglets weighing up to 30 jin cost about RMB 1.3 per jin, and ones of about 50 jin cost about RMB 1.5 per jin. Six or seven months later, a 300-jin pig could be sold in early 1989 for RMB 2.15 per jin.

The profit made depends largely on fodder costs and is perceived as depending almost entirely on this one factor, since labor costs are not calculated. Virtually every household has labor available to tend pigs that probably could not be used in any other income-earning activity, except tending some other type of animal that would also require fodder. By the summer of 1989, the price of fodder was rising, and this was the actual limiting factor on the number of pigs a household could raise, because it was not economically attractive to feed pigs with purchased fodder.

A common cropping practice in Huaili (subject to crop rotation) is to plant winter wheat and summer corn on a portion of a given household's land. The wheat provides the household's tax and food grain; the corn provides fodder. Households purchase fodder for their pigs only as a supplement to household-produced supplies. The cost of fodder (including that raised within a household) is deducted from the price each pig brings, but still allows for a net income of RMB 100–200 for each pig sold.[18] Thus the capacity of each household to raise pigs is normally restricted by its level of corn production. In 1989, the Huaili household most active in pig production, with nine pigs to raise at one time, relied heavily on wild grass collected by the adult woman of the household. This was also the choice made by a household heavily engaged in raising goats, although the small herd of goats was also taken out to graze along the sides of paths and streams by the senior man in that household.

In short, pig-raising is attractive to residents of Huaili, but limits on affordable fodder in the area prevent it from becoming an avenue for significant expansion. The same restriction applies to other large animals, including draft animals. Chickens pose less of a fodder problem but are vulnerable to diseases. This restricts most households to only a few chickens, rarely more than twenty at a time. Courtyard animal husbandry is widely practiced and can contribute noticeably to household income but lacks the conditions that could make this a promising avenue for expansion. It is likely to remain a mainstay of domestic economy, but no more than this.

The other very common commodity produced in Huaili households is vegetable produce. Virtually every household in Huaili gains some income from vegetable production, but the range is more variable than in pig-raising. The area of land formerly used in Huaili as "private plots" (*ziliudi*) is still allocated and cultivated in much the same way. It is now called "vegetable land" (*caidi*), but little has changed except the encompassing context of increased market potential. Households almost always use this plot of land for vegetable production, to meet their own needs for vegetable consumption and to provide some additional cash income.

The extent to which additional income can be generated from the production and sale of vegetables is less uniformly restricted than in the case of animal husbandry. The intensity of cultivation, especially the number of vegetable crops in each year, is variable. Additional land may be put into vegetable cultivation, either if less grain or cotton is grown on the household's main land allotment, or if the household has a cultivable courtyard that is not being used for some incompatible purpose. (Goats and chickens preempt courtyard vegetable cultivation unless securely penned.) Commodity production of vegetables is an area in which many households in Huaili still have some underutilized potential. Courtyards vary in suitability for cultivation, and households vary in the intensity with which they take advantage of this possibility. A focus of recent economic initiatives through the Women's Federations has been to mobilize rural women who lack other favorable income-earning opportunities to cultivate their courtyards in vegetables, and to do so intensively.

Huaili is unusual in possessing a highly marketable resource in *xiangchun* trees. The leaves of this variety of tree are an edible delicacy. Huaili is in the favorable position of being able to market its leaves with the claim that the Dowager Empress Cixi found that Huaili xiangchun were the best in China—she would eat only Huaili's xiangchun. Xiangchun cultivation requires some room, and thus competes with animals and vegetables for space in courtyards, but the trees do not require extensive care. They produce edible leaves three years after planting, so Huaili's recent organized effort to increase xiangchun planting will soon result in a dramatic increase in production. Many households in Huaili have xiangchun trees, most of which are grown in courtyards, although this remains a resource that can be developed further. It is not presently a significant contributor to most household incomes because even households with mature xiangchun often choose to use their limited supply for their own consumption and for gifts.

Some indication of the variation in these small forms of household commodity production is provided in Table 4.1, which gives 1989 figures for cultivation of xiangchun trees and courtyard cultivation of vegetables in Huaili for the three categories of household already discussed. Although some instances of nonactivity reflect lack of suitable conditions (such as a fertile courtyard) or use of the courtyard for domestic animals or for another space-consuming economic pursuit (such as producing sesame oil), increases in activity could be obtained, especially in xiangchun cultivation in nonspecialized households. The case of state-recognized specialized households is different. A few of these

TABLE 4.1

Xiangchun *and Courtyard Vegetable Production by
Household Category in the Village of Huaili, 1989*

Courtyard product	Household category								
	Nonspecialized households (n = 18)			Self-defined specialized households (n = 13)			State-recognized specialized households (n = 9)		
	Y	N	DK	Y	N	DK	Y	N	DK
Xiangchun trees	13	5	0	8	2	3	0	1	8
Vegetables	7	8	3	2	5	6	0	7	2

NOTE: Xiangchun is a variety of tree whose leaves are an edible delicacy. *Self-defined specialized households* are those that informally defined themselves as specialized on the basis of their small form(s) of household commodity production; thus this is an intermediate category between non-specialized households and *state-recognized specialized households*, which include only those households formally recognized by the state as "specialized" on the basis of meeting state criteria for significant and successful specialization in an area of economic activity. Y = yes, N = no, DK = don't know.

households could expand in these areas but prefer to concentrate on more profitable pursuits. More commonly, these households use their entire courtyard for their specialized endeavor and have no extra space; alternatively, if the household has both a shop and a separate home, household members are in actual residence in a living area attached to the shop and only rarely in their own homes. The intermediate category of self-defined specialized households resembles that of nonspecialized households in these fields of sideline production.

Nonspecialized households' activities in the commodity economy are not entirely restricted to production. Most adult men engage in some amount of "purchase and resale of vegetables" (*fancai*) in local markets on an occasional and small-scale basis. Women, especially young unmarried women, often sell the household's own surplus vegetables in the market in a neighboring village. Larger-scale commerce also occurs in the countryside but is not usually within the range of the ordinary rural households.

The commodity economy activities discussed thus far are not ones that imply restructuring of the rural economy. Because these activities are now taking place within a political context that encourages them, and within a commercial context that has greater marketing opportunities than in the past, there has been room for quantitative growth. This growth was visible in Huaili in the 1980s, although it was stalling toward the end of the decade as the overall Chinese economy encountered setbacks. To achieve greater prosperity and to establish it on a sound basis, the residents of villages such as Huaili require more than enhanced marketing opportunities for familiar household sidelines. One of the significant possibilities for qualitative change available in the 1980s was to transform a household-based economy both by developing additional types of economic endeavor, still on a household basis, and by carrying out these activities on a larger scale. Huaili particularly encouraged this economic choice on the part of a large number of households in the village.

Following the 1984 division of the land in Huaili, there was a rapid growth in the number of households that carried out some type of independent nonagricultural "project" (*xiangmu*). In 1985, there were 38 households with their own projects; in 1986, there were 52; in 1987, there were 81; and in 1988, there were 92. Toward the end of the decade economic conditions did not favor the initiation of new projects, although a few did go forward, some households successfully shifted from one to another line of business, and there were a few cases of expansion. Most household enterprises were managing to continue, although with less profit and more difficulty than in the mid-1980s.

The range of projects involved in this expansion of commodity production and commerce included: running retail and wholesale shops selling nonstaple foods; setting tables out by the roadside selling everyday goods (cigarettes, liquor, soap powder, candy); running restaurants and hotels; making false teeth; repairing watches; repairing bicycles; butchering meat; photography; making decorative (painted) mirrors; beekeeping; processing food products (bean curd, dried noodles, sesame oil); peddling clothing, shoes, or household goods in rotating markets; sewing; providing mechanized transport (by tractor); and growing mushrooms. Some of these activities can be performed on a range of scales and are not necessarily full-time activities for a whole household, or even for some household members. Others can only be carried out by a household that has made a substantial commitment of time and material resources and that has removed itself from agricultural labor (or that eventually reaches that stage). The latter are specialized households, one of the significant new forms in the emergent rural commodity economy.

Specialized Households

Specialized households represent an organizational vehicle through which *some* rural households are mobilized (more than others) as a force in developing a rural commodity economy. Specialized households are based on the same organizational and ideological supports that encourage the wider development of household-based commodity production, but mark a move toward increased specialization in economic activity and increased orientation toward the market.

The institution of state-recognized specialized households has been intended to harness the energies of the economically strongest rural households. By dissolving collective institutions and allowing households to compete and prosper in market milieux, this policy has been a pillar of the program of stimulating rural economic growth through allowing some "to get rich first." This is based on the premise that specialized households are more effective entrepreneurial units than are collectives. Official assumptions are made that their prosperity will create a degree of economic growth that, even if uneven, will have "trickle down" effects for nonspecialized households. Official confidence in this approach has been materially demonstrated by some (variable) programs of state economic incentive for households that could meet (again varying) official criteria for becoming specialized.

Specialized households are, most simply, those that have successfully specialized in one particular rural economic pursuit, and that have been officially recognized as having done so. Some state-recognized specialized households are agricultural, usually producing one particular crop on a comparatively large scale and on a disproportionately large portion of land. However, most specialize in nonagricultural pursuits, which are less constrained by land shortages and are usually more profitable than farming. Specialization and economic success are necessary but not sufficient conditions for categorization as a state-recognized specialized household (*zhuanye hu*). It should be no surprise to find that the state is once again involved in the definition of rural socioeconomic units, and especially ones that have a major role to play in reform economic policy. An officially recognized specialized household has a different relationship to the state than does an ordinary rural household—a relationship expressed primarily in economic terms, through different provisions for taxation and access to state economic resources.

Beyond these general principles for defining the character of specialized households, official guidelines have been established for clarifying the boundary between specialized households and nonspecialized households. These boundaries have not, in fact, remained clear, but an example may nevertheless serve to indicate the criteria used. A decision of the Rural Policy Research Office of the Chinese Communist Party Secretariat, dated October 13, 1984, decreed that state-recognized specialized households were those that met the following criteria: (1) most of their labor power is concentrated in a specialized production project, or such production takes at least 60 percent of the household's labor time; (2) income from the specialized endeavor must account for at least 60 percent of the household's gross income; (3) the commoditization rate of the specialized production must be at least 80 percent if nonagricultural, or at least 60 percent if agricultural; and (4) income from the sale of goods or services must be at least twice that of the average rural household in the household's county ("Zhonggong" 1985: 1).

Discussion and analysis[19] of specialized households has not, unfortunately, been possible in such clear terms—both policies and statistics based on them have been uncertain and shifting. Still, the general scale of the phenomenon and its relative importance in Shandong can be fairly indicated by Conroy's tabulations for 1983–84. These indicate that 13 percent of all rural households in China were recognized as specialized or key[20] households in January 1984, and that the comparable percentage in Shandong was 20.9 percent in June 1983 (Conroy 1984: 14). State-recognized specialized households are even more significant than these considerable proportions indicate, of course, because they are the wealthiest and most entrepreneurial in this household-oriented commodity economy.

The phenomenon of specialized households has raised questions of growing economic inequity in rural China. This is a problem that is openly admitted, officially and unofficially, within China, although it is commonly discussed under the rubric of "polarization" (*liangji fenhua*), a term that obscures as much as it reveals. Polarization adequately, and even strongly, expresses the growing differences in wealth now appearing, for the most part (but not exclusively) legitimately, throughout China in the reform era. The term does not, however, imply or lead in any clear fashion to an analysis in terms of socioeconomic structure, either in terms of class or of gender.

During my second visit to Huaili, in the summer of 1989, I investigated household commodity production and specialized households with the general object of furthering such an analysis, and with the specific purpose of examining the implications of the local Women's Federation initiative of involving women more intensively in commodity production. The 40 households in my sample during that year included households following the full range of economic alternatives available in Huaili at that time.[21] The sample specifically included all the state-recognized specialized households (n = 9). A senior member of each household in the sample was asked to identify his or her household as being specialized or not. Members of households with thriving economic projects preferred to identify themselves as specialized households, and this led to my identification of a category of self-defined (but not formally recognized) specialized households (n = 13). The remaining households (n = 18) were unambiguously nonspecialized.

I also included in the sample of 40 all households (n = 12) in which there were women who were especially active in the commodity economy, and all households (n = 6) in which there were women who were active in the political life of the village. The latter women are relevant because their political involvement in every case consisted of activity in the village women's organization—activity revolving around increasing the participation of women in the commodity economy.

According to current local standards, as expressed by village officials, state-recognized specialized households are those which are so specialized and successful in nonagricultural pursuits that they have given up their land allocations and pay a nonagricultural tax in place of the agricultural tax attached to land allotments. The large number of villagers who reported themselves as belonging to specialized households *not* included by these criteria led me to question the significance of the official boundary. Examination of the data, however, resulted in my concluding that there is a meaningful difference between state-recognized specialized households and self-defined specialized households, and that this difference extends beyond factors deriving directly from official recognition. The boundary is, nevertheless, somewhat arbitrary by at least one major criterion: some of the wealthier households in the village are not officially defined as specialized, essentially because they are still significantly involved in agricultural work.

The households in Huaili that are state-recognized specialized

TABLE 4.2

Landholdings of, and Labor Hired by, State-Recognized versus
Self-Defined Specialized Households in the Village of Huaili, 1989

Project(s)	Land[a] (mu)	Hired labor[b]
State-recognized specialized households		
1. Restaurant	0	4
2. Mirror production/restaurant/shop	0	2
3. Wholesale	0	6
4. Wholesale/factory manager	0.5/0.5	1 (wholesale)
5. False teeth	3.5/3.5	0
6. Mushrooms	3.0/2.8	2
7. Hotel/shop	3.0/3.0	0
8. Restaurant	3.0/3.0	5–7
9. Sewing/cycle repair	1.5/1.5	2 (sewing)
Self-defined specialized households		
10. Shop	3.0/2.0	0
11. Shop	5.8	0
12. Noodles	5.5	0
13. Chickens/pigs	4.2/4.0	0
14. Beekeeping	6.0	0
15. Tractor transport	7.2	0
16. Aluminum goods peddlar	4.1	0
17. Shop/lunchbar	2.3	1
18. Sesame oil/shop	6.4	0
19. Sesame oil	5.85	0
20. Cycle repair	7.6	0
21. Clothes retail	3.7	0
22. Building contractor	9.7	34

[a]The first figure for land is the total number of mu allocated to a given household; the second figure is the amount of that total which was temporarily contracted out.
[b]The numbers of hired laborers are approximate and should be read as maximum figures: most of the labor hired varies with season and levels of business activity; few are hired for the full year.

households are presented in Table 4.2 in the order in which they were originally cited by village officials. This order would appear to represent a progression from unambiguous and established specialized-household status toward somewhat more marginal status, as measured by landholdings. The list of self-defined specialized households in Table 4.2 is in purely arbitrary order.

Certain of these cases immediately appear unusual or even anomalous. Household 13 should, by the prime criterion of landholding, be classed with the state-recognized specialized households, and I suspect that it had been so classed the previous year. I visited this household in both 1988 and 1989; at the time of the first visit, it was a conspicuously successful household that had developed a small but growing chicken factory in storage buildings within the household courtyard. This enterprise had peaked at 1,000 chickens in 1988 and had then been discontinued due to a combination of problems with supply of chicks, fodder costs, and chicken disease. At the time of fieldwork in 1989, the woman of the household was raising nine mature pigs, largely fed by wild grass that she collected, and her husband was seeking attractive business opportunities in which to invest the earlier profits from the chicken enterprise.

This case is indicative of several significant elements in the configuration of state-recognized specialized households. The most firmly established are those that have definitively renounced their access to land in the village land allotment. Households take this step cautiously and prefer to begin by contracting out land on a temporary basis; business is always a risky matter, and the late 1980s were years of an increasingly unstable and unfavorable business climate.

The most successful rural entrepreneurs were those who were able to keep a close eye on business trends and to shift from one endeavor to another at the most rewarding time. Household 4 had quickly become one of the wealthiest households in Huaili by starting early in the wholesale business, but by 1989 it had left wholesaling (volume and profits were declining). The husband had accepted a position as a factory manager, while his wife had retired from business and was consolidating the household's position in the community through generous gifts of her time to the village women's organization and through granting interest-free loans to fellow villagers for both investment and personal purposes.[22]

Other specialized households, both state-recognized and self-defined, have also made recent changes, but their decisions to expand in 1988–89 (Household 3 opened a second wholesale outlet; Household 7 opened a hotel) were risky and may prove less advantageous than the retrenchment chosen by others. Household 10 is a retail shop that expanded (to become a shop) in recent years. Retail is a highly competitive area of commerce with a low profit margin, so it is unlikely that this shop will be able to expand further in the immediate future. The quantity of business for the village's skilled seamstress in Household 9 has been dropping, too, in recent years, in response to more ready-made clothing on the market and to the general downturn in business. Her own response has been to hire fewer apprentices and not to keep any past their term of apprenticeship.

The hiring of labor is a highly significant factor that in most cases coincides with the distinction between state-recognized specialized households and self-defined ones. The glaring anomaly here is Household 22, which would very likely be officially recognized as specialized were it not that the specialized activity in the household depends wholly on the husband, while the wife makes a significant contribution to the household's income by working an unusually large amount of land almost entirely by herself. The particular nature of the household's specialized activity is one in which she cannot fully share, given conventional patterns of gender division of labor, and she has not taken the early retirement option chosen by the wife in Household 4.

The large number of hired laborers cited for Household 22 (an approximation of the most recent seasonal maximum) is less an indicator of its scale of operations than of its particular character. This household enterprise is essentially one of labor contracting, based on the household head's own trade as a carpenter and on his organizational ability. He has no means of production or capital that he deploys in his enterprise, so it does not strictly meet the definition of a capitalist enterprise in which labor power and means of production are brought together by the owner of the latter, who is then able to appropriate the surplus value produced by the laborers he has hired. Instead, his enterprise is one of contracting strictly for the labor involved in building. Local people intending to build a house or shop procure the building materials themselves and call upon whatever labor resources they can. The remainder, including the skilled carpentry and masonry work, is then contracted to someone such as this man, who appears to have all the village's business. The contractor hires skilled and unskilled workers according to the contracts available, and pays them subject to the condition that payment is received from the contracting party. He is never in the position of advancing either materials or wages. The men he hires could all seek work elsewhere, but may receive more and more reliable work by staying with him. Hence his capacity to provide steady employment and his own trade as an artisan are the basis of his enterprise's income. This provides him with a better income than he would earn working as an independent carpenter, but may not be as lucrative as the profits to be made in more thoroughly commercial sectors of the commodity economy.

The other employers of hired labor in Huaili are more straightforwardly engaged in petty capitalist production than in petty commodity production. The hiring of labor and appropriation of surplus labor are intrinsic to the economic viability of the productive or commercial capitalist enterprises involved, and each of those enterprises has means of production on which the hired labor is dependent. This can be underlined by reference, again, to the households that appear exceptional in Table 4.2.

Household 17 is especially illuminating because both its enterprises are run by the woman household head, whose husband is in nonagricultural employment outside the village. The very small retail shop is open irregularly and, as usual with such small endeavors, is not very profitable. It runs for the most part on the labor of the woman's elderly but still able father, who lives with her for half of each year. The more interesting enterprise is the lunchbar that she opens seasonally. Here she is taking entrepreneurial advantage of the chance location of her home next to an open space that serves seasonally as a cotton depot. During the season when cotton is being transported to and from this depot, she hires a part-time cook and turns the shop into a lunchbar to serve simple, convenient meals to the people fortuitously brought to her doorstep. The woman herself is the prime entrepreneurial agent behind both the shop and the lunchbar, but she has no special skill and does not work in either enterprise except in a managerial sense. This household is similar in economic character to the state-recognized specialized households that hire labor, but its enterprises are very small; moreover, the household still works land and makes the most of courtyard vegetable production in a diversified move toward greater prosperity.

With two exceptions, all the state-recognized specialized households hire labor in their enterprises. Household 7 does not hire labor but would have to do so if all its recently expanded hotel space were being utilized. The present scale of its hotel business and small shop does not exceed what the household can manage with its own labor. The other officially defined specialized household that does not hire labor is Household 5, whose enterprise is entirely dependent on the artisanal skill of the woman of the household, who was trained by her father, through several years of apprenticeship, to make false teeth. She still undertakes a considerable amount of his contracted work and is not yet in a position to take on apprentices even if the scale of local business warranted doing so. The household has managed some expansion because her husband has taught himself to do extractions, as well as marketing his wife's work and doing some of the less skilled work for her, but this enterprise is too dependent on limited expertise to lend itself to hiring labor (in marked contrast to the potential for hiring labor in the building trades).

The hiring of labor on the part of some households in Huaili, especially state-recognized specialized households, signifies a qualitative change from petty commodity production to petty capitalist production. The households hiring labor are incorporating capitalist relations directly into their productive (or commercial) enterprises and are not involved in capitalist relations solely within the sphere of reproduction. This shift is not one that is commented on in the village or in the households themselves. The terms in which the commodity economy are discussed in China at the present time do not include this distinction. Participation even in petty commodity production can be, and has been, denounced as capitalist in the recent past. The step toward hiring labor appears to be viewed in the village as a matter of expanding an enterprise, and perhaps of achieving some lightening of the work load of household members (especially women). There is no sign of a conscious decision to promote this qualitative change, although growth in household projects and the health of the commodity economy are accepted and encouraged as contributing to prosperity.

A review of Table 4.2 shows several characteristics of household commodity production as found in Huaili. Unlike the situation in some other localities, there are no state-recognized specialized households that are concentrated in agricultural production. This is related to the relatively common rural plight of a severe shortage of agricultural land and a distinct surplus of labor. The core of Huaili's strategy in commodity production has been to promote nonagricultural household-based projects that could utilize un- or underemployed household labor to increase household income. Although I heard some comment from officials at township and county levels about the desirability, in their eyes, of adjusting landholdings toward a pattern of greater concentration (so that some people would have more land while others would have less, or none), there is little movement in this direction in Huaili and no indication that it is a major objective of village economic policy.

But neither is there an emphasis on state-recognized specialized households as employers of extrahousehold surplus labor. The employment generated by these households is not significant in terms of the numbers of people employed, wages, or security. Indeed, many of those employed come from outside the village (some are matrilaterally related to the employing households), and except in the case of skilled workers, all are young and temporary. The building contractor does provide stable employment for a number of men, some of whom are Huaili residents, but his enterprise could easily be run by the village itself, as comparable building teams are in Zhangjiachedao and in Qianrulin. At the village level Huaili does run another, less skilled labor-contracting enterprise (transport), which absorbs much of the less skilled surplus male labor in the village. In short, specialized households are favored not as avenues for creating employment but as avenues for creating self-employment.[23]

Members of both state-recognized and self-defined specialized households firmly stated that they received no official business incentives. This was evidently a genuine sentiment, and accurate in the sense that former special provisions to aid state-recognized specialized households were no longer in effect. These households considered themselves to be on their own economically, and although the point was not made in quite such explicit terms, state-recognized specialized households may even have been at a distinct disadvantage compared with the others, in that their status made it more difficult to practice tax evasion.[24]

Nevertheless, commodity production is given significant direct and indirect economic support at the village level. The indirect support reaches all village households, but disproportionately favors those with nonagricultural projects by relieving villagers of all tax obligations other than the agricultural tax due to the state (or the nonagricultural tax paid in lieu of it by the few landless households). The village meets all its expenses through income from small enterprises, such as a grain mill and a restaurant, which it either runs directly or contracts out to village households. This has the effect of allowing all village households to engage in commodity production without facing any village tax levy. This is, at least formally, an economic subsidy and encouragement to households to engage in commodity production, and is cited as such by the village leadership, but it was never mentioned by any household.

One form of significant direct subsidy was admitted by some of the households receiving it. Households that chose to invest in turning a very deep ditch between the village and a paved highway into commercial property could have 70 percent of the cost of doing so covered by the village. By 1989, almost all this promising commercial property had been developed and only a few less-well-located gullies remained. The households that had taken advantage of this opportunity were generally viewed as having benefited, although comments on the subject referred less to the subsidy than to their early occupation of valuable commercial land. It is both accurate and widely recognized that rural entrepreneurs can benefit enormously by taking a successful risk to enter a new field ahead of competitors.

Regardless of recognition granted or not granted to the village's economic leadership, it is clear that Huaili's leaders decided not to expand the village's own economic enterprises but to forgo the taxes this would have required in favor of allowing and encouraging households to use those funds to set up their own household projects. The village retains, from its collective past, some property and an organizational basis that allow it to directly subsidize (in a few cases) or indirectly find work for (in many more cases) households unable to take advantage of this policy. Huaili's economic approach mobilizes popular initiative at the household level in a manner consistent with national economic policy and trends, while preserving some elements of a collective safety net.[25]

The enterprises listed in Table 4.2 are conspicuous in the types of economic activity they represent; that is, there is remarkably little production involved in this commodity production strategy. The economic activities involved are primarily service and commercial ones. Most of the exceptions involve persons with some particular skill, usually acquired from the father of one of the principals involved, such as making false teeth (this woman's father chose to train his daughter as well as his son), making sesame oil, and carpentry. The village's only beekeeper learned this skill and began her enterprise through the help of her younger sister in another village. The seamstress and the painter of decorative mirrors are unusually skilled in their crafts, although these were not acquired within their families (but the latter is now training his son). The most interesting case of entrepreneurship in production is that of the young man who heard of a course being offered for a fee elsewhere in Shandong in the techniques of commercial mushroom-growing, took it, and has been extremely successful.

Aside from these instances, and simpler forms of commodity production resembling domestic sidelines, the commercial focus of village projects is related to the moderately favorable location of Huaili near a

paved highway, a standard market, and a township seat. It is also related to the fact that commerce is more profitable than production.
Fluctuations in business conditions and differences between specific
areas of commerce and production tend to obscure this pattern and to
render it somewhat more complex, but the generalization does hold.
The profits to be made from one's own labor and the sale of its products can rarely compete with those to be gained from the astute purchase and resale of commodities. On a larger scale, substantial profits
can certainly be made in rural factories, but these require more investment than Huaili households can provide. The wealthiest households
in Huaili are those that have proved especially adept in commerce. Recent economic conditions have resulted in large numbers of rural factories going bankrupt, especially in 1989, so there has been no encouragement for households that have prospered in commerce to move into
production.

The greatest profits do not, in fact, occur in the context of any of
these regularized specialized endeavors. Rather, they are the result of
risky but, when successful, highly profitable dealings in the purchase
and resale of scarce, highly valued commodities, especially wood (for
building purposes), fertilizer, and insecticide. All these are in short
supply and high demand. Although they can be traded on the free
market, much of the production and sale of these commodities origi-
nates within the state sector at controlled prices. Enormous profits can
be made by procuring any of these from the state sector and reselling
them on the private market. This practice has been one of the most serious economic problems plaguing China's transition from a planned
to a market economy and its continuing efforts to maintain a dual-track
(state and private) system in some sectors of the economy.

Although everyone in China agrees that this practice creates serious problems, they also agree that it is often impossible to buy essential or highly desired goods except through the channels that create these
super-profits. This area of economic practice is a gray one. It is not entirely proper, but since much of the produce from state enterprises is
now marketable as part of the autonomy granted state enterprises, it is
legal to engage in such trade. The gray areas are those of establishing
the connections that allow entry into this lucrative area, and here
questionable business practices are at issue; nor are all the commodities of this character on the market legally. Despite these considerations, there is a respect and prestige associated with the men who en-

gage in this commerce, both for the wealth it brings and for the ability in business dealings that it signifies.

Most dealings of this nature that were cited as occurring in Huaili in the late 1980s involved wood. Wood suitable for building purposes is very scarce in China and falls far short of the enormous demand generated by rural house construction. The same men who traded in wood might also trade in fertilizer, although that was less profitable. Insecticide was cited as a further possibility, although no one I spoke with said that he personally had traded it. Men in 8 of the 40 households in my 1989 sample reported having recently traded in wood. Some volunteered the information that this trade had been easier to engage in during the mid-1980s, and it is possible that a larger number of men in the sample had been involved at an earlier time. Two of the eight households definitely involved in this trade are state-recognized specialized households, and one is an especially prosperous self-defined specialized household. All but one of the remaining households are well-off; the exception is a poorer household brought into the trade as a partner by a wealthier, agnatically related household.

There is no connection whatever between the specialized projects of these households and the trade in wood. The trade does, however, require business skill, connections, and investment funds, and all these factors favor economically successful households. Five of the eight men involved in this trade were current or former cadres, and one more had a related link through his extravillage employment. Connections outweigh investment funds as a factor in access to this business. It is not, however, a regular and normal activity for any of these men. Trade in such commodities involves one or a few episodes of negotiating a sizable one-time shipment from a supplier far from the village, often in another province. Men do this individually or in ad hoc partnerships that do not extend into partnerships in other economic activities and that do not necessarily involve kin. All the people involved in this occasional trade, which is the peak of local business activity, are middle-aged men. This is part of a wider pattern in which long-distance trade is usually restricted to men, but it represents a further limitation to only those men with connections and current commercial knowledge.

These profitable occasional ventures into comparatively large-scale commercial activities form a part of the economic context in which specialized households are emerging, and although there is no necessary or demonstrable association, such ventures may be a source of investment funds.[26] This type of trade is a significant element in the socialist commodity economy in which specialized households operate, but for the most part it is external rather than internal to their operations. Nevertheless, it is worth underlining that the commoditization of rural China involves not only economic activity oriented toward markets but also activity linked with remaining collective and state sectors. The connection between these is important for rural commerce, as it is for the urban and national economies.

Changes in the large-scale political economy have allowed household enterprises to operate and continue to condition the terms of their operation. But not all households are equally well placed to make effective use of these new opportunities. There are several relevant differences among households.

Cadre or former cadre status. There has been some attention given in the scholarly literature to the advantage that current or former cadres have in the rural commodity economy (Oi 1989). The evidence from Huaili tends to confirm that *some* cadres have succeeded in transforming their former political status into economic leadership or advantage during the economic reform process. The forms that this economic advantage take are varied, however, including continued service as a cadre, factory management, and trade in scarce commodities such as wood.

Current cadre status is effectively incompatible with running a successful household-based enterprise as these operate in Huaili. One man in his thirties who has built up a growing household enterprise holds a junior leadership position and is under pressure to be groomed as the successor to the aging Party branch secretary (the village's foremost official).[27] He finds this demand difficult to reconcile with his time-consuming household responsibilities, and others in the village have commented that it would be especially difficult to do both because his very capable wife is illiterate and therefore unable fully to replace him in managing the enterprise. It is significant that he is the only member of either a state-recognized or a self-defined specialized household in Huaili who is in this situation. It is more common for such households to include former cadres, such as a man who served as an accountant for over twenty years and who now runs a wholesale business, but the data do not permit any conclusion beyond the one that this transition is possible.[28]

Special trade or skill. This is extremely helpful. Some trades are restricted by long apprenticeship and limited access, which may depend on being born into a family practicing the trade. This is the case both for the maker of false teeth and for the carpenter in the village. Both come from family backgrounds where their trades were practiced when political circumstances allowed, and their fathers trained them through apprenticeships lasting several years. Huaili's producers of sesame oil all report having learned this simpler skill through the agnatic line as well. Producing sesame oil is technically less demanding than a trade but does require skill and equipment; depending on current prices (very favorable in the late 1980s), it can be quite profitable.

Some other skills can be acquired through combinations of briefer instruction, reading related books and journals, and practice. In the case of Huaili, these include beekeeping, mushroom-raising, and folk dentistry. A few of the specialists in the village practice in areas where knowledge is more widely dispersed (sewing, cycle repair, tractor driving), so their enterprises depend on higher levels of skill than usual and, to varying extents, on the ownership of more or better equipment than others. In some cases, owner-drivers of tractors in Huaili learned their skill as tractor drivers during the collective era.

Entrepreneurial ability. This is a factor in the success of some specialized households, especially the more commercial ones. It has been important to identify a promising area of commerce and to enter it ahead of the competition. Managing good relations with suppliers, especially those supplying scarce goods, with customers, and with local officials, as well as the astute management of credit (both obtaining it and granting it), also contribute to an enterprise's success and are among the factors cited locally in assessing an entrepreneur's ability.

Entrepreneurial ability has been especially important because the growth of specialized enterprises in Huaili has not been dependent on access to large sums for investment. Each of these enterprises started with small sums (typically a few hundred RMB) from the household's savings or loans from relatives, and grew with revenue generated from the enterprise. Commercial loans were rare and virtually unobtainable by the late 1980s. The main instances of earlier loans were those involving substantial property that could guarantee the loan, such as a new tractor or hotel buildings on good commercial real estate. Access to funds was probably not a major factor in determining who initially ventured into commodity production and commerce in Huaili, although it may come to have a differentiating effect in the future, now

TABLE 4.3
The Highest Level of Education Attained by Members of the
Core Mature Couple in 40 Households in the Village of Huaili, 1989

Level of education[a]	Household category					
	Nonspecialized (n = 18)		Self-defined specialized (n = 13)		State-recognized specialized (n = 9)	
	F (n = 18)	M (n = 18)	F (n = 13)	M (n = 12)	F (n = 9)	M (n = 9)
None	10	2	3	0	1	0
Primary	6	8[b]	8	11[b]	0	2
Lower middle	2	5[b]	2	1[c]	4	3
Upper middle	0	2	0	0	2[c]	3[b]
Higher	0	1	0	0	2	1

NOTE: The one exception to a core mature couple occurs in Household 21 in Table 4.2 (a self-defined specialized household), where the key economic figure is the eldest (unmarried) daughter of the household. She is included in these figures in place of her mother and stepfather. This exception to the general pattern holds throughout the following tables in this chapter and accompanying discussion in the text.

[a]In each case these levels should be read as "at least some education at this level." The higher education is teacher's training in three cases and paramedic training in one case.

[b]One person in this category has also received further education during army service.

[c]One person in this category has also completed an apprenticeship.

that households are much less equal than they were in the 1980s and credit is harder to obtain.

Education. Education levels are generally low in Huaili and illiteracy is common even among young adults. Many of the trades and skills that form the basis of Huaili's specialized enterprises require literacy and numeracy or can be enhanced by an ability to read the numerous publications that provide advice on rural enterprises. Bookkeeping is rudimentary or nonexistent in the smaller enterprises but necessary to the larger and more commercial ones, such as wholesale businesses and restaurants.[29]

Table 4.3 indicates the highest educational level attained by members of the mature couple[30] at the core of each household's economy in the 40 Huaili households in my sample. This table suggests that a higher level of education may be a factor enabling a household to move into specialized production or commerce, and that the educational level of women is more salient here than that of men.

Labor. Larger household size has been noted as a feature of more affluent Chinese households in earlier times, and although this larger size may be viewed as a consequence of affluence rather than a cause

TABLE 4.4

Household Size and Labor Power in 40 Households in the Village of Huaili, 1989

	Household category		
	Non-specialized (n = 18)	Self-defined specialized (n = 13)	State-recognized specialized (n = 9)
Average household size	5.05	5.00	4.67
Average household labor power	3.22	3.65	2.44
Ratio of household size to labor power	1.57	1.37	1.91

of it, questions have been raised about the contribution of a larger number of working people to a household's prosperity (Croll 1987b; Zhou Qing 1988). On the assumption that the three categories of household economy considered here are associated with wealth and with the type of economic endeavor that makes wealth possible, they can be compared in size, labor power, and the ratio between household size and household labor power. Table 4.4 indicates that the expected relationship does not exist in Huaili. This may be associated with the available option of hiring extrahousehold labor.

Family type. Family type has been proposed as a factor, in that extended (or joint) families might be better able to mobilize and allocate labor among diverse tasks or endeavors, as exemplified by the Taiwanese family studied by Margery Wolf (1968). Extended families are almost unknown in any of the three villages studied, and there is a strong feeling in Huaili against enterprise partnership with close agnates. This may be the result of the dissolution of the few recent attempts at cooperation on an agnatic basis, either in agriculture or in nonagricultural enterprises. In fact, a tendency in the opposite direction is suggested by Table 4.5.

Labor intensity. If households do not have more labor power available, do they work the labor power they do have with more intensity, as has been observed among households striving to establish their own enterprises in Taiwan (Niehoff 1987)? Estimates of the work load of the members of the core mature couple in each household in Table 4.6 do not support this argument. There is no indication here that members of specialized households are working harder than others in order to build enterprises. In addition, I found no indication that the heavier work load carried by some members, especially women, in the non-

TABLE 4.5

*Family Type in 40 Households in
the Village of Huaili, 1989*

	Household category		
Family type	Non-specialized (n = 18)	Self-defined specialized (n = 13)	State-recognized specialized (n = 9)
Nuclear	9[a]	7	8
Stem	5	3	0
Aggregate	1	2[b]	0
Extended	1	0	0
Other	2	1	1

[a]Division in progress in one household.
[b]Division in progress in two households.

TABLE 4.6

*Estimates of Labor Intensity of Members of the
Core Mature Couple in 40 Households in the Village Huaili, 1989*

	Household category					
	Nonspecialized		Self-defined specialized		State-recognized specialized	
Labor intensity	F (n = 18)	M (n = 18)	F (n = 13)	M (n = 12)	F (n = 9)	M (n = 9)
Un(der)employed	0	0	1	3	1	1
Full work load	3	13	2	8	4	7
Heavy work load	1	3	3	1	3	1
Double burden	12	0	5	0	1	0
Not determined	0	1	0	0	0	0
Retired	0	1	0	0	0	0
Retired early	2	0	2	0	0	0

NOTE: Unemployed = no work; underemployed = significantly less than a full work load but not a situation of retirement; full work load = the local norm of substantial but seasonally variable amounts of work on all days of the year except customary holidays; heavy work load = significantly more than a full work load; double burden = approximately twice the full work load, in domestic labor and an income-generating activity; retired = no longer working and at or past the gender-specific retirement age; retired early = no longer working and below the gender-specific retirement age.

specialized households was intended to enable their households to establish enterprises of their own. Instead, it is an indicator of a lower living standard and a need to labor harder at less remunerative work than in households with thriving projects. The difference in work load is most striking among *women* in the different categories of household.

Consideration of these data strongly suggests that it is not access to labor power in a quantitative sense that determines the likelihood of a household successfully running its own enterprise. Rather, the striking distinguishing factor lies in *access to labor of a high quality*, and the greatest difference is apparent among women in the three categories. When this observation is combined with the data indicating a predominance of nuclear families among specialized households (see Table 4.5), this argument resonates with those in Chapter 5 regarding the shift in internal family relations toward an increasing emphasis on the economic partnership between husbands and wives. Where brothers and other agnates are not preferred, or are even avoided as partners, the role of the conjugal couple acquires enhanced significance. The emphasis on household boundary maintenance and on secrecy regarding household finances strengthens this partnership. It may even be possible to see a transformation of uterine strategies expressed here, in the form of an exclusion of the husband's agnates through a strengthening of the conjugal economic role.

Table 4.7 presents an assessment of the relative contribution of each member of the core mature couple to a given household's enterprise, and in some cases indicates in parentheses a complementary contribution made in agriculture. Subtracting 2 cases of retirement of older wives, who formerly did agricultural work and have now been replaced in that work by younger members of the household, and 3 other cases where the comparison cannot be made, 17 cases remain. There are *strong couples* in 6 of the 9 state-recognized specialized households. The couple relation is a prominent issue in each of the remaining 3 cases: Household 2, an unskilled widow who remarried a widower and occupied a position resembling a hired laborer; Household 8, an illiterate woman who worked hard but whose lack of education was openly commented upon as holding her husband back; and Household 5, a young man striving through self-education to reach equal footing with his wife and uncomfortable about his lack of success.

Among the self-defined specialized households, only 2 couples enjoy this favorable balance, although 5 more enjoy a more widely construed complementarity in which the partner less involved in the household enterprise concentrates on agricultural labor. The division of labor that might otherwise have been expected between brothers in an extended family is in both situations readily apparent between husbands and wives.

TABLE 4.7
*The Relative Contribution of Each Member of the Core Mature Couple
in State-Recognized and Self-Defined Specialized Households in the
Village of Huaili, 1989*

No.[a]	Wife	Husband
	Contribution to household enterprise	
State-recognized specialized households		
1	Critical	Partner
2	Hard worker	Critical
3	Partner	Critical
4	Partner	Critical
5	Critical	Assistant
6	Partner	Critical
7	Partner	Partner
8	Hard worker	Critical
9	Critical (sewing)	Critical (repair)
Self-defined specialized households		
10	Critical	Assistant
11	Assistant (agriculture)	Critical
12	Critical	(Agriculture)
13	Not clear (in transition)	Not clear (in transition)
14	Critical	(Agriculture)
15	(Agriculture)	Critical
16	Retired	Critical
17	Critical	Not resident
18	Partner (agriculture)	Critical
19	Partner (agriculture)	Critical
20	Semi-retired (care of grandchildren)	Critical
21	Critical	N/A[b]
22	(Agriculture)	Critical

[a]The occupation(s) of these 22 households are listed, in the same order, in Table 4.2.
[b]See note to Table 4.3 re Household 21.

It is also strikingly evident from Table 4.7 that women make important, and in many cases decisive, contributions to their households' enterprises, and not only in subordinate or supporting roles. In 8 of the cases I ranked the woman's contribution as the one decisive to the enterprise; in 6 more she is an important partner in the enterprise. The role of women in the economic restructuring accompanying commoditization is a hidden element that requires closer attention.

Gender and Class

Women's role in the rural commodity economy has not been entirely ignored by the state. Davin (1988) is surely correct in her view that the rural economic reform program was designed without explicit attention to the interests of rural women. However, this lacuna does not imply that the state has taken no interest in the role of women in the reform process. The most overt form of official interest and mobilization has been on the part of the network of Women's Federations. This interest has been complex, related *both* to the official, mass-organization character of the Women's Federations as a transmission belt from the Party to women *and* to the strengthening view within the Womens' Federations that they might become more feminist and more vigorously advocate the special interests of women. The ground on which these two interests have converged is that of women's role in commodity production—and, indeed, the role of the Women's Federations themselves in commodity production. The Women's Federations have moved toward an explicit, practical advocacy of increasing women's participation in commodity production, specifically in the spheres outside former collective or state economic structures (see, especially, Liang Weiling 1988).

Here the Women's Federations are building on a long history of women's involvement in domestic sidelines both before and during the collective era (I. Crook n.d., M. Wolf 1985, Judd 1990). Unlike some women-in-development approaches that treat women's economic role as separate and apart from the mainstream of economic activity by focusing on questions of subsistence and welfare (Kandiyoti 1990), this approach assumes that women are, or should be, centrally involved in the dominant economy of the time. Questions can be raised regarding the advisability or efficacy of promoting women's participation in a commodity economy, and such questions are being raised within the Women's Federations. However, as one of their cadres observed, "Commodity production is not ideal, but there is no other 'way out' [*chulu*]."

Involvement in commodity production extends throughout the Women's Federation hierarchy, although it is not supported, or not supported equally, by all. Running enterprises of their own is a method some now recommend that various Women's Federations use to compensate for limits and cuts to their state-provided funding (Wang Qi 1988). The impact of the official position is restrained by the weakness of the Women's Federations in the countryside, where they typically have no more than one cadre in a township, much of whose time may be assigned to general political work not related to women's issues. The impact of the Women's Federations on women in the rural economy is therefore restricted to the general legitimacy and occasional support (such as training programs) offered to women participating in the commodity economy, or to particular efforts at mobilization.

One such effort at mobilization is directly relevant here and has had an immediate impact on Huaili and a number of other rural communities. This is a small campaign to promote the "courtyard economy" (*tingyuan jingji*). It achieved some success in the rural suburbs of Tianjin in 1987 (Wang Qi 1988) and was actively promoted in Dezhou Prefecture the same year. This approach builds on women's established and accepted role in what were, and still are, termed "domestic sidelines," but tries to build on them through intensified expansion into courtyard vegetable production explicitly intended for the marketplace. This approach has adequately identified courtyard space as an underutilized resource that can profitably absorb increased amounts of labor. It may also be commended as an approach that is sensitive to the economic needs of the poorer rural households, which lack ready means to take full advantage of the opportunities unevenly offered by the commodity economy. Through this channel it is intended that even relatively poor households with only agricultural skills will be able to participate more intensively in the commodity economy and thereby raise their incomes.

This policy may also improve the relative status of women within their households, to the extent that through it they contribute more to the household's revenues, although this is not a major claim or objective of the minicampaign. It is also evident that courtyard production of market vegetables will not introduce structural change into the economy or the pattern of gender relations in the countryside. What it *does* specifically offer is increased income. Increased incomes are both needed and respected in rural China, and in this sense the Womens' Federations are certainly in touch with their constituency. The focus on income is also a realistic and sensitive response to the immediate needs of the poor, for whom longer-term structural change may have little to offer and be perceived as beyond peasant control and potentially threatening.

The success of this campaign has been real for a small number of households that have put their courtyards under intensive vegetable cultivation. Huaili was a village targeted in this minicampaign, and it received much more than the usual help in promoting it, in the form of a substantial time commitment from one county-level Women's Federation cadre. This cadre is very able and business-oriented, and Huaili was marked as one of her particular successes. It was surprising, therefore, to find that courtyard vegetable production is far from standard in Huaili (see Table 4.1).

Some of the reasons for this are readily evident. Many households have much more attractive economic avenues in which to invest their time. In this respect, Table 4.1 supports the interpretation that the courtyard strategy is primarily designed for households with limited resources. When I visited households that I would have expected to be engaged in this cultivation but that were not doing so, my inquiries elicited two main types of explanation. The first was that the quality of land in the courtyard was not good enough for vegetable cultivation. This is consistent with local official explanations that some portions of the present village were recently built over good agricultural land, while other portions had long been housing sites. Although even the latter could presumably be turned into vegetable plots with sufficient inputs of labor and materiel, this was evidently not regarded as an attractive or economic proposition. The other reason commonly given was the incompatibility of courtyard vegetable production with the raising of domestic animals. This does not refer to pigs, which are kept securely penned, but to chickens, geese, goats, and sheep. The fowl could be penned, at some expense, but sheep and goats may pose a larger problem. In a few other cases, the problem was said to be poor sunlight in the courtyard.

Although it was not mentioned directly by villagers, I would propose an additional factor to have been highly influential. It is one obliquely implied in the responses citing domestic animals. If the older domestic sideline of small-scale animal husbandry can be used and perhaps expanded to provide additional income, it will certainly be income gained with much less time and effort than through intensive vegetable cultivation. A major obstacle to the greater spread of the "courtyard economy" is precisely this consideration of labor. Though labor is not explicitly considered as a cost in Chinese peasants' calculations of the profitability of enterprises, opportunity costs of differential deployment is a factor in their economic decision-making. The enormous labor demands of intensive vegetable cultivation (nonintensive cultivation on such a small area would yield little) in comparison with animal husbandry must also be considered. Any of several members of a household with a little extra time each day can feed a few animals. This is considered such a negligible demand on anyone's time that I had to make a special effort to ensure that it was reported at all in my queries regarding household-labor time allocation.

The view that labor is a factor is confirmed by the greater response in Huaili to the call to plant xiangchun trees. Xiangchun require labor only for picking leaves at intervals in the spring and can potentially provide good returns in the marketplace. The call for women in particular to engage in courtyard vegetable production is especially problematic when labor is considered. As Table 4.6 indicates, mature married women in households without their own specialized projects are very heavily worked. Whatever surplus labor exists in Huaili is not to be found in this category. Thus what was in other respects a carefully considered program was limited by the low rate of un(der)employment in the specific target group. In fact, the most intensively cultivated courtyard I saw in Huaili was cultivated primarily by an aging but still vigorous grandfather. The courtyard economy approach may be more effective in areas where married women are less fully employed, as is the case in poorer regions of the countryside, provided these regions are not too far from markets.

From the perspective of examining changes in the relations of gender and class that are accompanying the development of the commodity economy, state-recognized and self-defined specialized households are of greater significance. These are the households that represent the emergent social forces which the rural economic reform program is trying to mobilize; they also embody some of the values implicit and explicit in the commodity economy. From the point of view of policy leaders at the highest levels (Jiang Zemin 1989), and through to the Women's Federations (see Liang Xuguang et al. 1989), the promotion of people of high "quality" (*suzhi*) to generate economic growth and social transformation is a major element in reform policy. From the point of view of the rural people, it is evident that "ability" (*benshi*), especially in the spheres of business and politics, is recognized and valued as a key to prosperity.

In connection with this emphasis, policy leaders also strive to draw upon popular initiative as a human resource for development by allowing more room for household-based economic activity than under the collective system. In popular eyes, the new economic policies have gained much of their legitimacy through the implicit offer they make of increased household and personal autonomy, insofar as the power of levels immediately above the household is comparatively weakened. Whether viewed from above or from below, the phenomenon of household enterprises—especially successful ones, as represented in specialized households—is one of the forces and one of the symbols of the emergent rural commodity economy.

Specialized households are a small scale but significant element in the restructuring of rural class relations on a partially market-oriented basis. It would be misleading to conceptualize class in China as a purely economic matter, for it is substantially determined by political relations that permeate the fabric of life in rural China. The re-formation of class in rural China very largely involves questions concerning rural industry (state, collective, cooperative, or private) and rural state structures. The phenomenon of household-based economic differentiation and its contribution to class formation must be placed within this broader perspective.

In itself, the emergence of successful specialized households generates immediate inequalities in wealth, which may then become inequalities in access to at least some types of means of production. For the present, it does not appear that nonspecialized households are in danger of losing access to land (although this may be a different matter in regions with agricultural specialized households), but they can be viewed as being in the early stages of losing access to nonagricultural means of production. At present, this is a straightforward matter of differential access to the liquid capital for investment. This is an especially serious matter because nonspecialized households have for the most part also missed the opportunities for exceptionally high rates of profit available to (some of) those who started household enterprises early, while the rural economy was flourishing.

It will not be easy for late arrivals in the rural commodity economy to overtake already established specialized households. As a result, it can be predicted that inequality will deepen. To the extent that the specialized households move from petty commodity production to petty capitalist production, their growth will be accompanied by the growth of a class of rural hired laborers. As long as these hired laborers retain access to agricultural land allocation, as they now generally do, they cannot strictly be termed a proletariat, but a tendency toward proletarianization is implicit in the specialized household phenomenon.

Specialized households may also enjoy special relations with the state. This is not accentuated in the current situation in Huaili, but it is an element that is at any moment subject to adjustment by local and higher levels of the state. Specialized households are potentially vulnerable to a shift in the political winds, but they are also potential recipients of further state support to the extent that the state chooses to consolidate the commodity economy in the countryside on a household-oriented basis.

It may also be possible to detect an association with specialized household status when examining a dimension of state power that is directly and internally connected with households—namely, household registration. In the 40 Huaili households in my 1989 sample, there are only 16 adults with nonagricultural registration. Ten of these are members of 6 of the 9 state-recognized specialized households in the village; none are members of self-defined specialized households; and 6 are members of 4 nonspecialized households. Examination of the individual cases indicates that nonagricultural status is not a direct consequence of being a member of a state-recognized specialized household, although the two youngest nonagricultural registrants under consideration may possibly have been aided in acquiring nonagricultural status by virtue of their households' economic success. In the other cases nonagricultural status has been inherited or acquired through work in an urban setting, with no connection to the household's specialized or nonspecialized status and often prior to the existence of this distinction.

That such a large proportion of persons with the preferred registration are members of state-recognized specialized households suggests that different lines of differentiation are reinforcing each other. The specialized / nonspecialized distinction is a relatively new one. If it persists, and if the current strong salience of registration status also persists, it can be predicted that state-recognized specialized households will disproportionately acquire nonagricultural registration for their younger members.

Gender enters as a factor into this process of class re-formation because, as the previous section indicates, the role of conjugal couples and of women in conjugal couples emerges as a major factor in the advantage that specialized households enjoy compared with nonspecialized ones. Women—not simply as laborers, but as especially skilled or able persons—are often decisive in enabling a household project to flourish, either by virtue of their own particular abilities or by virtue of their capacity to act as effective partners. Whereas women's economic contribution in the countryside was previously much more even and much less differentiated than that of men, women's economic range has widened to the point where it enters as an independent factor in household stratification.

This is most evident with respect to married women. Marriage occurs early, at present very close to 20 years of age, and is virtually universal for women. Combined with the move to another village that this usually entails for a woman and a divorce rate below 1 percent, this means that women find their economic futures closely tied to the households into which they marry. A woman's life and her children's futures are intimately tied to the well-being of this household, and much of her mature life is spent consolidating its welfare.

The economic activity of younger, unmarried women may succeed in opening the doors to nonagricultural registration and subsequent marriage out of the countryside, but this occurs only in a small minority of cases. Otherwise, a young woman's premarital work experience is unlikely to continue directly in her marital community. It is not unusual, for example, for women who were teachers in their natal villages never to be offered a teaching position in their marital villages. Most young women work, if the opportunity is available, in the factory or service sector and contribute substantially to their natal families' finances during several working years prior to marriage. They are unlikely to carry funds or skills acquired from such work into their marriage, although their incomes may indirectly help their natal families provide good dowries. Significant structural change in women's role in the rural economy depends on change in the roles they occupy through most of their lives as mature women, not on opportunities only temporarily available in their youth.

Nevertheless, young unmarried women are a strong element in the contemporary rural work force and are regarded, with considerable justification, as better workers than young unmarried men. (Relatively little seems to be expected of the latter.) For example, one young woman working in a rural factory elsewhere in the county was called home to join her household's growing noodle enterprise. Together with her mother, she is the household's main producer of noodles, and her family has arranged an extended engagement for her so that she will be available to their household enterprise for a longer time than usual without detriment to making a good match.

Another young woman is even more unusual. She has established herself as a successful retailer of ready-made clothing in local rural markets. Both married and unmarried women engage in buying and selling in their local standard market, so this is not itself a new departure. What is new is that this woman, and the three young women with whom she travels, must make regular purchasing trips to Shijiazhuang in neighboring Hebei Province to acquire their goods. This is unusual in two respects: women do not normally engage in long-distance trade (it is only the travel in a group that makes this respectable and feasible), and women do not normally engage in economic cooperation beyond their own household.

It is not accidental that this small group of young unmarried women represents the only instance of women's economic cooperation in Huaili.[31] The endeavor in which they are engaged could be built up with small investments that, although part of their natal households' assets, would not directly or wholly commit those households in the sense that would be the case for married women. A married woman would find it much harder to distinguish her economic pursuits from those of her husband, and very often is too committed to joint economic activities and to the care of her children to be able to operate in an autonomous economic fashion. Further, this activity on the part of young women is unambiguously temporary and will cease as each marries. It consequently poses no noticeable challenge to existing patterns of gender division of labor or to the maintenance of household boundaries. The young women's initiative and ability in a respected area of enterprise (commerce) are valued, as is the income generated, but this does not imply any structural change.

One of the highly significant and persisting elements in the gender division of labor is that *women generally do not engage in interhousehold economic cooperation*. If allowance is made for the obvious exceptions—the work of young unmarried women, and married women's relations with their natal families—this difference may be more precisely stated: *men do, and women do not, engage their households in economic relations with other households or with suprahousehold forms of organization*. Women only do so when the absence of a husband places them in the role of household head.

This general restriction on married women's economic role beyond the household severely limits the economic possibilities for women in a political economy in which households have only a limited and relative autonomy.[32] Suprahousehold economic units may well grow in importance in coming years; to the extent that this occurs without further extension in the limits of women's acceptable economic roles, it will be to the disadvantage of women.

Contrary to some predictions (such as Davin 1988), the reinforcement of the rural household economy has not been wholly detrimental to the specific interests of women. The argument expressed by one Women's Federation cadre that women can obtain a greater degree of autonomy and more effectively pursue their own interests in units of smaller size, such as the household, appears to be confirmed by this investigation. If women's work groups outside the household have disappeared, married women show no sign of missing them. As Margery Wolf noted (1985), the participation rate of married women in collective work was low, and they often preferred to spend more time on domestic sidelines. The collectives may have offered less liberation to rural women than has been supposed outside of China.

Conversely, interhousehold and suprahousehold organization during the collective era showed indications of strengthening primary groups formed around cores of male agnates (see Croll 1981). Patriarchy may have lost ground in the weakening of organizational levels immediately above the household, and it often may be easier to deal with on a household basis. Chinese women have long practiced skills for the informal management of households (see M. Wolf 1972).

Women are active agents in the processes that are reconstructing class in the Chinese countryside, but they are *not* acting in an organized or conscious sense *as women*. They may be a collectivity *in itself*, but they are not a collectivity *for itself*. Indeed, as barriers of class deepen and become more tied to the economic contributions of women (rather than being derived primarily from the contributions of their fathers and husbands), even the existing basis for mobilizing women will be weakened by the divisions among them.

If women have gained some more room to exercise their abilities and to enjoy autonomy within the commodity economy, they have not acquired it equally, and they have not acquired it as an identifiable consequence of a movement in the interests of women. Those who have gained have done so on the basis of openings provided by policy decisions taken by powers remote from their lives, combined with their own personal abilities and the potential available in their marital households. Their strength is based on *individual* and *household* factors, and the strategies they have effectively pursued have been *household* strategies. These contribute further to strengthening the already profound barriers separating households. It is in this sense, *a sense specifically and internally related to the active agency of the most able rural women,* that the household forms the greatest obstacle to organization and change in the specific interests of women.

CHAPTER 5

"Households": Between
State and Family

Households have been a central concept in discussions of rural China since the early years of the rural reform program. The production responsibility system, as initially presented, could have utilized many different forms of social organization and, in fact, did so for a brief period of time. But within a few years, by far the most common unit of production responsibility was the household (Watson 1984). Within China, 1980s official discourse on rural society and economy was pervaded by positive references to the household as a social institution and as an economic actor. This discourse referred to the household both in the broad sense in which every rural resident is a member of a household[1] and in the narrower sense in which some households, especially state-recognized specialized households, are prioritized in reform economic policy.

Researchers outside China quickly recognized the significance of the revitalization of the rural household and examined it as a major issue in the study of contemporary rural China. Despite the persistence of unresolved questions about the entity referred to as the "household," its significance has been confirmed repeatedly since the institution of the rural reform program.

The devolution of immediate responsibility for production from collectives to households in the form of contractual obligations was followed by measures to lengthen the term of contracts on agricultural land, and thereby to strengthen the household as a unit controlling the primary means of production in the countryside. Government policies and pronouncements generated during the early years of the reform were designed to encourage popular confidence that the reforms would be long-lasting and that cultivation practices and economic planning should be made with a long-term perspective. There were particular concerns that the fertility of the land should be maintained and that increased rural income should be invested in production and not wholly devoted to raising standards of living.

These policies also arose from a political imperative to strengthen the government's and the Party's legitimacy in the countryside and to encourage independent entrepreneurship. Household-based economic initiatives were officially sanctioned as a major economic force that the reform program was intended to unleash and to legitimate. The acceptability and emotive power of the household—closely associated with the family, the most reliable of social ties in a profoundly unstable social world—operated to obscure the extent to which the proposed policies diverged from past orthodoxy. This made it somewhat easier to advocate or to implement policies that would previously have been denounced as capitalist. The terminology also obscured the sensitive issue of bourgeois individualism by embedding the new entrepreneurship within a small but legitimate social entity. In addition, and this may have been an unintended implication, it obscured significant issues regarding the restructuring of gender relations.

The household in rural China remains a critical nexus of cultural construction and social relations in the practical world of everyday life and in the official political economy. It is deeply enmeshed in a larger, complex world in which the role of the organized state is preeminent. The villages studied here are in every case characterized by strong suprahousehold organization,[2] primarily operating in a governmental or quasi-governmental mode at the village level. The suprahousehold organization now in place in rural China combines a continuation of long-established lines of power stretching from the state to the rural people with a greater role and enhanced relative autonomy for the household level of social organization.

Some aspects of the relations in effect are expressed in China by the metaphor of the household as a biological cell (see Li Yunhe 1985). In this metaphor the household appears as the fundamental building block of rural life and the unit with which larger-scale social organization is constructed. The larger constructions are of a complexity much greater than that of the cell, and are hierarchically structured. Equally as interesting as this larger-scale organization is the question of the internal organization of the cell or household. This question is not posed by Li Yunhe, nor is it often posed by other scholars, Chinese or foreign. The household is treated as the lowest analyzable unit of rural Chinese society. It is imbued with the qualities of an agent, not necessarily an agent in a corporate sense but in the sense of a person, in such concepts as "peasant household individualism." It is common in the study of rural China, and of rural societies elsewhere, that households are reified and, by obscuring intrahousehold dynamics, implicitly identified with presumptively male household heads (see Yanagisako 1979: 190–91, Barlett 1980, Rogers 1980: 63–69).

Within Chinese culture, and in terms of a discourse familiar to all Chinese, there is a conceptual structure available that illuminates certain relationships obscured by a more limited focus. The central "five relationships" (*wulun*) of the Confucian social order for men were those of emperor and minister, father and son, elder brother and younger brother, husband and wife, and friend and friend. With the exception of the last relationship, which is horizontal and also the least culturally elaborated of the five, the wulun constitute an explicit hierarchical pattern of homologous relationships reaching from the apex of the state to the immediate relationships of family life. The emperor is conceptualized as paternalistic and the father/elder brother/husband as authoritative. Men are expected to order their relationships within and beyond their households in accordance with this framework.

The place of women within the Confucian social order is simpler and is adequately covered by the "three obediences" (*san fucong*), which stipulate that a woman should obey her father before marriage, her husband when married, and her son when widowed. There are no prescriptions for women's behavior in the world beyond the household because ideally she has no connection with that world except through a related male. Women are occasionally still referred to as "inside people" (*neiren*), which succinctly expresses this restriction.

These are everyday terms of a long-established and still-thriving model of ideal social relations, and are internal to the operation of the multiple lines of relationship revolving around the household in rural China. The cultural construction of the "household" and of its relation with other cultural constructs in the Chinese countryside is a necessary part of the examination that follows.

Conceptualizing the Household

Households, families, and domestic groups in general have been among the prime subjects of anthropological study (see Yanagisako 1979) and cross-cultural comparison within other disciplines (see Burch 1979). There are numerous variant conceptualizations of these available for use. The discussion that follows does not depart from any of these scholarly conceptualizations, but is based on the conceptualization that is embodied in social processes of constructing the household in contemporary rural China.

It will quickly be seen that many aspects of this conceptualization are similar to aspects already present in the scholarly literature. This very similarity may have obscured those features of the contemporary rural Chinese household that are less well represented in the literature—specifically, the role of the state in directly and indirectly constructing both the household and the unofficial domestic groups associated with it.

In analyzing the microlevel dynamics of social practices and cultural representations surrounding everyday life in the villages of Zhangjiachedao, Qianrulin, and Huaili, the role of the state emerges as a major determining element. This has not been more closely examined in the past because most studies of Chinese households were done when the state was somewhat weaker than it has been for the past several decades. In-depth studies were made in pre-1949 China, Taiwan, Hong Kong, and overseas Chinese communities, but only more limited studies have been conducted in the past decade in China proper, due to the constraints of fieldwork there.

The discussion that follows has been influenced by sinological scholarship directly addressing the role of the state in rural social organization and kinship in a concentrated fashion (especially Croll 1981). The larger literature debating the impact of the 1950 Marriage Law (such as Johnson 1983) or, more recently, the impact of the state's one-child family policy (such as A. Wolf 1986) also forms part of the background to the following analysis. The strongest influence, however, derives from a less obviously related but highly pertinent source, Arthur Wolf's 1978 study of the Chinese state's cultural penetration of rural society through its permeation of systems of belief and ritual, including ancestor worship, with representations of state power.

The conceptualization of the household effective in rural China at the present time is similarly constructed from within by the operations of state power. Some aspects of this construction are largely implicit continuities with established practices of gender and patriarchal authority. Others represent more recent mechanisms through which the household and other, nonofficial domestic groups are defined by state power. I do not focus on official restrictions and regulations (such as those regarding birth limitation campaigns), which are imposed on domestic groups and which have already been intensively studied. Instead, I approach the problem by examining means through which state power operates to define the household positively, both through such direct measures as the household registration system and through the less direct measures of culturally legitimating and privileging a political economy based on the household. The role of the state is evident where members of households, as officially defined, operate in explicitly sanctioned ways, and also when the same people nourish other forms of domestic group and relationship, and engage in creative practical strategies and responses outside the official ambit.

Household Registration

The concept of the household in contemporary China is one of deceptive simplicity. The household (*hu*) is present in China in terms compatible with a variety of cross-cultural conceptualizations of the household found in the anthropological literature (see Yanagisako 1979). Every Chinese person beyond early childhood is familiar with the term and able to talk about his or her household and who belongs to it. There are also ample official records pertaining to households and a body of indigenous as well as foreign research centered on the household as it is agreed to be constituted in China. The preferred starting point for an analysis of the Chinese household is therefore the household (hu) as it is "officially" (see Bourdieu 1977) constructed in contemporary China.

Although the rural Chinese household could be presented in familiar terms as a specific set of variations on a co-residential, kinship-based unit of economic production, consumption, and reproduction, these attributes are secondary to its construction as an element in a politico-administrative system of population control originating outside the villages but permeating the structure of rural social organization.

The state's promotion of households as the basic level of resource management and production in rural China is highly significant in this official definition and control of rural households. This is a relatively recent development but one that substantially strengthens official practices of the collective era in which households, rather than individuals, were both the units receiving distribution of collective income and the primary units of consumption. To the considerable extent that households coincided with family groupings, they were also the organizational vehicle for providing social services not provided by the collective or the state, including care of the young, the elderly, and the infirm. Current policy adds management of resources, production, and investment to the economic responsibilities of the household, and households increasingly are direct taxpaying units.

In all these aspects of economic activity households are granted a greater role, but this role is substantially defined by the state and realized through a multiplicity of relations with governmental and quasi-governmental bodies, including numerous tax-collecting agencies; several levels of government with control over such resources as land, water, energy, and transportation; and a myriad of bodies providing credit, regulating markets, and running agricultural extension and other services. People may and do seek to evade or circumvent the state in some of its manifestations, such as collecting taxes, and they may, where feasible, choose strategies to optimize a favorable relationship, as in the allocation of scarce resources, but they cannot choose to disregard it.

Nevertheless, however important the economic considerations, they are not the primary means through which the state defines and regulates households. The formal mechanism through which this is organized is the household registration system, which has been used with considerable effectiveness since the 1960s to maintain surveillance and control over the national population. Each person is recorded as definitively belonging to one household in a specified locality[3] and to a specified category (agricultural or nonagricultural). Officially registered membership in one household results in every person being unambiguously able to identify the household to which she or he belongs; it also precisely defines the boundaries of each household. *Actual* residence is more variable; moreover, *family* and family ties (both patrilateral and matrilateral) are more ambiguous than the household and are less tightly controlled by the state.

Registration in a specific locality implies access to its resources (such as land)[4] and services (such as welfare). Those not so registered cannot make claims on the locality for either. A right to a specific registration is variously acquired by birth, marriage, or government policy. Policies regarding household registration are intricate and somewhat discretionary, but the guiding principles of the system can be outlined briefly. Children born in the countryside usually inherit their *mother's* registration, and this is normally that of her *marital* community. This will also be the registration of the *father*, if he has agricultural registration. As one of its measures to restrict rural-urban migration, the registration system does not grant nonagricultural registration to the children of a man with such a registration unless their mother also has nonagricultural registration. Most married women with nonagricultural registration are living in cities, but there are substantial numbers of men with nonagricultural registration whose wives and children have agricultural registration and who consequently remain in the man's home village, even if he is working at a remote location and able to visit only infrequently.

In such cases, the officially registered household in the countryside includes only those members with agricultural registration in that locality, even if there are members commonly present who hold nonagricultural registration. The latter have no rights to resources or services but are in no sense prohibited from living in the locality. This situation of split households generates a significant number of recorded female household heads, whose actual circumstances vary from being virtual head of what resembles a single-parent family to being nominal head of a household in which her husband is fully present and active.

Men born in the countryside commonly retain their original registration throughout life. A woman's registration commonly changes shortly after marriage to that of her husband, if agricultural, or, if not agricultural, to that of her mother-in-law—in other words, to that of her rural marital community (also see Judd 1989). Nonagricultural registration is not granted by virtue of marriage, but agricultural registration can be changed from one locality to another through marriage. In the case of uxorilocal marriage, which is not common in any of these villages, the woman retains her original agricultural registration and the man changes his, if his registration is agricultural. However, a common current pattern is for men entering uxorilocal marriages to hold nonagricultural registration.

Both men and women may change their registration later in life, in association with permanent employment in a town or city, higher education, military service, privilege accorded to relatives of cadres, and a host of other reasons. It is nevertheless very difficult to change from agricultural to nonagricultural registration. This change is often a major objective of rural young people, and of their parents on their behalf, but it is one that most have no chance of accomplishing.

In a formal sense, the household registration (*hukou*) system bears a striking resemblance to the family registration (*baojia*) system still familiar to older villagers from the Republican era (see M. Yang 1945), and its depth in the contemporary countryside is based on a long historical tradition of state mechanisms for population control. The household registration system does not have a hierarchy of decimal-based groupings (the ten households of the *jia* and the ten jia of the *bao*), although households were formally subsumed under their production teams and are still grouped in village or subvillage units that are responsible for the households which compose them. The household registration system is less preoccupied with control of political opposition and crime than was the baojia system, but withdrawal of registration, and especially of nonagricultural registration, is a sanction that has been extensively used. Many recent changes in household registration involve the restoration of previous nonagricultural registration status to persons *and members of their households* who lost it on political grounds between 1957 and 1977.

Thus the household registration system continues an underlying principle of state control of the rural population through mechanisms based on the household and applies this principle to contemporary circumstances. It constitutes a comprehensive household-based data base on the entire population that the state can use for multiple purposes of social control. At present these purposes include implementing state birth-limitation policies, restricting rural-urban migration, and controlling access to economic resources and social benefits. Household registration is a major subject of concern for people in rural China and one that is invariably discussed in serious, often troubled tones.

Tight control of household registration, primarily as a move to restrict rural-urban migration, became effective in Shandong from about 1964. Rural-urban migration had been a less serious concern in the 1950s. Many migrants who left rural areas during that decade lost their urban employment in the economic crisis of the early 1960s and returned to their previous rural homes, or, in the case of those from Shandong, tried to make new homes in undersettled areas elsewhere, especially in the Northeast. In the years of economic recovery controls were tightened, and they remained tight through to the reform movement of the 1980s.

During the rapid economic growth of the early and mid-1980s, increased rural-urban migration was tolerated, although primarily in the form of temporary contract work that did not imply a change in registration status. A small proportion of jobs classified as temporary can be reclassified as permanent, according to varying and unpredictable state quotas, and so lead to nonagricultural registration, but in the overwhelming majority of cases nonagricultural registration is a prerequisite for permanent employment in a town or city. This arrangement facilitates control of the enormous reserve labor force in the Chinese countryside by allowing migration where and when economic conditions are favorable while guaranteeing access to resources and services only at the rural locality of registered residence. The primary concern most rural residents have with the household registration system is precisely this restricted access to urban residence and employment for themselves or for their children.

The possibility of altering records locally to resolve registration problems is controlled by the practice of reporting changes annually to higher administrative levels and of turning over the previous registration book to the Public Security Bureau when a new book is needed, which happens roughly every decade. The accuracy of a person's current registration is therefore subject to confirmation at any time by reference to extravillage state authorities.

Household registration is first recorded in a book usually held at the village level. This is a loose-leaf binder with a page for each household, held within a solid cover of the red plastic commonly used for official identification documents. The most recent compilations for the villages studied here were done in the early 1980s, which may be a national constant connected with the 1981 census. Households were grouped in units, which at this time might still be those of the dissolving collective system; there was a page listing households in the unit by number and by the name of the household head, who is the senior male unless he is very elderly or registered elsewhere. The entry for each household allows space for a few characters in each of the following categories for every member of the household:

Household head/Relation to household head
Name
Former name
Sex
Birthdate
Precise place of birth
Native place
Ethnicity
Religion
Education
Work unit
Profession
Marital status
Other places of residence in this city or town
Date of moving (registration) here and from whence
Date of moving (registration) elsewhere and reason
Comments

I carefully examined the registration book for Huaili and found detailed information and official stamps in it for persons—and in a few cases entire households—who had acquired nonagricultural registration and who in some cases had left the community since the book was compiled.[5] Acquiring nonagricultural registration is a process that requires official documentation. Other changes more common in a rural community were rarely recorded: births, deaths, marriages in and out, and household divisions. Moreover, the volume was still organized according to the five production teams of the collective era; it had not been reorganized to match the village's postcollective restructuring into three agricultural groups. None of these changes requires immediate documentation for any practical purpose, so they could be left until the next large-scale revision of the registration book.[6]

Household Composition

The household is essentially defined by this politico-administrative system and reinforced by its actual and official role as a co-residential economic unit. But its utility as a mechanism of population control is intrinsically connected with its being almost identical in composition to the family, although the family (*jia*) is a much more flexible and ambiguous social entity.

Households in China are, in the sense this term is now used in the villages, wholly composed of families. There are cases of single-person or partial households, and there is no absolute requirement that persons of any specified relationship must be in the same household, but households nevertheless exhibit some very consistent patterns of familial composition. Unrelated persons are *not* considered part of a household. Hired laborers may live and eat in a household as part of their remuneration, but they are not considered part of it. Even hired laborers who are related are not considered part of the household—their hired status sets them apart in economic terms, and their registered household residence will be elsewhere.

Close family members—a spouse, unmarried child, or married child who has not divided (*fenjia*) out of the parental household—may be in the ambiguous position of having formal household registration elsewhere. Such people are not officially members of the household, and their usually nonagricultural status introduces complications, but they *are* included in rural residents' view of who belongs to their household, regardless of the extent of their actual presence there. In this sense considerations of family membership prevail over the official concept of the household—these persons are informally described as being members of the "household" (*hu*), a more restricted term than "family" (*jia*). Their participation in the unofficial household may nevertheless be limited if they are usually absent, working at a distance. Young people in this situation[7] are often on their way out of the household and perhaps out of the village. Husbands who have long-term employment at a substantial distance retain some of their earnings for their separate lives and, if they are rarely at home, may not have a significant place in their village homes.[8]

The boundaries that define who is in a household are quite explicit and often deep, despite the significant points where ambiguity is possible. The essential consideration is that of whether or not the household has divided (fenjia). (The term used in this context is "family"—but family as used here is identical to household, except for the possible addition of persons with nonagricultural registration. This could also be referred to as household division.) Fenjia is a formal process in which an estate is divided and a household splits into two or more households that live and eat separately, although they may do so in the same courtyard and with continuing very close relations.

The process of division is a formal one that is now presided over, in each of the three villages studied, by a village-level official who, along with other significant responsibilities, acts as the village mediator (*tiao-jieyuan*). Village leaders are continually involved in family matters in their community: arranging marriages, seeking solutions to major household disputes, and presiding over household division are only the most obvious occasions for this involvement. In most cases of household division, the details are worked out informally within the household before it meets formally with the mediator. His usual role is to provide public sanction for the private arrangement, but he can also play a more active mediating role.

The formal procedures with the mediator are considered to be the defining feature of a household division, and here the entry of the state into the household is again clearly manifested. Nevertheless, many divisions are incomplete or ambiguous in everyday life, and this is common enough that there is a standard fixed phrase, "the division is unclear" (*fenjia bu qing*), to describe it. Households that have not (yet) divided often show signs of gradually moving toward division before it actually occurs. On one level, household division is a clearly bounded official event; on another, it is a flexible and ambiguous process.

Household division is ubiquitous. Although each of the three villages has what villagers describe, in highly positive tones, as "big families" (*da jiating*), this actually refers to "families of four generations" (*sidai tongtang*). This generational depth is the local criterion for a large family, which is not necessarily an extended family in anthropological terms. In fact, only two of the three villages had even one household that could be described as consisting of an extended family.

The household closest to the model of an extended family had a cohesion based on the personality of a warm and vigorous widowed matriarch (who had herself been a daughter-in-law in an extended family for fifteen years). Nevertheless, it manifests certain qualifying features that are also found among larger stem families in these villages. The second son and his wife actually live in the nearby township seat where they work and hold nonagricultural registration, but they both return to his mother every day—she cares for their child—and they contribute economically to the household managed by his mother. Not including this couple's home in the township seat, the household has two houses in the village. The oldest son lives in one with his wife and two children. These children are also cared for by his mother, but she lives in the other house with her unmarried son and daughter. In one respect the household is unusual, and this may also have some bearing on its continuing unity. The deceased husband of the present matriarch originally came to the area as a minor cadre in 1956, leaving his family in the Jinan area; in 1962 his family came as economic refugees to this village, close to his place of work, and they have remained there ever since. The matriarch speaks positively of the welcome the family received in the village, and the household is well-respected, but it is the only household of its surname in the village, which may contribute to its exceptional cohesion.

The other household that appears to consist of an extended family is structured in a similar fashion but is further from the model. In this case the pivotal person is an elderly widower who is blind and physically frail but in full possession of his mental faculties. His middle-school education is unusual for a man of his generation (b. 1908), and his military service in the War of Liberation and subsequent position as a cadre in commercial management have not lowered his status. As a retired state cadre he receives a pension, which most rural residents do not, and he therefore still contributes to the household economy. The members of his family who live with him, and other members of the village as well, are proud of his undivided household of three married sons and nine grandchildren. Nevertheless, two of the sons are working and living in the distant city where their father was formally a cadre and are too far away to return frequently, nor are their children living in the larger household. The household has not formally divided, in deference to a respected father, but it is less of an approximation to an extended household than the first one cited. The distant location of the first and third sons' employment and their greater ages are factors moving this household further from the extended family model.[9]

It is unquestionably the norm in all three villages that households with more than one son divide. Sons often remain within the parental household for a time after marriage, although they may do so in a separate house. This is partly an elaboration on the separate quarters customarily provided a newly married couple within the parental household; it is also an adaptation to space shortages and housing regulations that make it difficult or impossible to add to an existing house. A second house provides a solution and also prepares the ground for the division that will follow within a few years. One of the three villages, Huaili, also shows signs of a new rural pattern: weddings do not take place until a house has been built for the new bride. In Qianrulin the wedding may take place, but the bride is unlikely to take up continuous residence with her husband until a separate house is built and the household divides. In Zhangjiachedao it remains common for a young couple to occupy part of the husband's parents' house in their early marital years.

A feature of the current demographic situation in rural China is that the generations that have recently married, or that will soon do so, are ones born before any significant official move to reduce the birth rate. The sibling sets of grooms often include brothers, and this will continue to be the case for some time. The present pattern is for older sons to divide out of the parental households one at a time, within a few years of marrying. This is an accepted and expected occurrence. Whether the youngest son also divides out is less certain: some do and some do not.

Villagers disagree on this situation, and their responses appear to present the choice made in each household as the preferred and normative one. Many parents in or approaching this situation clearly prefer that the youngest or only son remain in the household. This is evidently not the only possible choice, and some of the alternatives are harmonious and attractive, such as division but continued sharing of the same courtyard and daily close association and cooperation, or a similar arrangement with houses at a slight distance (often as a result of houses being built at different times, with resulting site constraints).

All three villages also contain households composed solely of a senior generation (a couple or even a widow or widower) with married sons or daughters in separate households in the same village. In such situations, the combined force of affective ties, cultural expectations, social pressure, and legal requirement ensures that the material needs of the senior generation are taken care of by the households of their married sons or, in some cases, their married daughters. Official prescription requires, but stops at, familial economic responsibility for the care of the elderly: it does not prescribe co-residence. Popular village norms are shifting but still encourage co-residence, as indicated by a continuing large number of stem family households.

Table 5.1 provides some information in schematic form on samples[10] of households in the three villages. The conventional categorization into family types is limited in the information it provides, but at least serves to indicate the high incidence of nuclear family households. I am confident that the extended family households in the samples are the only extended families in these villages. Without implying that the readily

TABLE 5.1
Sample Distribution of Family Types in Zhangjiachedao (1986),
Qianrulin (1987), and Huaili (1989)

Village	Family type				
	Nuclear	Stem	Extended	Other	Total
Zhangjiachedao	61	13	0	10	84
Qianrulin	17	14	1	1	33
Huaili	23	10	1	6	40

NOTE: These samples overrepresent the proportion of extended families and atypical family or household forms, because they were constructed to explore the range of kinship organization in each village, so atypical households were included to the maximum extent possible. Those families categorized under "other" include single-person households, those composed of a widow with children, stem or nuclear households with added individual relatives, a household that has reincorporated a divorced daughter and adopted her son, and composite households arising from remarriage.

categorizable households all represent unambiguous or homogeneous forms of relationship, it is worth commenting on the households categorized under "other." These represent a wide range of additional possibilities, some of which are at least partially assimilated to the other three categories but which are nevertheless distinctive. They include: single-person households (all in the sample are elderly), households each composed of a widow with children, stem or nuclear households with added individual relatives (a husband's younger sister, an orphaned nephew who is informally adopted, and an aged uncle of the household head), a household that has reincorporated a divorced daughter and adopted her son, and composite households arising from remarriage.

There is much more flexibility in familial relations than indicated by the clear boundaries of the household system, or even by actual residence. After division, the newly formed households vary in the degree of separation they maintain, but some do stay very close and may even constitute aggregate families, a type of family consisting of more than one household (Croll 1987a).

Expressed popular views on the subject of desired family form are varied, contradictory, and in flux. There is a continuing high valuation put on a large multigeneration family living together in one harmonious household. Such households are consistently referred to in positive tones, which can be interpreted as showing both respect for the social achievement they represent and admiration for the double good fortune of children and long life. Whether because the good fortune cannot be counted upon or because the social achievement is increasingly difficult, people do not necessarily, and do not openly, aspire to a large household.

The most obvious aspiration in this direction is the sometimes expressed and evidently deeply felt wish that the youngest or only son will not divide out. This preference is very real but may not be universal or universally strong. It is moderated by the intensely close relations between the households of parents and sons that often follows division, relations that may include young grandchildren spending every day with their grandparents and even daily commensality. In Qianrulin, for example, it is considered normal and expected that *every* divided-out son and his wife make a daily visit to his parents.

Division may allow for very substantial continued cooperation and care, and the parental generation is just as likely to be giving as receiving. The losses implied by division are consequently limited, and they are balanced by advantages that are valued by some, if not by all and if not equally. Household division facilitates the enhanced personal autonomy that is now a legitimate goal to pursue in China, and that is notably pursued by younger people. Young men are no longer dependent on resources controlled by their fathers, although they can marry only with the help of both their parents and a wider circle of kin in meeting the heavy costs of a wedding and a new house. Young women can often reduce the tensions between mother-in-law and daughter-in-law by pressing for division, and even by spending lengthy periods of time with their natal families until a division occurs (see Judd 1989). Provided a young couple has access to childcare by one of their parents, preferably the husband's mother, they have the possibility of being otherwise independent economically. Cooperation and help will continue, but the possibility of relative economic autonomy even for a newly established nuclear family provides a basis for moving away from stem families.

This move is further complicated by the often conflicting effects produced by the different dyadic relations within a larger household. The daughter-in-law/mother-in-law tension receives most explicit attention in any discussion of this issue, and the handling of this relationship may determine whether a youngest or only son remains in a stem family or divides out. Other relationships may also prove tense, although they are more difficult to express openly and may indirectly surface through daughter-in-law/mother-in-law tensions. Certainly, where this or any other household relationship is difficult, division is available as a solution and is one whose harsher side can be softened by way of a wide range of close postdivision relationships between the two households and their members.

Division is more often welcomed by the younger generation and, within it, by the daughter-in-law, who is much more comfortable in her own home. Some village leaders in Zhangjiachedao were at pains to indicate that division is also preferred by the older generation. I am not convinced that their views were widely accepted among their peers in the village, but their arguments and policies are interesting. As one such leader pointed out, parents of young couples are often still vigorous, active adults and may be more affluent than their children. Despite the pervasive cultural emphasis on households remaining together to care for the elderly, the senior generation often supports the younger one well after the adulthood that normatively accompanies marriage. This leader, himself about sixty years of age, held that this promoted dependency among the young and hence was undesirable. He compared household division with decollectivization and the end of institutionalized collective practices of shared consumption without direct economic incentives, or what was known as "everyone eating from one big pot." In the same way that the breaking down of collectives into smaller units heightened responsibility and productivity, he held that the breaking down of large households into nuclear family households would decrease dependency and increase initiative on the part of the young. The village rehousing program provided for row houses suitable in size for a nuclear or a small stem family, and according to this official, the housing policy was intentionally directed toward promoting small families. Households could, however, arrange to divide formally yet live side by side, sharing a courtyard and, if their members wished, remaining in practice a single, undivided household. A spatially different but socially similar alternative that could be done without building more than one house at one time placed closely related households to the front or back of each other in separate rows that were constructed in different years. Similarly, in Qianrulin and Huaili one household might own two spatially separated houses.

The policies through which Zhangjiachedao encouraged smaller households did not imply lack of concern for the well-being of the elderly. The village enforced the legal requirement that sons contribute to the care of their parents; it also provided housing and financial support, at the average per capita income level for the village, for elderly persons without any children to care for them. Although daughters are also legally required to support their parents under the revised Marriage Law that came into effect in 1981, this is not considered enforceable in the same sense as it is for men, simply because the daughters may already live beyond the bounds of their parents' village. One elderly woman from Zhangjiachedao lives with her married daughter in a city in another province, an arrangement facilitated by an economic subsidy from the village. Indeed, sons in the village are fined if they do not support their parents; daughters outside the village receive economic aid if they do support them.

The remaining significant gender difference here concerns daughters who have not yet married out of the village. Village leaders have partly turned to intravillage arranged matches for one daughter of each set of parents without sons, where they can arrange it. Intravillage marriages have occurred in Zhangjiachedao in the past, as love matches, but have come to be seen as a solution for the care of the elderly, like uxorilocal marriage. Huaili shows similar signs of both intravillage and uxorilocal matches made for the care of a woman's parents, and also of active village-level official involvement in arranging these matches.

Household Boundaries

The households discussed here are not formal constructs derived from or designed for systematic cross-cultural comparison, so the question of what precisely constitutes a "household" has not been directly addressed. A Chinese household is what it is defined to be, and politically realized as being, within the household registration system, but it is also a somewhat more flexible and ambiguous concept as lived in the political economy of everyday life. It also bears some resemblance to exogenous anthropological conceptions of the household. An exogenous definition of the household would fall victim to the pitfalls indicated by Collins (1986) of substituting formal abstraction for lived relations, of missing historical processes through which new forms of household are created in the contemporary world, and of inadequately addressing relations that do not coincide with formal household boundaries.

I address the issue of household boundaries and boundary maintenance at this point not in order to seek means of imposing criteria for separating supposedly discrete social units, but because the dynamics of maintaining household boundaries is a critical process in the wider dynamics of relations within and between households. The exploration of household boundary maintenance is both a precondition and an internal component of the analysis of that wider social field.

Villagers with whom I spoke strongly emphasized the separation of their respective households from one another. Members of households, and especially the senior women in them, were emphatic about the independence of their own households. It is unquestionably the ideal that each household should be self-sufficient, even while it is tacitly acknowledged that this ideal is impossible. If the ideal cannot be attained, various strategies are nevertheless available to approach it and to affirm it on a symbolic plane, while simultaneously achieving the accommodation necessary for daily cooperation. A keystone in this pattern is the strong expression that members of each household properly adhere to norms of being on good terms with *everyone*, but on especially good terms with *no particular person or household*. The object here is a strategic balance in which a household can enjoy the benefits of diffuse neighborliness and cooperation without creating either special ties or jealousy.

The association between strong expression of household boundaries and the voices of mature women suggests that gender is an implicit but effective structuring element in the creation and maintenance of household boundaries. One older woman stated what was both an ideal and an approximate reality: "Each household has its own economy and looks after itself." Another older woman indicated even more firmly that "everyone deals with their own problems." A tone of affirming one's confidence and self-respect emerges from statements of this nature.

Households are closely associated with women, and the senior woman in each household has a real and felt responsibility for its well-being. She has typically left her natal home to enter a household in unknown social territory, and this is still the case for women marrying at the present time. This radical change upon marriage is a test each woman faces in the process of becoming an adult, and her success in handling it is a measure of her as a person. Her subsequent life is spent within the constraints of encouragement to tend to her household and not to involve herself in matters beyond it, whether community issues or the business of other households. New brides are expected to stay within their mother-in-law's household and not to associate with women in other households. Their only relief from this pattern is visiting their natal family—and the prospect of greater autonomy in the future as they assume the social role currently held by their mother-in-law. In later years mature women are expected to associate with the wives of their husbands' brothers and may also associate with the wives of other friends of their husbands and with neighboring women, but this does not imply or require particular closeness. Closer friendships may form, but this is discouraged and women prefer not to draw attention to such ties.

Women's visiting outside the home is quickly put in the pejorative category of "running around" (*chuanmen*), which implies neglect of one's proper business and idle meddling in the affairs of others. A young woman's morals and respect for her marital household (and mother-in-law) are put into question by such behavior. An older, mature woman will be viewed as neglecting her own household, where her responsibilities may be formidable, and as encroaching on the households of other women. The only contact with other women readily admitted for women in this age category is that of prescriptive and diffuse neighborliness or, in a few cases, being sought out within their own homes for help or advice by other women (but no woman says that she does this). Elderly women who have passed household responsibility on to a mature daughter-in-law may legitimately "run around," and they do so very actively. This is not only a question of relaxed controls on respectability for elderly women, although it may be phrased in that way; it is also a recognition that after "retiring" their contacts with other "retired" women do not threaten the boundaries of their own or other households.

This is not to suggest that household boundaries are so deep that they prevent women from forming informal networks.[11] The boundaries, which partly serve the particular interests of the senior woman in each household, discourage such ties and do isolate some women, especially those without ready-made networks of sisters-in-law (specifically, husband's brothers' wives; *saozi*). However, these boundaries are not the immutable entities implied by the physical metaphor of the word "boundary." Rather, they are one of the negotiable elements in a fluid and contested social field. The assertion of the existence of boundaries obscures ties that cross those boundaries, especially ties between women where those are effectively formed, while providing each senior woman in a household with a base protected from open encroachment. The legitimacy of household boundaries is not so much a fact as a strategic resource.

The chief agents in processes of household boundary maintenance are the senior female and senior male member of each household, younger and older members being less influential and consequently less in control of the household's place in the society outside the protective walls of the courtyard.[12] The ties women and men create beyond the household are strikingly different, and this difference is part of the explanation of household boundaries as an issue of strategic contention.

The fundamental concern here is the integrity, continuity, and control of a household's economy. Additional elements, such as privacy and the partial seclusion of women, are also involved and interwoven with economic issues, but it is the household economy that is central. Consequently, household economy is the subject of unspoken, gendered contention regarding household boundaries. Precisely because the boundaries are not rigid and fixed, and cannot possibly become so without threatening a household's access to wider networks of cooperation and help, the *management* of the household's boundaries is essential to the economic interests both of the household as a whole and of its various members. Moreover, although it is advantageous to preserve the resources of one's own household, it is also advantageous to gain access to those of other households. Rural life is largely determined by the enormous unpredictability of both natural processes and social processes (prices and policies determined elsewhere) beyond villagers' control, so they need to be prepared for all possible eventualities.

The balance of generosity and cooperation on the one hand with saving and secrecy about income on the other is a tactic deployed within the larger strategies of adjusting household boundaries toward each household's optimum. These concerns are presumably long-standing matters in peasant communities,[13] although they were moderated in the collective era, when households had a much reduced economic role and when incomes were more equal, open, and based on a small range of options usually controlled at levels above the household. Decollectivization and the revitalization of household-based economies have made household-oriented strategies much more significant. Household boundaries receive more emphasis and are more problematic in

Huaili, the village in this study with the most household-oriented economy, than in Qianrulin or Zhangjiachedao, with their more public economies centered on village industry.

The revitalized household economy is being created in a milieu qualitatively different from the household economy that preceded collectivization, despite some formal resemblances. Kin relations of various types are of continuing importance and may even be of greater importance than in the past. Families have become more stable than in times of higher mortality, migration, and economic hardship. They have also been affected by state structures that have, paradoxically, reinforced the family, both as a means of consolidating the state's political economy (by relying on it to provide social benefits the state cannot provide) and as a long- and short-term refuge from shifting political winds.

Moreover, kin relations in the countryside are now operating in an increasingly commercialized society and culture. Commercialization has a long history in China and is intrinsic to peasant societies, but the sudden shift toward a commercial orientation, together with the cash incomes generated by the thriving rural economy in the early 1980s, constituted a dramatic change from the circumstances of recent decades. The management of kin relations within this cash nexus is one of the current problems of everyday life in rural China.[14] In the past kin relations were not separate from economic considerations, but there was a less complicated economy to consider. In addition, relations with the community of those who were in a common accounting unit during the collective era add more people with a history of economic claims on one another. To the extent that suprahousehold organization persists, these ties continue in modified form into the present.

Kin, and to a lesser extent neighbors, expect generosity from one another, including (for kin) substantial help with such expensive and essential matters as the wedding of a son and providing a son and daughter-in-law with a new house. These are among the most inflationary items in a generally inflationary economy. At the same time that generosity is required, it is also important both to be prosperous and to be seen as being so. The latter is necessary not only for prestige but to ensure good marriage matches for one's children. Tight control of a household's economy and careful choices about obligations and generosity are unavoidable. To ensure its financial integrity and try to enhance it, a household is well served by careful negotiation of its economic boundaries. Social ties can easily become economic claims, so these must also be controlled. Secrecy in economic matters is essential to the practice of calculated generosity, and this is an intrinsic element in household boundary maintenance.

Every member of the household is normatively involved both in maintaining the desired good-but-even relations with members of other households and in protecting the interests of his or her own household. The most active agents in these processes are those primarily responsible for a household's well-being—most commonly a mature couple of husband and wife, but sometimes a widow and her co-resident son or a female household head with a usually absent husband. It is these persons who are able to determine in which directions the household may build specially close economic ties and perhaps allow the household's resources to "leak" beyond its boundaries. The exact possibilities here depend both on the internal relations within the household and on the various ties available beyond the household, but some common structuring features are identifiable, and these are connected with gender.

A primary point of leakage is with close agnatically related households within the same village. Close family ties and a possibly recent history of some members being in the same household may minimize household barriers if personal relations are good. Small children may provide a major channel for contact where a paternal grandmother is caring for a child who is not in her own household: she is the first choice for childcare, and young mothers almost always engage in income-generating work if it is available and if adequate arrangements can be made for their young children. In Huaili the agnatic bias in land-group composition adds a basis of economic cooperation. Close agnatic relatives expect help from each other for ritual occasions and in times of need. Ties through men are especially important here, although some of the actual arrangements are made by the mothers and wives of agnatically related men. Restrictions on women's extrahousehold ties and the social pattern of women marrying outside their own communities (but preferably not into a community into which a sister has married) help ensure that leakage of household economic resources in the village occurs within a confined agnatic grouping in which there are reciprocal obligations. Simultaneously, the intensity of obligation generates protective measures of boundary creation and maintenance.

Women's ties that generate competing demands for household resources are focused at first on their natal families (Judd 1989) but may later come to include married-out daughters. Most households assist a woman's natal family with the substantial expenses of weddings for its sons and building houses for the new couples; where relative circumstances warrant, they also provide additional help in the form of money, loans, or sometimes labor. Assistance to a married-out daughter most commonly takes the form of the maternal grandmother caring for small grandchildren where a paternal grandmother is not available. Some other forms of economic cooperation may also occur, such as providing loans for investment, but the localized nature of most rural economic activity, even when it is not agricultural, combined with the norms of village exogamy and patrilocal postmarital residence, make direct matrilateral cooperation in production impracticable. *This set of ties is best understood as women's ties of practical kinship, outside the formal discourse of patrilineal kinship relations.* Their husbands are also involved, but conceptualizing these ties as ones between male affines would misrepresent the character of the relationships involved and the gender and identity of their primary agents.

The Uterine Family: Children and Grandmothers

Beyond the cultural construction of household boundaries lies a fabric of social relations within and between households, much of which is woven from strands of official and practical kinship. Many of these relations are continuing elements of the culture, and there is no need to reiterate the classic features of prescriptive patriarchal authority, maternal nurturing, or mother-in-law/daughter-in-law tensions.[15] Yet there are emerging changes that prompt a reconsideration of some important aspects of Chinese family organization, and that even qualify the character of these presumed constants of patriarchal authority, maternal nurturing, and mother-in-law/daughter-in-law tensions. Despite reemphasis on the importance of the rural household, as Croll (1988: 99) has observed, relations internal to the rural household remain little studied. Further analysis of these relations is essential to understanding the household and to achieving a richer conceptualization of the field of relations in which it is an important nexus.

The critical changes here are ones of generation, interacting in complex fashion with preexisting patterns of gender difference. Most obviously, the economic base of fathers' patriarchal authority over sons has been weakened. The collective system had already weakened it by depriving household heads of control over the means of production, but the collective system had distributed individually earned work-point income in lump sums to households and had placed a high workpoint value on the labor performed by older men. Decollectiviza-tion may be said to have returned the means of production to the household, and some household heads do exercise formidable author-ity, but household division provides a young married son with access to a share of the household's resources—and hence to potential inde-pendence—based on those resources and on the income-earning abil-ities of himself and of his wife.

Norms valuing household independence and accepting the prac-tice of division facilitate early division and weaken the authority of the father and the significance of the father-son axis in the wider network of kinship relations. The father seems best able to retain authority and prevent division where he runs a nonagricultural household enter-prise dependent on his own skills, contacts, or management. Such in-stances were not common in these three villages. The trend is toward early division and the formation of loose relations of cooperation, as in land groups, which meet filial obligations but mute patriarchal authority.

The more interesting questions involve generation and the uterine family. The concept of the uterine family (M. Wolf 1972) expresses the relations of practical kinship in which women implicitly nurture fami-lies of their own descendants despite, and to some extent against, the patrilineal model, which officially appropriates lines of descent. Wom-en nurture sons to care for them in later years; they protect the inter-ests of their respective uterine families against the claims of the uterine families of other women in the same household; they rely on ties with sons in preference to ties with their husbands; they marginalize their husbands in the process of creating and consolidating uterine families centered on themselves; and they compete with their daughters-in-law for their sons' allegiance.

The concept of the uterine family is a major element in contempo-rary thinking regarding Chinese kinship, and is one of the most in-fluential concepts contributed by the anthropological study of China to other branches of sinology (see, for example, Johnson 1983) and an-thropology (see Lamphere 1974). It has not been significantly devel-oped since Margery Wolf initially created the concept, although the lines of analysis she applied to the dynamics of extended family households

in Taiwan, and with which she created the uterine family concept, remain productive.

The field of relationships in which the uterine family is located has
shifted sufficiently to pose questions about the form the uterine family
may take at present and in the near future. Certain of the specific features encouraging the uterine family in the form in which Wolf found
it are no longer prevalent in China. Most obviously, plural marriage has
long been illegal and seems actually to have disappeared, and extended families are relatively rare. These changes significantly reduce the
extent to which a mature woman is in a competitive position within
her own household in relation to other mature women.

The pattern of early household division and a degree of acceptability for youngest or only sons dividing out has an impact on a woman's
relationship with her married sons and with her daughters-in-law. She
may, of course, effectively use the ties of her uterine family to hold one
son and, in the best of situations, create a harmonious relationship with
his wife. This will permit a stem family to continue, and the situation
will in some respects resemble the familial model the mother-in-law
would have known in the years of her childhood, and in early adulthood as a daughter-in-law herself. There are nevertheless likely to be
some significant changes, both for mother-in-law and for daughter-in-
law.

The possibility that a daughter-in-law will prefer to divide out, even
if she is married to the youngest or only son, gives her a degree of informal but very real power in her relationship with her mother-in-law.
Young women would never mention this themselves, but both women
and men in senior generations spoke very matter-of-factly about this
change in the status of daughters-in-law. A good daughter-in-law re-
strains her show of this power and is respectful of her mother-in-law,
helping with cooking and other domestic tasks and not removing herself from her mother-in-law's household without permission except to
return to her natal family. Formerly the latter, too, required the mother-in-law's permission, and whether it still does is a question not settled in every household. Nevertheless, daughters-in-law in these villages do have their natal homes as places of relaxation, refuge, and often indulgence during the early days of their marriage, and may also
use prolonged visits at their natal homes as a means of signaling a wish
for or forcing an early division. All the same, a proper young woman
has a good relationship with her mother-in-law and, in the modern de-

finition of model young womanhood, such a relationship is especially expected of a woman Party or Young Communist League member.

In short, daughters-in-law have a vastly improved status vis-à-vis their mothers-in-law than their mothers-in-law experienced when they were young daughters-in-law. Older women who are now mothers-in-law readily observe that their daughters-in-law have a much easier existence than they had at the same point in their lives. The older women are able to accept this change with some grace because their own lives have also become easier than they might earlier have expected.

Young daughters-in-law may retain their own income earned outside the household. A woman's marital family is reluctant to claim a woman's income after she is married and before children have fully incorporated her into her marital household. And, even if she is spending much of her time with her natal family, her income no longer belongs to it. The period between a woman's marriage and the birth of her first child may be one of the most pleasant periods of her life, despite the stress of transitions to adulthood and to a new community, provided that her relations with her new husband are smooth. She may be temporarily relieved from work outside the home and be pampered by a natal family concerned to ease her departure, as well as by a marital family desiring to establish good relations with a daughter-in-law who has the power to provoke a division.

The arrival of a daughter-in-law has some benefits for the mother-in-law. The economic anxieties that intensified a woman's dependence on her sons have been eased by general economic improvements, at least in these communities, and by effective legal and customary obligations on sons for the support of their parents. Personal considerations and social adjustments to a son's marriage and to the addition of a (prescriptively restrained and timid but helpful) strange woman to the household remain unavoidably difficult, however normal and expected. Women do not expect to know their daughters-in-law before marriage, and some women I spoke with whose sons were engaged were unable to tell me the name of the fiancée and might not have met her. I presume that the prolonged absences of new daughters-in-law visiting their natal families are as much a pleasure for the mothers-in-law as for the daughters-in-law. However, when the initial period of adjustment is passed, even the most indulgent mother-in-law will find her workload considerably lightened.

The arrival of a woman's first daughter-in-law may provide her first substantial relief from a double burden carried through the course of many years, including years of much more difficult economic circumstances. (Growing daughters may also help, but they are more likely to be working long days in any income-generating work outside the household that can be found, and hence may not be asked to do domestic work as well. They will also be marrying out of the household within a few years.)[16]

As Croll (1979: 47) has noted, the work load for women in a multi-woman household is much lighter than in a one-woman household. Qianrulin shows a distinct pattern wherein women tend to retire from the agricultural work they have done all their adult lives when their household takes a daughter-in-law, who then replaces the older woman, now in her forties, in agricultural work. This is evidently not simply a matter of household composition, and is dependent on some modest economic margin, but it also indicates the greater extrahousehold economic value of the daughter-in-law, who is physically stronger and, given the pace of generational change in modern China, usually more educated and possibly more skilled. The mother-in-law will then look forward to caring for her son's children. This constitutes a division of labor that is economically advantageous to the household and generally welcomed by the mother-in-law.[17] By this point, the situation of the daughter-in-law is less comfortable than in the early days of marriage, and she will likely benefit from the help of her mother-in-law with childcare and domestic labor.

The conditions under which the strategies of the uterine family can be deployed have shifted significantly. The young mother will likely still be providing substantial care for her infant and young child, but the primary caregiver is usually the paternal grandmother. Young mothers have acquired—or have had imposed—a greater role as extra-household income earners than they previously had, and a much greater role in this respect than that included in the basic uterine family model. They lose some contact with their young children in the process, but the mother-child tie is implicitly assumed to hold. The interesting element here is the conditions provided for *a shift in uterine family strategy to the paternal grandmother–grandchild relation*. The daughter-in-law's work outside the home allows the mother-in-law to form close ties with her grandchildren, and *through them with their parents*.

This strand of relationship was rarely commented on spontaneously, and not in such explicit terms, in the formal or informal discussions I had with villagers, but the role of paternal grandmothers in caring for grandchildren was readily apparent, openly discussed, and accepted without controversy. Indeed, the paternal grandmother is the first choice to care for children, even when it may mean sending them to another community and hence causing more or less lengthy separations from their parents. Where the stem family continues, older children may find themselves sharing a room and a bed or sleeping platform (*kang*) with a grandmother or grandfather. Where the stem family does not continue, or where division preceded the birth of a child, childcare by the paternal grandmother remains preferred and provides a framework for daily interaction between the two households, because the child is (usually) delivered to and fetched from the grandmother's home on a daily basis.

This shift in the identity of the primary agent in uterine family strategies from mothers to grandmothers is consistent with Margery Wolf's (1985: 206) later findings that older urban women emphasized uterine family strategies more than younger urban women did. She did not comment on the grandparental variation that I am identifying here, but she was referring to urban women for whom the uterine family strategy may have become less significant. Wolf did not identify either a reduction or an adaptation of uterine family strategies among rural women in her 1980 study (M. Wolf 1985), although I would argue that these can be identified as emergent in the countryside on the basis of the findings reported here. To some degree this represents an extension to some rural areas of relational patterns more typical of urban China. Adaptation of the uterine family strategy to changed rural conditions is also apparent in grandmothers building future security for themselves through care of their grandchildren. This is a creative response in the absence of other economic means, such as pensions, and in circumstances of extended life expectancy and widespread household division.

The Uterine Family: Women's Work

Restructuring uterine family strategies is intrinsically implied within the entire range of production and reproduction issues now centered on rural households. The analysis of this restructuring can be effectively approached through closer examination of the connection between the care of children and the economic role of rural women in a shifting pattern of division of labor.

That children have a highly valued place in Chinese culture is a point that requires no emphasis, although it does underlie the importance of issues involving childcare.[18] Every married couple (and their parents) in rural China aspire to the early birth of at least one child.[19] In the communities studied here, there is sufficient affluence to occasionally allow early retirement on the part of women over 40 and a sometimes lighter work load for household members in general, but rarely an affluence that can support the removal of young mothers from income-generating work. Besides, many people have chosen to make the most of favorable economic and political conditions to work harder and earn more.

I met only one young mother in these three villages who had voluntarily removed herself from the work force. Together with her husband, she had built a highly profitable wholesale business that had made their household one of the wealthiest in Huaili. When the couple responded to changing economic circumstances by leaving the wholesale business, the husband went into factory management outside the village and the wife did not immediately seek other income-generating employment. She did, however, take an active role in her village through interest-free loans to other households and through unpaid work in the village women's organization. She could be viewed as actively pursuing local political avenues to make her household's conspicuous affluence acceptable and secure. This is evidently not a choice available to many rural women.

Many areas of China have been unable to provide full employment for the rural population, with the result that women have been marginalized in the labor force even in the highest economic growth years of the mid-1980s. The villages studied here are in somewhat better economic circumstances, and hence represent rural communities in which extrahousehold economic opportunities are present for both women and men (also see Judd 1990). Women may retire earlier and may perform hard labor for low pay, as in agriculture, but in these communities they do have the opportunity to earn income outside the household if they can make themselves available for such work.[20]

In the village of Huaili, 25 out of the 32 women in my 1989 sample who were married and under the age of 40 were fully occupied, and at

least 12 of these could be viewed (and in many cases identified themselves) as carrying the classic double burden of full work inside and
full work outside the home. The remaining 7 women either represented a range of exceptional circumstances, such as personal physical dis-
ability or temporary care of a seriously ill relative, or they were new
daughters-in-law who had not yet assumed a full role in their marital
households.[21] In Qianrulin, 17 of the 21 women in my 1987 sample who
were married and under the age of 40 could be considered fully occupied. One of the exceptions was a new daughter-in-law who had not
yet assumed work in her marital home. The 3 others combined agricultural and domestic work and may have been less than fully employed. They all had mothers-in-law resident in their households. In
Zhangjiachedao, 27 of the 32 women in my 1986 sample who were
married and under the age of 40 were judged fully occupied. Of these,
19 had identifiable employment outside the household and 8 combined agriculture with domestic labor. The remaining 5 combined agriculture and domestic labor as well, and 1 of the 5 was also engaged in a
part-time domestic sideline; all 5 were involved in income-generating
work, but they were not constrained by the relatively inflexible hours
of extradomestic employment and may have been underemployed. All
5 were the only adult woman in their respective households.

There is no doubt that young married women seek income-generating work when they can obtain it. In Qianrulin and Zhangjiachedao,
the most attractive income-earning opportunities were outside the
household in rural industry. In Huaili, the best opportunities were in
household-based commerce and commodity production, activities easier
to combine with childcare than factory work. In all three villages, small
amounts of agricultural land made agriculture a possible full- or part-
time activity. Young married women in all three villages expected to do
income-generating work while they were young mothers; they also expected that their households' standards of living would suffer if they
did not do so. Their mothers and mothers-in-law had all faced the same
demand and had worked for workpoints during the collective era.

Childcare arises as an issue only in this context of determining
availability for work. The time spent in childcare is essentially invisible
time,[22] and is apparently absorbed into the time every woman spends
in social interaction with members of her household and community.
Even relatively small children are not thought to require any care once
they are able to attend school, at six or seven years of age.

TABLE 5.2

Childcare Arrangements Mothers Reported for
39 Sibling Sets in the Village of Huaili, 1989

Primary caregiver[a]	Number of sibling sets
Paternal grandmother	13
Paternal grandmother; mother	9
Maternal grandmother	2
Maternal grandmother; mother	2
Paternal grandmother; maternal grandmother; mother	1
Paternal grandmother; paternal grandfather	1
Mother	8[b]
Orphaned nephew; mother	2
Mother's classificatory younger sister; paternal grandmother	1
Total	39

[a]Where there is a combination of primary caregiver, this represents a sequence and was usually the result of a grandmother's decease or illness.

[b]Of the 8 cases where the mother listed herself as the sole primary caregiver, 4 explicitly indicated the unavailability of both grandmothers.

Kindergarten may also be viewed as obviating the need for childcare, although the day-only childcare available in Zhangjiachedao was not adequate for meeting the needs of shiftworkers in the village's main factory, and Huaili's kindergarten had recently lost its sole teacher and had closed indefinitely. In any event, kindergartens have a limited clientele, as the definite preference is for care to be provided by a grandmother. Also, kindergartens do not care for infants or toddlers, although mothers will undertake work outside the home within three or four months of giving birth if a grandmother is available to care for the child.

Table 5.2 shows the childcare arrangements mothers in all living generations reported for 39 sibling sets in Huaili. Where there is a combination of primary caregiver noted, this represents a sequence and was usually the result of a grandmother's decease or illness. Of the 8 cases where the mother herself is listed as the sole primary caregiver, 4 explicitly indicated the unavailability of both grandmothers due to death, illness, or (in one case of a maternal grandmother) excessive distance, and 1 more said that her paternal grandmother was still having children herself.

The first preference for childcare, and a uniform preference expressed by everyone I met (except for one atypical grandmother),[23] is
for the paternal grandmother to care for her son's children, whether or
not she lives in the same household. This is not an absolute obligation
but in most cases she is willing to give this care, provided she is able to
do so. It is also the most effective contemporary means of maintaining
her uterine family. Depending on her own household's circumstances,
the paternal grandmother may either combine childcare with other forms
of work readily performed in the household (domestic labor, animal
husbandry, or domestic sidelines) or she may cease other activities and
make the care of one or more grandchildren her entire contribution to
her family.

Usually children's mothers will care for them outside their own
working hours, but even so, children may spend virtually all their
waking hours and take most or all their meals with their paternal
grandmother, even if she is living in another household. In some cases
children will be almost wholly cared for by their grandmothers (paternal or maternal), as when both parents are working in a town or city
and do not have access to childcare. Small children may then live in the
countryside in the grandparental home until they begin school.

Paternal grandmothers are not always available to care for their
grandchildren. Although the standard pattern of early marriage and
early parenthood makes most women grandmothers in their forties,
early death or ill health may nevertheless intervene. Several descriptions provided by mothers of their history of childcare arrangements
indicated a shift in care from the paternal grandmother to the mother
during the grandmother's final illness. Women in China very often
continue to perform childcare and domestic labor as long as they are
able to do so, which may extend into their eighties. There is much less
evidence of older people in the countryside "retiring" from work than
the culture's explicit value on age would seem to indicate.

Some of the middle-aged women interviewed described an additional constraint when they were raising their children during the 1960s
or 1970s: their mothers-in-law might still have been working in the collective for workpoints and unable to afford to stop doing so to care for
grandchildren. Changed economic conditions have for the most part
removed this constraint in these villages, because of increased rural incomes and because the allocation of land to households removes the
previous incentive for extended work hours, provided that the house-

hold has enough other labor power to work its land allotment. Another pattern which has disappeared is that of a woman's mother-in-law being busy raising her own younger children when she first becomes a grandmother. As previously mentioned, one woman told me that rather than being helped with childcare by her mother-in-law, she had helped her mother-in-law.

The invariable second choice for childcare is the maternal grandmother. She is less commonly available because her paternal grandchildren have prior claim, and grandmothers are not expected to care for an unlimited number of grandchildren. In some cases distance is a problem, since daughters have usually married out of their mother's marital village. But the distances involved are rarely more than a few kilometers, and small children can be, and are, readily transported by bicycle to and from their maternal grandmothers on a daily basis. This practice is not culturally elaborated but is a common and explicitly acceptable arrangement. It is one of the elements of a complex of practical kinship revolving around women and their natal families, which are always referred to as a woman's "mother's family" (*niangjia*). In addition to the other aspects of this complex, which I have discussed elsewhere (Judd 1989), some questions can be raised here about the implications of this customary practice for an understanding of the uterine family.

Maternal grandmothers figure more prominently in mothers' childcare considerations than Table 5.2 might suggest—in a number of the cases where women said that they cared for their children themselves, or where they sought less usual arrangements, they made the point that the maternal grandmother as well as the paternal grandmother was either deceased or seriously ill. The mother's mother appears never to be excluded from consideration simply because she is the maternal rather than paternal grandmother.

Daughters, too, are part of a woman's uterine family and, at least in the areas of Shandong reported on in this study, the ties of caring and economy between a woman and her natal family typically last as long as either of her parents is alive.[24] Besides the visits daughters make to their natal families, mothers make visits to their married daughters, often by themselves. The distances are usually not great, and even when a daughter may live in a remote city, as far away as one of the Northeast provinces, her mother will visit her if at all possible. The ties between mothers and their married daughters have been greatly under-

estimated in the scholarly literature, although I doubt that they are un-
derestimated in the Shandong countryside.

Daughters (and their marital families) customarily give some assistance to their natal families, where absolute and relative economic conditions warrant; moreover, the provisions of the revised Marriage Law
that came into effect in 1981 make a daughter's support of her parents
obligatory. The legal change is too recent to explain the niangjia complex, but the customary economic ties and affective-moral ties are well
established. *The nurturance of daughters* is a part of the building of a uterine
family, even if sons and their families take precedence. Mother-daugh-
ter ties may also serve as a uterine balance against the mother-in-law/
daughter-in-law stresses to which both are subject, albeit from different quarters and different perspectives. It should not be surprising that
this strand of the uterine family can extend to a woman's care of her
daughter's children.

As indicated by Table 5.2, where a grandmother is not available,
other relatives may be sought to care for a woman's children and thus
enable her to work outside the home. Grandfathers do sometimes do
this, where there is need and where their health permits. The two separate instances of orphaned "agnatic nephews" (*zhi*) caring for younger children continues, in slightly modified form, an earlier pattern of
older children caring for younger ones. This pattern was often referred
to in another context, even by relatively young married women in their
thirties, as a reason for their never having attended school. In earlier
decades older children, especially daughters, would often care for
younger siblings and perform domestic labor so their mothers could
contribute to the family income.

This arrangement is not unknown in parts of China at present, but
I found only one instance of it in these villages. Several factors have
contributed to this change. The obvious ones are improved health care,
which results in grandmothers being more readily available, and improved access to at least primary education. Less obvious, but equally
or more important, is the value of the labor power of teen-aged girls.
When younger they may be valuable in the home, but by the time they
are about 16 they are likely to be employable in rural industry or capable of generating income through agricultural or small-scale commercial work. If very young women are removed from school for economic
reasons in these villages, they are more likely to be working outside
the home than enabling their mothers to do so. Preferred childcare ar-

rangements involve persons who do not have even moderate remunerative opportunities in other fields.

The practice of engaging young rural women as nannies (*baomu*), which became common in the cities in the 1980s, is rarely workable in these communities because it depends on a sufficient difference between the mother's income and the nanny's wage to make it attractive to both mother and nanny. This is difficult in many cases even in cities, where urbanites complain of the shortage of rural women willing to work for a nanny's pay.

Women in rural communities who do not have access to an older relative to care for their children may have no choice but to remove themselves from the extradomestic work force for a few years. But a woman who does so may still be able to contribute to her household's income through work performed in the home, such as various types of cottage industry on a "putting-out" basis, raising animals or vegetables in the courtyard, and types of household-based enterprise to which she can contribute without leaving the home.

As all this indicates, women's economic roles and changes in them are determining factors of household and familial relations and strategies, including the construction of uterine families. Most discussions of rural women's economic role in north China depart from Buck's (1964) massive survey conducted in 1929–33. The figures he obtained for women's and men's agricultural work in north and south China have been cited and reanalyzed widely, and are often construed as indicating a low level of participation by women in the rural economy. Thorborg's examination of Buck's figures shows participation rates of 16–23 percent for women in the rural economy of the north by a narrow and purely agricultural definition, and 20–27 percent by a wider definition that includes subsidiary occupations (Thorborg 1978: 585).[25] These figures are sufficiently high to call into question the common wisdom of northern Chinese women being predominantly nonproductive, but even these figures must be questioned. The proportions are biased downward by an inclusion of all women between the ages of 15 and 59—the lower limit may well be too high, but the upper limit is certainly unrealistic.

In addition, it is unlikely that Buck's survey, conducted long before recent feminist critiques, succeeded in avoiding all the pitfalls that tend to render women's work invisible (see Rogers 1980). The argument for the latter problem is significantly buttressed, at least for Shandong, by

Martin Yang's (1945) detailed description of the standard rural division of labor in Taitou. The oldest generation of women I interviewed in all three villages consistently stated that they had worked in agriculture in their natal villages before marriage, except in a few cases of exceptional wealth or exceptional poverty. There is little reason to view women in rural Shandong as new entrants to the sphere of income-generating work, although some of the specific circumstances have changed in the intervening decades (see Thorborg 1978, Judd 1990).

I will not attempt at this distance in time to reconstruct early twentieth-century patterns of division of labor or of balancing reproduction and production. It is sufficient to observe that the most comprehensive data base available can be interpreted as confirming women's significant role in production in rural north China at least as far back as 1930. Women in rural north China may in that era have used the uterine family strategy to enhance their position in their families and hence their own security, but they had other, economic strategies available to them as well. The household-oriented rural division of labor described by Martin Yang (1945) for a community of small-landholding peasants in the early part of the century amply indicates some of the possibilities in households with real but modest resources.

Collectivization altered this division of labor by making the primary cooperative and productive unit a large, suprahousehold one, whether at production team or at brigade level. Women were active in the extradomestic work force during this era (see Thorborg 1978, Judd 1990); however, as with men, the precise work performed was not coordinated at the household level, and it figured in the household economy only in terms of the value of the workpoints thus earned.

With the reconstitution of altered terms of household-based production, the issue was no longer simply that of workpoint contributions from household members but one of constructing a division of labor in production within the household. Of course, where the issue is solely urban-style employment and the earning of cash income, this may not arise, but such is rarely the situation in the countryside. Those with agricultural registration must either grow their own staple food or purchase it on the free market, because they are outside the state supply system. Although some rural households are sufficiently prosperous to abandon agriculture, the vast majority, including the overwhelming majority in Zhangjiachedao and Huaili,[26] must strive to combine food production in agriculture with one or more cash-earning endeavors. In principle, agriculture can also generate cash income, but none of these villages has a favorable ratio of agricultural land to population, and the area that can be sown to cash crops is limited. As is common throughout rural China, these villagers seek cash income in nonagricultural pursuits, and if they are unusual, it is in their comparatively good access to such opportunities (primarily in rural industry and commerce), despite the fact that none of the villages has the advantage of a suburban location.

The arrangements made within households to apportion their available labor power among various economic pursuits are complex and dependent on the opportunities available in each locality at a given time, as well as on whether the members of a particular household are positioned to make use of them. Various aspects of the economic problems this poses have been discussed in Chapters 2, 3, and 4. Here the particular point to be made is related to the virtual disappearance of the extended family, even among the wealthy, and the predominance of nuclear families. A consequence of this is that a household division of labor between adult males (father and son[s], or brothers), as described in Margery Wolf's (1968) classic study, is no longer the solution. Indeed, I observed a near absence of such relations.[27]

Moreover, in the agricultural and commercial village of Huaili, where such cooperation might be most expected, my interviews in all the self-defined and state-recognized specialized households revealed a strong aversion to the idea of partnership with brothers or other relatives. Nobody I spoke with expected such an arrangement to be free of conflict. Younger relatives (patrilateral or matrilateral) might be hired, and loans or some form of help might be given, but enterprises were strictly household affairs and none of the households involved was an extended family household.

A corollary of this situation is that the husband-wife economic partnership assumes particular importance. In a sense, the partnership of fathers and sons, or of brothers, is rendered nonessential because wives are full-time income-earners. This is most feasible where an older woman is available to care for children and perform domestic labor, but in her absence many wives effectively carry a full double burden. Thus the *division of labor between related men* that is familiar in the literature can be, and actually is, replaced by a *division of labor between husband and wife*.

The role assumed in the household by a wife who is her husband's primary economic partner is distinctly different from the role of a more dependent wife, and such a wife may be much less reliant on the strategy of constructing and consolidating a uterine family. Moreover, despite the continuing practice of arranged marriages, the husband-wife dyad is strengthened. This is not only the case for poor rural households—greater relative equality of husbands and wives in poorer families with little to rely on but their labor power has long been noted—but also occurs in rural households that have done well in the economic diversification and commercialization of the 1980s. It is an indication of a probable long-term trend in the countryside.

The uterine family strategy is more strongly evident, in its innovations as well as its continuity, among the present generation of grandmothers than among younger mothers. A strategy that has worked well and has much to recommend it will not necessarily be abandoned by these younger women, but it may come to assume a less central role in a wider repertoire of strategies.

In this process, new dynamics emerge within households that formally and superficially resemble earlier forms of nuclear or stem family, but that actually represent emerging new forms of household and family.[28] At the same time, relations are created across household boundaries that are as essential to the operation of households as are relations within them. The small size and limited internal complexity of the rural household pushes it and its members into close relations that transcend its simultaneously carefully maintained boundaries.

Between Households

Households are not wholly adequate units to perform many of the activities associated with them. The household is best viewed as only one significant nexus in a field of diverse relations and activities (see Yanagisako 1979). A cultural and currently ideological emphasis on the household, together with a history of formal analysis of households in cross-cultural comparison, have put excessive emphasis on the household. Yet households are important units of analysis and represent a significant unit of experienced rural social life. Households have a locally unavoidable place in the political economy of rural China because of their construction as powerful and legitimate social entities by state mechanisms, because they nearly coincide with nonofficial family units of social organization, and because they are the central units of corporate estates.[29]

In protecting the integrity of the household estate and in maintaining their household boundaries, villagers repeatedly emphasized that they cooperated with those outside their household "only when necessary." This explicit approach of avoiding cooperation and the fact that cooperation is very often necessary are the warp and the weft of the fabric of interhousehold cooperation.

A large portion of the interaction that transcends household boundaries, and that simultaneously internally constructs households as social units, consists of relations between households and suprahousehold organizations of either governmental or quasi-governmental character. The most important of these, in relation to households, operate at village level and have been the subject of sustained discussion in earlier chapters. If relations involving suprahousehold organizations are excluded from discussion, the activities and types of activity that involve households in relations beyond their bounds can be summarized as follows:

(1) Households may require some form of regular or occasional cooperation in the course of *production*. This varies in accordance with several considerations, especially the type of production in question. This aspect of interhousehold relationship has already been discussed in Chapters 2, 3, and 4.

(2) Households may *distribute* some of their income beyond household boundaries, usually to patrilateral or matrilateral kin.

(3) *Consumption* and *investment*, unless involving extrahousehold production links (such as pumps shared by land groups), rarely require cooperation with other households.

(4) Legitimate *reproduction* in rural China requires both legal marriage registration and a customary wedding ritual, and usually implies a conjugal tie within a household. There is some ambiguity about this if the members of the couple do not have the same household registration, but the unofficial, customary household does include both members of the couple. The significant interhousehold ties often involved in childcare by grandmothers in separate households have already been discussed.

(5) The household and, more importantly, the larger and more ambiguous unit of the family are responsible for providing most forms of

social security in the countryside. A few benefits may be generally provided by the village, but this is variable and many benefits, such as medical and hospital insurance, have been weakened since decollectivization. Economic support of persons unable to work on grounds of age or infirmity is provided by local government only if there are no relatives to assume this responsibility and if no other private arrangement can be made (see Palmer 1988). The most common ties this generates between households involve economic support rendered to healthy but elderly parents who are living separately from divided-out sons,[30] and to a married woman's natal family.

(6) All rural households are involved in various relations of *mutual aid*, involving either firm customary obligations or more optional and occasional cooperation. The most fixed of these ties involve obligations to aid patrilateral and matrilateral kin—with money, labor, or both—when they confront the major expenses of building a new house or celebrating the wedding of a son.[31] Help on the occasion of funerals is similarly obligatory. Other forms of cooperation may be mutual or asymmetrical and may involve major life decisions (such as acquiring nonagricultural registration) or small, everyday acts of cooperation (such as loans of cooking ingredients).

Those aspects of interhousehold relations closely connected to household and family relations and to the negotiation of household boundaries require particular attention. The following discussion focuses on activities not addressed in detail in other chapters—namely, distribution and mutual aid beyond the household.

Villagers widely expressed two different versions of the nature of interhousehold cooperation or, more accurately, of what they viewed as the prevailing norms: that every household looks after itself, and that everybody helps everybody else. This denial of cooperation or help,[32] together with the assertion of generalized assistance, may seem paradoxical at first glance. However, the combination can be understood as an accommodation to the reality of mutual interdependence that infringes on no household's proper position of respect and allows the fiction of evenness in social relations to be maintained.

Much of the extrahousehold distribution of money and labor occurs in contexts that, ideally, mute differentiation. The most pervasive, prescribed, and, for most households, significant distributary occasions are those of house-building, weddings, and funerals. Expectations and obligations vary with precise economic circumstances, and amounts of money or labor given or loaned by each household are noted, but these are circumstances every household expects to face, so more or less balanced reciprocity within the circle of agnatically related households is expected, provided that the households involved have a fair demographic balance and that each household is able to, and actually does, carry its weight. Neighbors are involved to a lesser extent in helping with the same occasions, and here, too, balanced reciprocity is roughly attainable. The continual repetition of this reciprocity provides a basis for the diffuse solidarity within the village to which residents of Huaili particularly point.

The same important occasions are also the time for some asymmetrical gift-giving, which is less predictable but still very common. A married woman and her marital household ideally contribute to the same occasions within her natal family, although the scope of this obligation is limited to her immediate natal family. Her natal family does not directly reciprocate. One might view this as a form of generalized reciprocity, although it occurs within such a large and dispersed marital area that it is less a vehicle for social solidarity than an additional resource that households facing major expenses may be able to utilize. Some households deny giving any such assistance, and in other cases the money or labor provided may be purely symbolic. The relative wealth of the natal and marital families is explicitly referred to as a conditioning factor, whereas it is not mentioned in the parallel agnatic context even if it actually is a factor.

The more problematic issues in interhousehold ties involve cooperation beyond the scope of customary or roughly symmetrical obligation. Despite the fact that many households require some assistance from others at some time and may always wish to have the possibility of this security available, every household would prefer not to be receiving assistance, or to be able to balance or justify this assistance in some legitimate manner. The result is a complex set of interhousehold obligations, the most significant of which involve what may be broadly termed scarce resources[33] and differential access to them.

I am referring here to relations other than those involved in the forms of economic cooperation that are normal and expected. For example, land is scarce in Huaili and is normally fully worked by the household to which it is allocated; moreover, the village has mechanisms to reclaim such land where it is not used by a given household, with the result that agricultural land for lease is very scarce. It is therefore a form of special consideration when one household leases land to another. This is not an unmentionable matter because it is understood that almost every household would prefer to have more land, and usually the leasing household does pay rent in cash or in grain.

However, the leasing of land is not a purely commercial transaction. The scarcity of land implies that it is not readily available on the market and that the opportunity to lease it is itself a matter of privilege. Thus it is something normally provided to a closely related household, usually through agnatic ties and usually within the same village. In addition, although some households in Huaili indicated that they leased some of their land to kin for less than the standard rate at which the village itself rented out its small amount of discretionary land, no household indicated that it charged more. Agricultural land has been commoditized to some degree, but it has not been removed entirely from the context of kin- and community-oriented considerations, nor is its price determined according to supply and demand. Consequently, access to surplus agricultural land is a means through which other-than-commercial ties can be reinforced.

Another instance in which atypical exchanges take place across household boundaries involves households that are short of labor power for agriculture, usually because one or more adults in the household is working far from home. The most common situation is that of an absent husband whose wife and children form a separate rural household.[34] The wife will have difficulty doing all the agricultural and domestic labor on her own, especially while her children are young. In this situation she is likely to receive a considerable amount of assistance in agricultural labor, especially during the busy seasons, from her husband's male agnates. This is considered help and is in the nature of a gift between households, but that does not preclude gifts in return. The absent husband and his household will seek means to reciprocate: his work elsewhere may, for example, provide him with access to resources that are scarce and valued in his village. Exchanges of this type are not spoken of as exchanges, especially because of the ambiguity surrounding the increasing commercialization of social relations in the countryside, but neither are they a source of embarrassment.

It is always easier to speak of only one side of such an exchange, and preferably the side in which one's own household is the giving party. Members of households with no other resources may be generous with the labor they contribute to other households, in agriculture or in house-building, and willingly speak of this as their contribution to a wide-spread network of reciprocity in the village, while leaving other aspects of the network unmentioned. Similarly, members of households that have been conspicuously successful in commerce willingly speak of the loans they provide for investment or for family needs to relatives and neighbors.

Through these mechanisms, the rich and the poor engage in strategies designed, for different reasons and in different ways, to mute and to negotiate the conflict generated by the increasing economic differentiation and inequality that has accompanied the reform program. The efforts at equalization more characteristic of the collective era have been replaced by maneuvering for relative advantage within a more thoroughly and explicitly unequal and hierarchically structured social order. Conflict between newly rich and poor households is suppressed and managed rather than harnessed to fuel a program of political change.

Not all the significant relationships between households established in these ways are readily presented, or actually occur, between households as units. The more obligatory relations typically do apply to entire households, but other, more optional ties often exist between persons in different households. These unavoidably impinge on the households to which the individuals belong, but are distinguishable from ties that involve whole households. Here gender differences are conspicuous.

Women and men both enter marriage with a set of kin ties, but these are different for women and for men, and the difference is confirmed by the everyday ties of patrilocal postmarital residence.[35] Kinship relations have become more significant in the wake of decollectivization, but the resulting pattern of kin relations is not directly predictable from either genealogical principles or preferential postmarital residence. Kin ties are drawn upon in selective, optional ways and often involve matrilateral ties wherever advantageous. Non-kin ties are also drawn upon to whatever extent possible, to aid a household in negotiating its way in an increasingly commoditized and fluid social world without depending solely on commercial relations (see Wang Sibin 1987). Although the commercialization of social relations is a pervasive trend, commercial ties are not perceived as reliable, so the object is to mobilize all available social ties and obligations in order to survive and thrive in this commercialized social milieu.

The significant everyday ties of most men are with their close male agnates,[36] and their wives are expected to have their closest everyday ties with the wives of these men. Where men's ties are not agnatic—these are often referred to as ties with neighbors—the wife is again expected to find her friends among the wives of her husband's friends. In this form of asymmetry, a wife's extrahousehold contacts are subsumed within her husband's, whether the exchanges that take place involve the members of the couple together (such as husbands helping to build a house while wives cook together for the builders) or separately (such as helping to sew a quilt or loaning a plow).

The subsumption of women's extrahousehold ties under the umbrella of their husbands' lifelong village ties restricts the realization in social interaction of conflicting or simply differing interests on the part of wives vis-à-vis husbands. This reinforces a separate effect generated by processes of household boundary maintenance. The priority of the household and its estate in determining the well-being of household members limits the extent to which members with differing interests can act independently beyond the household's bounds to realize their particular interests. Whether manifest or latent, the extent of difference or conflict within a household is variable and to some extent open to personal influence or control, but the restrictions that operate to contain these differences within the household are shared elements of the culture and social structure. This is not to suggest that such restrictions are absolute, but they do effectively restrict women's strategic means to pursue interests that diverge from those of other members of the household. This operates in favor of the interests of men being identified and realized as the dominant ones within a household, but it may also operate in favor of a mother-in-law vis-à-vis a daughter-in-law.

The extrahousehold links of husband and wife also show asymmetry where they diverge. Work within the village rarely provides the occasion for people to form especially close ties, especially since much work is now organized on a household basis, but there are exceptions, especially for men. Those men who have work outside the village, especially work that provides good political or commercial contacts, nurture such contacts. They may also have extravillage contacts formed while serving outside the village in the army or in some other, usually political, capacity. Within the village, the men who demonstrate the closest non-kin-based relationships are those who are cadres (and often also Party members) or, more commonly (now that there are fewer positions to fill), those who formerly worked together as cadres. These men not only have a shared experience that sets them apart from other villagers and that may have involved them in close cooperation on difficult matters, they may also have exceptionally good access to resources beyond the village. Some of the most lucrative commercial dealings in the countryside are carried out by former cadres on the basis of knowledge and contacts acquired while they were cadres. Extravillage political contacts can also provide a channel for the resolution of political or administrative matters resistant to resolution through any other means, such as a change in household registration.

Women less commonly have close ties with other women formed through work relations within their villages. Many women simply do not do work that brings them into contact with women outside their own households. Where they do, as with men, this does not necessarily lead to the formation of especially close ties. However, and again this parallels the situation for men, they may form such ties where their work is in some way distinctive. The two most prominent cases of such ties in these villages were each distinctive. One was between two women involved in small businesses that were conspicuously successful and that isolated them to some extent from other women in the village, both because of their wealth and because they were constantly tied to their business premises, located across the street from each other.

The other such tie was a type that might occur more often, although it would only be found among young unmarried women. Unmarried women in Huaili actively engage in small-scale rural marketing where it does not require long-distance travel. In an acceptable variant of this pattern, a group of four young women cooperate in traveling together to Shijiazhuang in Hebei Province to purchase clothes that they then sell independently in local markets. Travel and business, which they could not carry out on their own, they can engage in as a group. This type of female work group is one that will disperse with the marriage of the women who compose it.

Young married women are substantially constrained in their social interactions in their marital villages. As one of the later ritual stages following a wedding, the bride is formally introduced to women in other households related to her husband's, ideally by a woman married to an elder brother of her husband, but she is discouraged from contacts beyond that range by lack of opportunity and by strong social pressures against "running around."

Women do not often have access to extravillage ties through the work and political channels available to some men. Rural women rarely join the army, rarely serve as village cadres, and, if they work outside the village, usually do so before marriage and use this work as a channel to leave the countryside.

Women's extravillage ties, in contrast, are with their natal families. While men's kin ties rest predominantly within their community of residence, women may be positioned to make use of the existence of close extravillage kin ties, ties to which their neighbors and their husband's sisters do not have access. A woman's natal family is therefore a varying resource that differentiates agnatically related households. Her natal family will not, except in rare circumstances, provide her with direct economic assistance, but the level of its affluence will determine whether or not she and her marital family are obligated to give assistance, and this in itself has an indirect but significant differentiating effect. The only important form of labor provided to a married woman by her natal family is possible childcare. These few considerations do not, however, exhaust the resources available to her from her natal family. The range of possibilities here has no a priori limits and may encompass any assistance possible in the locality. Some may be valuable: one woman introduced a new cash crop to her marital village after learning of its profitability from her natal village; another woman learned beekeeping, a new and remunerative enterprise in her locality, from a younger sister who had married into a different village.

Some of the most significant help from women's natal families flows from older to younger generations—namely, the valued and rare resource of direct access to nonagricultural registration, or access to a job that is likely to lead indirectly to nonagricultural registration. This change in official residence status is essential to a secure exit from the countryside. Except in the case of older people having nonagricultural status reinstated after losing it in various political vicissitudes, or the occasional rare case of change in status for the household of a nonagricultural registrant, change in status occurs in early adulthood. Thus the aspirations of mature rural residents toward a change in residence status take the form of hopes and efforts to obtain nonagricultural registration for one or more of their children. Retiring grandparents (usually grandfathers) who have already taken care of their children's futures may be able to pass on their jobs and registration to a grandchild of their choice (inheritance of employment is standard practice in factories and offices), or may be in a sufficiently senior position to introduce a number of grandchildren or various other relatives and connections to employment that may lead to nonagricultural registration. The status and personal connections of senior relatives—matrilineal as well as patrilineal—are major factors in determining the life possibilities of rural young people.

Most villagers have no promising channel available to them; some may have a slight prospect in the form of someone's pending retirement; and a few have much better prospects deriving from well-placed senior relatives. Parents activate all such avenues available to them in the interests of their children. Because the object is to expand such possibilities to the furthest possible official limit, and because these limits are arbitrary and changeable, access to this critical resource is variable and unpredictable. Certainly fathers take care of their sons first, but the range of assistance an influential person may be able to extend more widely is less determinate. Some are able to assist even their daughters' children. From one perspective, this implies that well-positioned persons and households can extend their political and economic advantages to their descendants through both male and female lines, and that a degree of bilaterality in this type of inheritance is associated with positions of power or privilege. From another perspective, it implies that *some* women are able to gain access to such valued resources as preferred registration status for their descendants by way of their own natal families.

CHAPTER 6

Women and Agency

Writing about the lives of women in China moved some years ago from accounts of extraordinary successes to troubled accounts of a revolution postponed or unfinished (Andors 1983, M. Wolf 1985). The current consensus acknowledges changes for the better as well as persistent and contemporary structural obstacles to change. A major focus of discussion is the mixed effect of a succession of official policies and political movements. As the limits of these have become increasingly apparent, there has been a partial shift in attention toward examining the importance of a familially based patriarchy (Johnson 1983, Stacey 1983). This direction has been encouraged by concern about the implications of the rural reform program of the 1980s.

I will contribute to this discussion by presenting a point of view based on two central propositions. First, I start from the proposition that a wholly or even mainly top-down strategy for revolutionizing the status of women in rural China has been, and continues to be, intrinsically impossible. Movements for such fundamental change have been important and influential since early in this century, and policies regarding women's status have been part of the Chinese Communist Party's program since the 1920s. Although I would not wish to underestimate the role of these movements and policies, their capacity to effect change in the countryside has been limited and largely indirect. The national political context has provided varying degrees of support and has conditioned what has been possible for rural women, but the changes have been ultimately dependent on the opportunity for rural women themselves to gain access to support networks and to realize possibilities through their own active agency.

Second, I do not view patriarchy as essentially or even primarily based in a familial or domestic context, although that is one significant sphere of its manifestation. Patriarchy is here seen as one strand in a wider complex of hierarchical relations in China.

Official Policy and Its Limits

Since 1949, the effective public structures on women's issues have been the linked ones of Party, government, and Women's Federations, together constituting the structures of the state in this field. The leadership of the Chinese Communist Party ultimately determines policy in all spheres, although aspects of its power are delegated and it is far from being a monolithic organization. The government at all levels operates under Party guidance and with considerable overlap of leading personnel. The Women's Federations form one network reaching from national to township levels and with local women's organizations included in its scope. It is both a mass organization led by the Party and a quasi-governmental body responsible for women and, in some provinces, for young children. There are few women in Party and government leadership, and since the Thirteenth Congress of the Party in 1987 and Deng Yingchao's retirement, there have been no women at the highest level of the Party.

The structure of the Women's Federations is that of a "mass organization" in Marxist-Leninist terms, a "transmission belt" from the Party to the particular constituency of women. Much of its work has consisted of mobilizing women in support of current Party policies, whether or not these are of specific concern to women. In addition to this top-down work, it has also tried to represent its constituency's interests in down-up directions, either by influencing official policy or by providing support to women on issues directly affecting them, such as implementing the provisions of the Marriage Law of 1950 and the gender equality provisions of the Constitution of 1982. The Women's Federations are not universally viewed as highly effective. They lack political clout and human and material resources, are called upon to organize women on many issues other than those directly in the special interest of women, and relate so broadly to the interests of all women that they are often not recognizably feminist. Indeed, the structure is that of a broad umbrella organization for women.

Rural women's experience with organized change within this framework has passed through several stages during the lifetimes of women still living in China's villages. During the pre-1949 era, women in war zones where the Communist Party was active joined in support work and often replaced men who had left as soldiers, including replacing them in some rural leadership roles. This may be viewed as mobilizing women for causes that were not gender-specific but that were in their interests. The 1950 Marriage Law more directly addressed specific needs of women in its opposition to the traditional patriarchal family structure, as did the subseqent campaign to propagandize it. This law opened the way for women in especially difficult marital circumstances to seek and obtain divorces, for young people to resist unwanted arranged marriages, and other similar steps, although it was rarely at all easy for individual women to take such actions effectively and without incurring heavy social costs. Although this law is viewed in the literature primarily as a law for women, it was in fact a general reform of marriage and family law, and was also directed toward benefiting children and young men. Subsequent movements have similarly been mixtures of broad movements for change, sometimes with elements of particular relevance or benefit to women. The most recent example is the Campaign to Criticize Lin Biao and Confucius in the late Cultural Revolution period, which, as it unfolded in rural areas in 1974–75, consisted largely of attacks on aspects of Confucian tradition that are detrimental to women.[1]

In the 1980s there have been no campaigns specifically designed to further the interests of women, although some statutes do contain provisions that favor such interests. The Marriage Law that took effect January 1, 1981 (see *Marriage Law of the People's Republic of China* [1981], 1982) is in some respects more bilateral and gender-balanced than the preceding one (*Marriage Law* [1950], 1975); the revised Constitution of 1982 (*Constitution of the People's Republic of China* [1982], 1985) includes provisions for gender equality; and the 1985 Inheritance Law allows daughters as well as sons to inherit their parents' property (Palmer 1988).[2] Also, the Women's Federation network has become more active in advocating equality for women in the 1980s. But these measures have had a less profound effect on the lives of rural women than the reform policies, even if the latter have been largely indirect or not intentionally designed to alter gender relations.

Each of the three villages in this study has a link with the official Women's Federation network, although that link ranges from minimal and fragile, in the case of Zhangjiachedao and Qianrulin, to relatively active but still fragile, in the case of Huaili. The link is not, in any case here or elsewhere, a matter of the direct presence of the Women's Federation network within the village. Although its primary sphere of activity has historically been the countryside—unions have provided the main vehicle in the cities[3]—the Women's Federation network is not organizationally present within villages. The personnel of the network can be found only as far down the administrative hierarchy as the township. Yet within each village there is normally at least one woman responsible for "woman-work" (*funü gongzuo*), as the work of the Women's Federations is known. This woman is called the "women's head" (*funü zhuren*), a title which implies that she is the head of an organized women's body in the village, although that body may have little if any organizational form or substance. All three villages studied had a designated women's head during at least some of the time of the study, although the activities of this person and the extent of any organization beyond the women's head were more variable.

Zhangjiachedao had an able young married woman as women's head in 1986. She had served in the same position in her natal village, and in both villages was also the village paramedic responsible for women's reproductive health. In her role as women's head, most of her responsibilities concerned promotion and implementation of the state's birth-limitation policy, a political role directly tied to her paramedic work. In the course of working closely with her in my investigations in Zhangjiachedao, I found that she was knowledgeable about all women of childbearing age in the village but that she hardly knew many of the older women. She said herself, and firmly, that her work as women's head was *only* "family planning" (*jihua shengyu*), which in the context of the time referred to the single-child policy. Although the Women's Federations formally hold that the birth limitation policy is the responsibility of a separate official organization, it is common in the countryside for women's heads to be responsible for this element of state policy.

More extended discussions did elicit information about her occasional mediation in domestic matters—for example, persuading a woman in her own natal village to drop opposition to her daughter's proposed marriage into Zhangjiachedao. Zhangjiachedao's women's head was evidently drawn into this matter not only because of her formal position but also because of her own networks and, I expect, her personal qualities. The informal aspect of her work in this area is probably essential to her effectiveness, but she presented it in the terms of normative official discourse—namely, as "education" (*jiaoyu*) that she sometimes engaged in to help resolve domestic problems when consulted.

Current official ideals of domestic relations are very close to traditional ones, including the ideal that a young woman is largely to be judged by her deference and success in maintaining a good relationship with her mother-in-law. There is no sharp contrast, in this respect, between the traditional, customary, and informal expectations that a women's head must meet and her obligations to promote officially approved social norms.[4] Nevertheless, Zhangjiachedao's women's head evidently saw the two as quite distinct. Her reluctance to describe her mediating activities as part of her work—and, when she did so, her use of conspicuously official terms—showed that she thought of her tasks as women's head as a form of official work. Women often seek informal channels to mediate domestic problems, and as a woman in the community she might become involved, but she did not view this as the same as doing official woman-work.

The only other formal woman-work she mentioned was that of providing general assistance with Party work in the village. She was not herself a Party member, although she was in the process of applying for membership. Her work for the Party was, in effect, work for the village level of the state, in which government and Party are combined, and was representative of the common situation of those doing woman-work in the countryside. Women's heads in the villages and Women's Federation staff in the townships regularly have a portion of their time appropriated for general political work. In the case of the women's head in Zhangjiachedao, this demand on her time may have indicated a degree of political confidence and a step toward her incorporation into local political work. This incorporation, preferably in the form of adding a place on the village committee for the women's head, is a measure promoted by the Women's Federations, but it is not official state policy.

In Zhangjiachedao, only this one woman had a formal role in woman-work; there was no supportive committee structure. All women in the village are called together for one meeting each year, but this meeting does not have any apparent importance. Married women of childbearing age are called together for a meeting every month, but this is specifically concerned with women's reproductive health and with the state's birth-limitation policies.

Qianrulin's women's head in 1987 was also a young married woman who had previously held the same post in her natal village. She worked as a teacher in the village kindergarten, a position linked to her role as women's head. She was a full-time employee of the village, with her position described as being two-thirds teaching, one-third work as women's head and for the village committee. She had joined the Party in her natal village, was one of only three female Party members in Qianrulin, and, perhaps most important, was married into a family influential in village political life.

Qianrulin reported having a five-member women's committee consisting of a head responsible for all aspects of woman-work in the village; a vice-head responsible for preschool education (the village's other kindergarten teacher);[5] a woman responsible for the older women in the village (the previous women's head, herself over 50 years of age); a woman responsible for unmarried young women in the village (of whom she was one); and a woman responsible for young daughters-in-law (of whom she was one). The primary activity reported in all these spheres was promoting political study, including study about the "five-good family" (*wuhao jiating*).[6] The women's head also said she did some work regarding the birth limitation program and some domestic mediation.

The structure described here, and the inclusion of the women's head in the Qianrulin village committee, represents a full formal organization of woman-work at the village level and is very close to what is officially advocated. Despite this full formal structure, however, there were no claims made by anyone in Qianrulin that woman-work was especially active or effective there, and some women made a point of informing me that it was not a strength in the village. The complete formal structure in Qianrulin is probably best viewed as an instance of overt compliance with prescribed forms on the part of a village whose continuing adherence to collective organization has made it especially sensitive and attentive to official expectations from outside the village.

Huaili was much more active in woman-work. In this respect it is less representative than the other two villages but indicative of the limits of what is possible. At the time of my first visit to Huaili in 1988, the women's head was an energetic woman in her fifties who had recently recovered her nonagricultural household registration and was preparing to join her husband in the city where he worked. By the time I returned in 1989, she had departed and the new women's head was a well-educated young married woman in settled residence in Huaili, her natal village. When I returned in 1990, this woman had obtained employment in a nearby town and, although she visited constantly, was no longer serving as women's head. A replacement had not yet been appointed and the village women's organization was inactive. The village Party secretary considered it obligatory that the position be filled and said that it would be filled by appointment by the village Party branch. He had a young woman in mind for the position who had not previously been involved in woman-work in the village, and a former schoolteacher with a highly supportive mother-in-law was also under consideration.

The position of women's head in Huaili was not combined with any other village duty but was remunerated on the level of a minor village official, such as a team head. It was in effect a part-time job, although it was not viewed as a very lucrative one. It was therefore not attractive to the women in the community who were occupied with demanding household enterprises. The element of remuneration is also important in another sense: the fact that the women's head is paid whereas others on the women's committee are not reinforces the definition of woman-work as a category of official labor rather than as a voluntary vocation (see also Judd, in press).[7]

Unlike Zhangjiachedao and Qianrulin, Huaili had a women's committee (*fudaihui*) that did carry out some activities. This committee was more stable in composition than the succession of women's heads might indicate. In 1988, it consisted of the head and four other women, one of whom became women's head shortly later—she was a young upper-middle-school graduate, the daughter of a retired village cadre, and worked repairing watches in local markets. Another was the only female Party member in the village, whose inclusion was directly related to this status. Her activity in the organization was restricted by her chronic ill health and the disadvantage of having missed an education in her youth while caring for members of her natal family. The two remaining women were each considered at different times as a potential women's head, although other names were mentioned as well. One was an ambitious small entrepreneur who ran a shop and seasonal snack-bar with the help of her father and hired labor. Her husband was a former soldier and a Party member, and she was being considered as a future Party member herself. The other woman had had exceptional success in recent years in a small wholesale enterprise, together with her husband. By the time of my fieldwork they had left that area of business, which was then declining. The husband had gone into factory management while the wife had retired to leisure and conspicuous affluence although only in her thirties. She was the most obvious philanthropist in the village, protecting the family wealth with generosity, as well as with a safe and guard dogs.

When the women's head left in 1988 and her successor was appointed, a replacement committee member was found in the person of Huaili's most successful woman entrepreneur, a former schoolteacher who managed the village's leading restaurant. A further addition was due after the departure of the next women's head, but no immediate action had been taken and the committee had been short a member for some months by the summer of 1990. The committee was then inactive in any event, pending the appointment of a new women's head.

The Huaili women's head and women's committee had two formal vehicles for reaching out to other women in the village: calling meetings and organizing activities. During the 40 household visits I made in Huaili in 1989, I systematically inquired about the involvement of every woman in this sample in women's activities in the village. This produced information on ties with the village women's organization on the part of 54 adult women.[8] The level of activity in this sample is certainly higher than in the village as a whole, because I included in my sample all the members of the village women's committee and all households with women active in the public life of the community. A total of 23 of these women reported no involvement whatever with the women's organization; 25 said they attended at least some meetings when called upon to do so but did nothing more. Of the remainder, 5 were the members of the women's committee (including the women's head) and 1 was a skilled seamstress who had run a sewing class organized by the women's committee in 1988.

The norms the women reported for attending meetings and becoming involved were that each household could be expected to send one woman to meetings when these were called. The meetings were effectively a state matter at the village level, with a degree of compliance expected on the part of mature women representing their households. Young unmarried women were not usually expected to attend, and women over 50 not only did not attend (with the exception of one woman of 54) but in some cases said that they would be objects of ridicule in the village if they did so.

The target group for the meetings is indicated by the mechanism used to call them: the meetings are announced in the village primary school, and school-age children are asked to inform their mothers. This is the same age cohort that supplies the members of the women's committee. In 1989 these women fell between the ages of 27 and 41. None of the women in the sample reported visiting the village's Women's Center (*funü zhi jia*), and I never observed it in use.[9]

The predominant focus of activity in woman-work in Huaili was related to improving the economic situation, specifically the income-generating capacity, of women in the community. This was consistent with national policy, with the orientation of Huaili toward a household-based commodity economy, and with the current priorities of the prefectural and county Women's Federations. In 1987, a vice-head of the Ling County Women's Federation made almost daily visits to Huaili, a lengthy trip by bicycle, over a period of six months, to organize women's activity around courtyard vegetable production and the cultivation of xiangchun trees. She chose Huaili as her focus because the village was suitable in terms of both its economic orientation and its women's organization, although the extent of organization and the level of activity in Huaili nevertheless owe much to her work.

The role of the Women's Federations in promoting income-generating opportunities for women in the villages is connected with a renewed emphasis in the 1980s on grass-roots organization and a departure, within some Women's Federation circles, toward having the Federations promote women's integration into the market economy. The Women's Federations network had not previously focused on economic issues, and even in the late 1980s those of its staff who did so were in a minority. Huaili benefited from the intensive presence of an able organizer who was willing to make a concentrated effort in this direction.

The specific type of activity advocated in Huaili in 1987 drew upon a model of courtyard cultivation in Tianjin. The brief campaign left a legacy of intensive courtyard cultivation in a modest number of Huaili households and marked the beginning of the village's organized efforts in this direction. It has been followed by training classes in sewing and seed selection, in an effort to find further means to improve the income-generating capacity of women in Huaili who lack other channels for economic advancement. Some women and households in the village have benefited—in addition to those who found other economic avenues without the aid of the Women's Federation—but there is general agreement that more needs to be done.

It was difficult to devise viable economic strategies for less advantaged women in the context of the declining economic opportunity prevailing at the end of the decade, and the township Women's Federation staff still in contact with Huaili were perplexed by this problem. The lack of anyone responsible for woman-work in Huaili exacerbated the difficulties, but the village's greatest success was directly connected with the earlier, temporary presence of a county-level Women's Federation organizer. Even if she had not departed for the south in late 1989, the county Women's Federation could not have continued to devote so much attention to one village. The strength of the Lingxian Women's Federation fluctuated during this period, but in 1990 the complete staff comprised fewer than ten women, and not all these were suitable for rural organizing work. The assistance provided to Huaili in 1987 was more than a village could reasonably expect, but was still not sufficient to create a village women's organization capable of continuing effectively on its own.

Formal organization on the part of women as women in the villages exists only as instigated by and connected with the formal structures of the state—namely, the institutions of women's heads and (sometimes) committees at the level of the village, and links between these and the national network of Women's Federations. Formal organizing of women as women is inextricably associated with the state, and especially with aspects of the state external to the village. This is true not only of the occasional local intervention by Women's Federation organizers but also of women's heads. These are locally appointed, but the institution of this political role is a national policy. Thus no formal organization of women as women exists in the villages outside state channels. Spontaneous organizing of any type has been politically suspect during most of the history of the People's Republic and has been effectively illegal since 1989. Even during the few years of relaxation in the 1980s, when spontaneous organizing did occur, including organizing of women's groups, this was an urban phenomenon. No such formal organizations were created in these villages, and woman-work remained a monopoly of the state.

State-authorized woman-work was designed to mobilize women for general social goals and, in some specific instances, to advance the interests of women as women. Both these aspects of woman-work are in evidence in the variety of work described for these villages. It is important to note, however, that the women's organizations in these villages did not work for any goals that could be described as women's rights or gender equity. Also, in each village the scope of work undertaken was restricted, and even within those terms the accomplishments were modest.

The women's organizations in each case operated with meager resources, even where working for the goals of national policy was concerned. Woman-work was viewed by all levels of the state as a low priority, while the majority of rural women viewed it as ineffective in working for their interests and as simply one more aspect of local political work. The elements of woman-work involving the birth limitation campaign and organized political study were unwelcome. Even the work designed to assist women economically reached only a minority of the women who could have benefited from it in Huaili.

This is not to suggest that women were passive or ineffective in making changes in their lives; rather, it is to suggest that their agency was not subsumed within the formal state structures designated for women.

Agency Expressed

Women in these villages with whom I was in frequent discussion showed a definite pattern in how they presented themselves as agents. In the majority of contexts in which they talked about their actions and decisions, they spontaneously referred to themselves (individually) as autonomous actors. There was no doubt that in the tightly knit context of a Chinese village, other persons were also being taken into account, but they conveyed no sense of passivity in the course of ordinary conversation. There were contrasting instances, of course, where I encountered women during household visits who hardly spoke, and then only when I made a point of bringing them into the interview. These situations always occurred when a given woman and I met only once, with several men present during the visit.

The women with whom I talked in more familiar, less constrained contexts spoke with matter-of-fact assurance about their everyday lives and their autonomy within them, but there was a silent, problematic supplement to this assurance because it was generally, if not invariably, associated with no mention whatever of men and their agency. When men were introduced into such a discussion, through some query on my part, the tone would often, although not always, shift to one that indicated at least uncertainty about—and often definite limitation of—the woman's sense of agency.

The point is not simply that rural Chinese women perceive and present themselves as active agents, and do so most effectively when men are neither participants in the discussion nor subjects of it, although this is part of the pattern. Rather, the following pages map out differences in women's agency in a range of contexts. A major structuring factor in the exercise of agency in the Chinese countryside is the separation of various spheres of activity, some of which are specifically separated by gender. I try to trace some of the implications of gender differences in agency in these different spheres. My argument connects at points with analyses of "weapons of the weak," as proposed by Scott (1985) for Asian peasant societies, but with adaptations designed to accommodate gender difference.

A useful departure point is a comment offered separately by two of the more conspicuously able women in Zhangjiachedao in 1986. Both the women's head and the one woman accountant in the village's weaving and dyeing factory independently asserted that "men are more able" (*nande geng you benshi*). Male leaders in the village declined any such interpretation, affirming that more women leaders should be fostered and that it was their intention to do so. Upon inquiry they did not indicate any concrete measures for doing so, but the village did have a number of policies that were indirectly favorable to women, such as a junior-middle-school graduation requirement for workers in its weaving and dyeing factory.[10] Such apparent discrepancies could be dismissed as simply ordinary and everyday. Here I would like to examine precisely such ordinary, everyday conceptions about gender and agency, and their attendant discrepancies, to explore what they reveal about the microdynamics of the social and cultural construction of gender in rural China.

When women who had already established themselves in the public sphere spoke very modestly of their positions and accomplishments, referring to men as having more ability (*benshi*), their statements held more than the apparent content. The ability they were referring to was not generalized, that is, there was no implication that men were simply better at everything. Rather, their superior ability was seen to lie specifically in areas of the public domain that are—and were in premodern China—especially highly valued, namely, the areas of politics and business. The recognized value of political leadership in China hardly requires emphasis, and since the 1980s leadership in business, whether in management of enterprises or in more independent commerce, has been highly and openly valued. It is true that there have been periods since 1949 when business was not valued, and equally true that it is not highly placed in the formal Confucian hierarchy of professional prestige. Traditionally, however, business has been recognized as a significant source of wealth and power. It has regained this status under the current drive to modernize, and those who have shown entrepreneurial ability are spoken of with noticeable respect in the villages.

When the women I spoke with claimed that men had more ability, the reference was to these specific spheres. Politics and business are not only the two most significant channels to power and prestige, they are also areas in which it is almost impossible for a woman to operate effectively, given the pattern of male networking from which women are effectively excluded. I was assured that although a woman might be able to manage a rural industrial enterprise, the outside arrangements crucial for supplies and marketing would have to be done by a man. An effective woman entrepreneur would either be operating on a very small scale, where such needs were not an obstacle, or she would require a male associate for the outside arrangements—an associate who would have to be a related man, given the pressures for "respectability." Household-based enterprises effectively give such opportunities to husband-wife teams, so women in favorable household situations may be much less constrained in household than in collective enterprises.

This respected ability in politics and business is to some extent associated with the high status in the public sphere attainable by some men within villages, either through leadership internal to the village or through activities that extend beyond it. Lest this seem too reminiscent of our own cultural model of the public-domestic divide (Rosaldo 1980), there is no requirement now that women be excluded from the public domain, although that was a feature of premodern Chinese culture. Women in rural China have a well-established public role in the economy of China's villages, especially in those villages that have the resources to approach full employment or that have a labor shortage (otherwise women may well be treated as surplus labor and excluded or marginalized). However, under normal conditions it is culturally acceptable only for women to hold leadership or management roles in relation to other women, not to men.[11]

The pattern that emerges is one in which women are active agents and perceive themselves as such, but can only express and activate this agency provided that doing so does not place them in competition with men. Certain areas, such as the women's organizations or minor enterprises with a primarily female labor force, such as sewing groups, may be defined as female preserves in such a way that the issue of male-female competition does not arise.

This underlying, unvoiced competition is another level revealed in women's statements about men having ability and in the modest statements village women leaders make about their own qualifications and work. It is proper and, in effect, prescribed that a woman should be modest and unassuming, but seemly modesty is only part of this more complex pattern (see Brandauer 1977). There is a strong prohibition on the expression of any view that could be construed as competing with male prerogatives. This especially affects the few women in leadership roles in villages, and their status and effectiveness as leaders depends on observing this prohibition.

A corresponding pattern exists at the household level, where women commonly hold substantial authority and are at least tacitly recognized as doing so, as in the common expression, "men are in charge outside, women are in charge inside" (*nan zhu wai nü zhu nei*). Again the pattern is one in which a woman will commonly and spontaneously speak of herself as running the household and making major decisions, such as finding a good marriage match for a child, but when asked about the role of her husband will also commonly show deference to his decision-making power. Similarly, conflict in households, if mentioned at all, is referred to as existing between women, typically mothers-in-law and daughters-in-law, but not between men and women. Men observed that some husbands are "henpecked"—men married to women's heads are especially open to such a judgment—and I heard jokes about this from men but not from women.

Whatever the real authority exercised by women in a household, and it is often substantial, it is not acceptable to express it openly unless the male household head is effectively absent. This qualification points to a significant segment of the rural population, however, for many village men have long-term or short-term employment that keeps them away for extended periods of time or allows them to commute home on less than a daily basis. This situation has created a large number of female household heads and has allowed some women to replace men in village positions as men take preferred positions elsewhere. Thus it may be viewed as partially advantageous to women in terms of enhanced rural opportunities, although at the cost of a disrupted family life.

Division of Labor

Women are actively involved in the public sphere through a pattern of relatively strict division of labor by age and gender categories (see Judd 1990). Assignment of work on the basis of ascribed or partially ascribed status[12] can be viewed as a strategy for reducing conflict within small communities and easing the difficulties of labor management. What is actually a social division of labor then appears to be a natural division of labor and can be spoken of as such, and this is indeed the usual vocabulary of discourse on the subject in China.[13]

This is not to say that such a division of labor is immutable, and change in it over recent decades is easily evident. For example, weaving in the Zhangjiachedao area earlier in this century was done as a cottage industry by male weavers, but working the looms is currently women's work in the village, following the now-standard pattern of textile factories of women tending looms and men doing mechanical, marketing, and managerial work.

In the precollectivization household-based rural economy, prior to the mid-1950s, there were also customary patterns of division of labor according to age and gender, and these varied with class, region, and household composition. Collectivization adapted these patterns and to some extent reduced differences both by absorbing women into public agricultural work and by making decisions about their work allocation at least potentially a public issue. Separate work groups and somewhat separate work assignments minimized conflict and ambiguity. Also, the period of collectivization was one in which the rural population was overwhelmingly involved in agricultural work; there were few alternative occupations available. Decollectivization, since the early 1980s, has implied more complex possibilities and, at the same time, a general weakening of official public authority to assign work. The present situation is highly fluid and variable—much depends on individuals finding or making opportunities for themselves and on the range of possibilities in each locality. The pattern of division of labor is correspondingly much more complex than in previous years.

Of the three villages studied, Qianrulin is closest to the previous model because it retains a collective economy which is essentially the same in structure as that typical of the collective era. The village and its three agricultural teams exercise authority over the labor allocation of their members. The division of labor in Qianrulin is a matter of village political management, within the context of local customs and conceptions of a natural division of labor. The arrangement currently in effect shows the following main features: Upon leaving school, young women and men are assigned work in the village, with the exceptions of a few (both female and male) who find work in towns or cities on a contract basis and a smaller number (all male)[14] who join the armed forces. Full employment is in effect for young people, and under- or unemployment in the public sphere is found only among older people, primarily women. The young women are largely employed in the village's large felt factory, which also employs a number of unmarried young women from neighboring villages. Smaller numbers of young women are found in other village enterprises, such as its furniture factory and small clothing workshop, and in agriculture, but there are none in its agricultural machinery and transport group. Young men have a wider range of possibilities: they may be assigned to any of the village enterprises, and there appears to be a village-level plan for training them for subsequent positions of leadership in all spheres. Younger married women tend to be assigned work in agriculture or in some of the village enterprises, such as the felt factory, the clothing factory, or as cooks in the dining halls the village runs for nonlocal workers.

Women in Qianrulin currently retire from employment in the public sphere when their daughters or daughters-in-law replace them in the work force. They remain active in the household by cooking, caring for grandchildren, and contributing to household income through raising domestic animals, but essentially remove themselves from the public sphere at a time when those men who have had leadership opportunities are assuming increased public responsibilities. This need not be viewed as a wholly disadvantageous arrangement for women, for it relieves them of a heavy double burden (much commented upon by women). Men do not have the same opportunity for early retirement, but may either rise to positions of public prestige and power or at least be assured of continuing employment to a late age. Although some older men contribute noticeably in raising domestic animals and, less often, in tending grandchildren, they have a less obvious domestic contribution to make, and the cultural pattern in this village strongly discourages it.

Men (but not women) tend to return to their workplaces in the evenings to socialize on a regular basis, and many have cots there where they sleep regularly, returning to their homes only for meals. This arrangement is suggestive of the men's houses found in the ethnographic literature of numerous other cultures, and although it does not quite reach that degree of separation, the divide between a male public and a female domestic sphere is especially marked in Qianrulin. It is also the village (of the three studied) with the least active women's head and the least public involvement of women.

The most prominent woman in Qianrulin in 1987 was an elderly woman who in her youth in the early 1950s had been the village women's head and received training as a midwife. This woman's prominence was due to her noted ability in an important, valued field from which men were definitely excluded. The current women's head, although an apparently able person and one of the three women Party members in the village, was not prominent; moreover, as a kindergarten teacher, she was not well positioned to play a leadership role in the community.[15] Two women (one also a Party member) who were in their early thirties and married to men in leading positions did have some responsibilities in the factories in which they worked, but their abilities appeared to be underutilized. One of these women made a point of characterizing the village as "ordinary" (*yibande*) in terms of its woman-work.

Women's limited access to Party membership is an important factor in restricting their role in public life, especially in the countryside. Party membership is effectively essential for significant participation in political leadership, although recent reforms have rendered it no longer a formal necessity. Women are at a particular disadvantage in connection with prevalent customs of postmarital residence, which usually require a woman to take up residence in her husband's community at or shortly after marriage. Acceptance into membership in the Party is granted only after a lengthy period of observation and consideration, and is not infrequently denied. It is usually preceded by a term in the Young Communist League, which is less exclusive, but a person's eligibility for membership in the League may expire without a successful transition to Party membership.

Two recent trends for women are pertinent here. Marriage age for women fell in the 1980s, and at the end of the decade was close to the legal minimum of 20 years of age. This makes it increasingly difficult for a woman to gain Party membership before marriage, and indeed, her natal community may be uninterested in encouraging someone who is expected to leave soon. Formally, one can enter the Party at 18, but age at entry is commonly higher. If a woman does not become a Party member before her marriage, she is not normally considered again until she has resided in her marital community for several years, becoming well known and respected. These are also the years in which she is likely to become a mother (even under current policies) and hence to have less time for public affairs. If she has moved to her marital village as a League member, that status expires between the ages of 25 and 28. Qianrulin's women's head, the only one in the three villages who was a Party member, had married in her late twenties, an unusually late age. A factor working in the opposite direction is an emerging trend for intravillage marriage, which is practiced in Zhangjiachedao and which has been reported in widely distributed regions of China in recent years.

In Zhangjiachedao, labor allocation is effectively a matter of village political decision-making rather than of isolated contractual decisions, although that is now the apparent form. The management of land in the village is indicative of this situation: about 1 mu of land for each person is allocated to households, and household members share agricultural work, depending on complex factors of household composition and employment, but there is a tendency for the prime agricultural worker to be a married woman who is restricted from employment outside the home by the unavailability of a senior woman to care for her young children.

Two aspects of this situation compare interestingly with Qianrulin. First, in Zhangjiachedao married women in the village, if they meet the junior-middle-school graduation requirement for employment, are welcome workers in the village weaving and dyeing factory, and this or employment in one of the smaller village enterprises, such as its clothing factory, is the preferred situation in the eyes of the village leadership. Indeed, the leadership prefers to deny that anyone other than the members of the agricultural machinery team is a full-time agricultural worker, although women did observe explicitly that there were women in this situation. Village policy can work either to expand or to reduce this feature of gender division of labor.

Second, both villages show a clear concern with inequality among households and an attempt to reduce it. Although in either case there could be some households exclusively or primarily engaged in agriculture, both villages have avoided this arrangement. Manual agricultural work is the least preferred rural occupation—it is unremunerative, physically demanding, and low in prestige. Both villages have met the necessity that some people engage in agricultural work (to provide food for the village and meet state quotas) by reducing its role in the village economy and by spreading it among households. In both cases this strategy to reduce inequality among households has been at the cost of increasing women's role in the least preferred economic sector.[16] In the case of Zhangjiachedao there is a village policy in place designed to spread this work more evenly, but it cannot in every case override factors of childcare or education.

Other aspects of the division of labor in Zhangjiachedao are less innovative. Women typically tend the looms and inspect the cloth in the weaving and dyeing factory, while men do machine maintenance and repair, transport and business, and almost all the managerial work; and women comprise the staff of the small clothing factory, with the exception of its male head. Generational differences in employment are present to a similar but lesser degree compared with Qianrulin. The chief differences are the mix of younger and middle-aged women in factory work and a less marked pattern of retirement by older women. Men predominate in public leadership positions in Zhangjiachedao, too, but the public sphere is less markedly separate and male than in Qianrulin.

Women leaders in Zhangjiachedao were conscious of these patterns but reluctant to speak about them. One woman worked for me doing a household survey in the village. She initially showed considerable hesitation and lack of confidence, but quickly acquired the new skills involved and ceased to find the job at all intimidating.[17] Another was adamant that she possessed no special abilities for her role as a factory accountant, but did concede that the work was less difficult than she had anticipated and, when asked in hypothetical terms, agreed that this was probably true of other positions in the factory as well, and that she or some other woman could, if called upon, even take on the role of factory head. These instances indicate both mystification surrounding male leadership roles in the countryside and demystification in the eyes of women who achieve some entry into hitherto restricted spheres—although it is not appropriate to voice this openly or to express confidence. Another dimension of the assertion that "men have more ability" is that it preempts backlash. Women leaders at the village level (always junior in status) are especially isolated and vulnerable.

Women in Zhangjiachedao did play a larger role in the public arena than in Qianrulin, and this is partly to be seen in the roles of women leaders. The village women's head was better placed, through her role as paramedic for women and birth control worker, to be involved in current issues of public policy than was the Qianrulin women's head, who worked in a kindergarten; she also had the advantage of doing this work in Zhangjiachedao, where there was a high level of compliance with official policy. She had an important role to play in the community, although it was not one that required her to lead or supervise men. This was also true of the other women with responsible positions in the village. The woman accountant had a position that was skilled and involved responsibility, but she was one of several accountants and had no immediate subordinates. She did, however, have a concurrent role as a vice-head of the Young Communist League in the village, which implied a minor leadership role in relation to both men and women. The wife of the weaving and dyeing factory's head ran the factory's dining hall and did have some authority over a very small staff, but this could be viewed as an extension of her domestic skills and as borrowing on her husband's status. A fourth woman acted unofficially as vice-head of the clothing factory, but this required only that she take responsibility for the premises and the other women workers.

Again the pattern for women in the public sphere in Zhangjiachedao was shaped by a requirement that male leadership prerogatives not be questioned, although this was less rigid than in Qianrulin. More generally and importantly, in Zhangjiachedao there were other mature women, not in leadership roles, who had skilled, well-paid factory jobs that were contributing to raising their status, and whose households benefited from the contribution these women made.

In Huaili, there is little village-level control over labor allocation and there are few public leadership positions to fill. The only formal village leadership position filled by a woman is that of women's head, but some of the village's more successful household entrepreneurs are women, such as a former teacher who manages the business of a restaurant while her illiterate husband, trained as a cook in the army, takes care of the cooking. Other women are involved in household efforts in which everyone takes part, such as producing dehydrated noodles on a commercial scale.

In 1987 the village women's organization, led by the county Women's Federation, began encouraging women in Huaili to become more active in "commodity production" (*shangpin shengchan*). Specifically, women were organized to use empty space in their courtyards for vegetable cultivation or for planting xiangchun trees, whose leaves are an edible delicacy. The women's organization succeeded in persuading some women to try this, and the first year produced profitable crops. This approach constituted a legitimate extension of 1980s economic policies to a particular underemployed category of producers.

This situation was distinctive in its use of the Women's Federations network for mobilizing women to engage in economic production on their own behalf. This is a change designed to bring the Women's Federations into step with the current national policies of economic development, thereby enabling them more effectively to address issues of women's economic status. The strategy is one of identifying underutilized resources and moving in directions that will increase household income without generating competition or conflict.

This strategy is also one entirely based on the household and the rural marketing system. Although it operates with the approval of the village leadership, the strategy circumvents the village level of social and economic organization. In particular, it avoids rural industry entirely. Despite concerns expressed outside China about the disadvantages for women of a household-based economy following decollectivization, there are indications that rural Chinese women find the household posing fewer problems for them than larger-scale productive units. Advantages that Western feminists see for Chinese women in all-women work groups in a collective economy do not seem to be valued by rural Chinese women, who did not experience these work groups as necessarily supportive or enhancing.

"Housewives"

The public sphere in Chinese villages is largely structured by kinship ties, and there is little within it that is not variously affected by linked dimensions of household organization. This can be seen in the organization of division of labor already described. For decades now, women have been major direct contributors to village economies in addition to their indirect but essential contributions within households. Nevertheless, married women in the work force in Qianrulin were consistently described to me by a (male) village leader as "housewives" (*jiating funü*): whatever they did in the public sphere was overridden by a more fundamental definition of them in domestic terms, at least in male eyes. Women spoke of their households as extremely important but did not refer to themselves as housewives; rather, that was an objectivizing term used by someone not in the same category. In short, work outside the home does not place a rural Chinese woman in a distinct public sphere or give her status in that sphere. A corollary is that she has little to lose by removing herself from the public work force, provided she has comparable or better income-generating possibilities within the household. Income, rather than work, is what is noticed and valued.

Relations between households are substantially framed in terms of kin connections and the relative generation of related males, especially in single-lineage communities, although everyday relations between households are commonly managed by women. Gender differences are especially marked in the process of forming affinal ties between households. Although coercively arranged marriages have long been illegal and the extent of arrangement has been gradually decreasing, the parents of a prospective couple—both fathers and mothers—play major roles in determining matches. Of special interest is the role of the

matchmaker, now termed "introducer" (*jieshaoren*), who still commonly introduces suitable partners and who is invariably called upon to
mediate and formalize arrangements even when they have been essentially arrived at by the prospective couple. In the minority of cases
where men play the role of introducer, the match is likely to be an advantageous alliance for the households and to involve men with ties
beyond their own village, or to be an especially difficult match to make
that involves drawing upon wide networks or facilitating an awkward
situation within a village.

Normally, however, women act as introducers. Women usually
marry out of their own communities and hence have detailed knowledge of households in more than one village. Yet women experienced
in this area denied that it was superior information which made them
preferred introducers; instead, they asserted that men lacked the understanding of social relationships necessary to play this role successfully. This was not an area in which women considered men more able.

It is significant that women's role as introducers in forging affinal
ties—important matters in a rural world largely structured by kinship
and marriage—does not give them any recognized advantage. Introducers are not professionals and derive little if any direct material advantage from their role. If they introduce a known woman from their
natal village into their marital village, as frequently happens, they may
gain some companionship, but introducers denied that this was ever
an overriding motivation, asserting that each woman's separate
household ties were of prime importance.

The major exception is the case of matrilateral cross-cousin marriage. This has been discussed in the literature as a traditionally preferred marriage form, on the grounds that a father would feel confident that his sister would be a good mother-in-law to his daughter. In
the case of one such marriage in Zhangjiachedao, where I met the
mother-in-law and daughter-in-law in question, the mother-in-law was
firm in saying that she had initiated the match because she knew the
younger woman and thought she would be a good daughter-in-law.
This avenue for women's initiative has, however, been closed by more
bilateral prohibitions on cousin marriage in the 1981 Marriage Law.
More autonomous matches decided upon by young people may reduce the role of introducers in the future, although rural young people
usually lack opportunities to meet potential spouses in other commu-

nities. Arranging affinal ties is a major area of women's effective agency but not one from which they benefit.

Within the household, the familiar model is one in which a patriarch is powerfully dominant. This model has caused much concern among Western feminist scholars as households have acquired increased importance in the Chinese countryside since decollectivization. However, this model is problematic on several grounds. It fits best with the formal ideology of Chinese social relations but noticeably less well with everyday realities of social existence. As Margery Wolf (1972) has argued, women have a variety of informal strategies that they can and do use to optimize their positions in households. Certainly, formidable women are amply recorded as a feature of Chinese domestic life.

Still more important is the context in which patriarchy in the household can thrive. It is less an independent phenomenon or a feature of household social relations than an institution founded on arrangements that extend beyond the limits of the household itself. The central pillars of the institution have been (1) control of household economic resources by a senior male acting as household head, and (2) male control of the public domain. Both should be viewed as under question. The exclusive economic control of the household head was initially challenged during the land reform, but this continued to some extent through the era of collectivization, when the earnings of all household members were commonly grouped together and distributed by the collective in a combined allocation to the household. The individual wages now earned by various members of a household may still be pooled, but at least they are received by the individuals who earn them.

This shift is loosening patriarchal power in the household in favor of younger members, both women and men, and resulting in larger numbers of nuclear families as young couples gain the economic independence to set up their own households at, or shortly after, marriage. None of the three villages studied had any extended families. Stem families are common and are likely to remain so in order to meet cultural and practical requirements for the care of the elderly, but young adults at the present time typically have several siblings each, so a mixture of stem and nuclear families is standard. Within stem families, the young—including young daughters-in-law—have greater autonomy than in the past. This increased autonomy is largely due to a shift in power between generations, rather than primarily a matter of changed gender relations. However, the consequences are especially marked for young married women and may have further implications in terms of gender relations as these women mature under quite different conditions from those faced by their mothers and mothers-in-law.

Male control of the public domain has been another source of men's power within households, but it, too, is in question. Elisabeth Croll (1981) found that collectives in the countryside used their authority, formal and informal, to reinforce traditional patriarchal norms, and this is still evident in Qianrulin. The more general issue at present is that of control over the vehicles of rural economic development. The more successful and larger village enterprises can play a role, similar to that the collectives once played, in reinforcing patriarchy both in the workplace and in rural households, through their hiring decisions and the consequences of those. Women's organized turn toward household-based enterprises in the 1980s can then be seen—as some in the Women's Federations claim—as more advantageous to women than employment even in relatively well-paid rural industry. The implicit statement is that male control beyond the household is stronger than that within the household. In the absence of stronger women's organization and networks at the village level, this appears to be accurate.

Freedom and Quality

A keynote in women's discourse and strategies in rural China in the 1980s has been the concept of freedom (*ziyou*).[18] Rural women themselves spoke of this in direct and practical terms in relation to choices they did or did not have available to them, for example, in relation to marriage and divorce. Women's Federation staff, or cadres, used the same concept but often in more theoreticized and politicized modes of discourse. They placed more freedom for women in the context of the political and economic opening of the era of reform. The Women's Federations officially welcomed the reforms as beneficial to women on the ground that, freed from previous constraints, women would be able to exercise initiative, demonstrate ability, and achieve success more readily. The reasons the Women's Federations have taken this position are complex, but the position need not be dismissed as merely an obligatory endorsement of state policy.

In the late 1980s this appeared to be a reasoned assessment of the history of the women's movement in China up to that time, and of current possibilities. Such a position did not imply an abandonment of women's organizations. Nevertheless, the advocacy of "freedom" in the 1980s contained some of the same problematic ambiguities as in the West, where it represents both liberating aspirations for autonomy and obfuscations of institutions and practices that restrict it.

An explanation for this view lies in the limited effect of top-down movements for changing the status of women over the past several decades, combined with some evident but uneven changes. The latter appear attributable to the combination of openings provided by official policy and exceptional initiative on the part of individual women who have thereby added to the range of legitimate options for rural women. These women acted as models to be emulated along lines familiar, legitimate, and effective in both the Confucian and revolutionary traditions. The issue in the 1980s was to find ways to make policies that included, but did not give priority to, gender equality serve as further channels for such initiatives.

The research reported here tends to confirm comments by women leaders about restrictions on women under the collective system, although these restrictions were at least partly matters of variable village policy. Women (and their households) had turned to household sidelines as an attractive economic alternative even in the collective era, when the market system was less active and alternatives more limited (M. Wolf 1985). The strategy of evading restrictions in more public and male-defined economic spheres in favor of more autonomous activity carried on in the household, usually by individual women, could be seen as a practical strategy spontaneously devised by rural women and later advocated by the Women's Federations as legitimate.

This strategy was similarly astute regarding the second component of the effective combination already mentioned—namely, the initiative of individual women. The Women's Federations network is understaffed; at best, it reaches only to the township level in the countryside, and then usually with only a single cadre. Organized action on women's issues that is reliant on organized support from the Women's Federations may be feasible in urban areas, but it is not a realistic alternative in the villages where the majority of Chinese women live.

At this point the issue of ability returns, but in a different form. Since the 1980s the Women's Federations have been actively advocating improving the "quality" (*suzhi*) of women (see Kang Keqing 1987).[19] This is largely a reference to the educational and economic disadvantages women commonly experience compared with men, but it is also a reference to political and personal dimensions of quality. One of the national propaganda efforts of the Women's Federations network is the promotion of what it terms the "four selfs": self-esteem, self-respect, self-possession, and self-strengthening (*zizun, ziqiang, ziai, zizhong*). The aim here is to suggest that women are as able as men, and to provide at least moral encouragement to the rural women whose sense of agency is critical to prospects for change in the countryside.

This policy of improving the "quality" of women does not directly confront the problem of gender discrimination; rather, it implicitly accepts the proposition that in some respects, such as formal education and economically useful knowledge, women are at a disadvantage compared with men. The emphasis of the policy is less on combating discrimination than on placing women in a stronger position to improve their lives. This is a realistic approach under conditions of entrenched patriarchy and women's organizational weakness in the public realm in the countryside. "Quality" is an issue because so much depends on relatively isolated women and their effective agency.[20]

China in the 1980s has been characterized by the impact of policies that have created some windows of opportunity in the public realm, both as the indirect, unsettling consequences of policy shifts as such and because of the specific nature of the reform policies themselves, which advocated and legitimated dispersed initiative, at least within ambiguous official limits. Although the reform program has had mixed implications for women's interests, many women, including at least some segments of the official Women's Federations, have responded actively to the new situation.

In terms of long-standing Chinese criteria for viewing the women's movement, this response can be seen in part as an implementation of the same reform policies that are being pursued in the society and economy as a whole. The strategy of improving women's status by involving them in extradomestic productive labor has long been a tenet of Communist orthodoxy and of Party policy in China. Women are now well established as present in the public economy, so the issue has shifted to one of improving their relative position, although discourse on the subject emphasizes increased income-generation rather than structural change. This offers the promise of increased household income to all household members and thus circumvents potential opposition.

The lack of priority given to gender equality, combined with official legitimacy for it, is conducive to prospects for quiet change. The relative weakness of women and their formal organizations requires that they be wary of overt challenges; however, under favorable conditions, it also permits covert challenges to be effective at times. Although the actions rural women take can be viewed as partly defensive and limited, there is also a sense in which they are the most effective means of subverting patriarchy in the countryside.

CHAPTER 7

Gender and Power in
Rural North China

The rural reform program of the 1980s initiated a reshaping of every aspect of life in rural China. The current shape of China's rural society is one that bears quiet continuities with multiple pasts—collective and precollective—together with recent vitality and unsettled concern about a problematic future.

The resurgence of aspects of rural social life that were constrained during the collective era has combined with an increased official tolerance for diversity in rural social organization. This has added significantly to the range of economic opportunity and social expression possible in the countryside. It is much more difficult now than in the collective era to generalize regarding even the formal structures of rural social life. This study has attempted to avoid, or not to place undue emphasis on, the idiosyncratic elements of the three villages studied, but to focus instead on elements that might be shared with other villages. Nevertheless, three villages in one province cannot do more than provide one of numerous starting points for a comparative study of rural social life in China. The empirical material and arguments presented in the preceding chapters are an attempt to provide just that. On this basis it is also possible to venture a few propositions that might prove useful in further investigation.

Two central threads run through the discussion as it has been presented thus far. One of these concerns the centrality of gender in rural social life and its contemporary processes of transformation. In this aspect of the study I have tried to sketch emergent formal and informal lines of structure, custom, and practice. Many of the significant features of gender in rural China are embedded in relations that anthropologists conventionally designate as "kinship." This is manifestly problematic in that the relations in question are simultaneously kin, economic, political, and virtually every other type of social relation at the same time. In China, furthermore, the idiom of rural social relations is largely that of kinship; consequently, kinship relations occupy a sizable portion of this study. The approach to gender in rural China taken here is also strongly concerned with the place of gender in relations of power, and especially in the workings of state power.

The second thread running through this study concerns the relations of power in rural China. These relations have been explored primarily in terms of several specific aspects of gender, and especially in relation to the practices and viewpoints of Chinese women. This aspect of the study has involved a reassessment of the nature of state power and a reconceptualization of rural power relations in which gender is central.

Gender and State Power

The historical starting point of this study is the rural economic reform program, that is, the initiation of a series of fundamental changes in rural economic and political organization *on the part of levels of state organization far removed from village life.* Whatever the changes made at the village level—and these have involved local initiative and moved in diverse directions—policy decisions at the national level have enabled and variously encouraged them. Indeed, these changes could not have happened without the post–Cultural Revolution change in national policy. This is not to suggest that there is any automatic or simple implementation of this policy at local levels. If that were so, there would be no need for local studies, and the shape of Chinese society and polity would be entirely different. The issues addressed in this study are all internally defined by the question of the relation of social life at the village level to near and distant state power, as concretely realized in the transformations of the rural economic reform.

The most dramatic change in this reform program was the institution of the "production responsibility system" at the beginning of the decade. This permitted local initiatives within some national guidelines and resulted in a variety of forms of decollectivization. In none of the three villages studied were there significant pressures within the village to decollectivize. The specific local responses each made consisted of devising forms both for preserving elements of collective life and for redefining the operations of state power internal to each village. These responses also involved an increased role for households and, more optionally, for intermediate and informal social groupings, such as Huaili's informal, unnamed "land groups." The importance of the household, based on small families, and of other ties involving kinship has correspondingly increased the importance of local ties that are, or appear to be, kin-based (see Perry 1985, Wang Sibin 1987). The resulting variations studied here all fall within the framework described by Philip Huang as a "mixed collective-family system" (P. Huang 1990: 220).

The long-standing basis of rural political economy in China has been agricultural production, and the reorganization of agriculture has been basic to the entire reform program. Qianrulin provides an interesting instance in its continuation of the collective structure despite the withdrawal of higher state support or encouragement for this form. The village (formerly a brigade-level accounting unit) acts as a bridge or hinge giving internal form and authority to collective formal organization within the community and integrating it into a wider decollectivized, mixed political economy. Households remain allocated to agricultural teams (formerly production teams) and have much the same relation to agricultural production as in the years when collective organization was the national norm.

There are two major distinctions from this past. First, Qianrulin's success in rural industry has drawn most of its work force out of agriculture, so that the preponderance of agriculture characteristic of the earlier era no longer applies to it. Second, women's labor has become the major component of ordinary agricultural work. This tendency could be found in earlier collectives where other employment opportunities were available and is not directly related to the collective-decollectivization divide, but it is a change characteristic of the greater rural economic diversification of the reform era, and one in which Qianrulin shares despite its otherwise atypical features. Qianrulin is distinctive in that work is still formally allocated; the gender division of labor is therefore a politico-administrative matter as well as an expression of cultural norms and a response to market forces and household demands.

Zhangjiachedao has formally decollectivized, but the village (formerly the brigade, and still referred to as such) predominates through the success and scale of village-level rural industrial enterprises and the village political leadership that made this recent growth and prosperity possible. The organization of agricultural production in this village has included widely different arrangements in a sequence of experiments determined by the village level of leadership. At the time of fieldwork, the arrangement was one that had land equitably divided among and managed by households. Considerations of household labor management resulted in some concentration of mature women in agricultural labor, although this received no encouragement from the village leadership. Zhangjiachedao's internal social organization revolved around the two poles of village and household organization, with little intermediate social organization.

Huaili is the most agricultural of the three villages studied and the one that may be most widely indicative of reform-era social organization in agriculture. The village decollectivized reluctantly and at a later date than most collectives. When it did so, it devised mechanisms and criteria at the village level to effect the division of collective agricultural resources. These mechanisms drew in the recognized male leadership in the village and produced means of assessing differences among the assets of the previous agricultural teams in order to arrive at an agreed-upon division of the proceeds from liquidating these assets, and to provide a modest economic base for the village (formerly the brigade), which in this case had been an economically empty level prior to decollectivization.

The process of decollectivization also involved setting criteria for the allocation of land. These focused on several contentious factors— differences in the quality of various plots of land, equitability, mechanisms to ensure (or at least encourage) the performance of public labor for water control, mechanisms to allow informal land groups to draw lots for land together, and provision of a reserve of land for discretionary adjustments in following years. The particularly interesting aspects of land allocation in Huaili are the explicit elements of gender inequity that prevailed—the gender differences in basic allotments, the provision that land allocations for public works be made only to men, and the lack of provision for adjustments of land allocations as women marry in or out.

National policy precipitated fundamental change in the local political economy, but then allowed it to be realized through local andro-centric political organization. Decollectivization has continued, in a somewhat altered form, the consolidation and incorporation of co-residential agnatically related groups of men also found in earlier periods in China. In the south this was associated with strong, localized corporate lineages in single-lineage communities prior to the collective period. During the immediate collective past of communities such as the ones studied here, and in China in general, the structure of collective political economy in the countryside made collectives into similar corporate units, although they were not necessarily single-lineage units and membership in a lineage was not an officially permissible criterion for membership. Nevertheless, widespread adherence to norms of patrilocal postmarital residence and lineage (or surname, or village) exogamy created communities based on one or more cores of agnatically related men, into which women were born and out of which they married into other communities structured along the same lines.

Collectivization made these communities corporate ones that shared an estate and held rights to allocate labor and apportion benefits within communities that had clear boundaries with one another, and that had formal ties and obligations to levels of political organization above the village. The corporate communities in question might be neighborhoods within villages or villages themselves. The boundaries and levels shifted at times during the collective era and in the process of decollectivization, but the underlying character of androcentric communities persisted through several changes in the specificities of political economy.

In the case of Huaili, it is possible to see this androcentry at work in relatively explicit and complex fashion—in formal village government, informal land groups, and household organization—but it is also a pattern evident in the other villages studied, where it is institutionalized primarily at the village level. Androcentric forms of organization are in each case part of the local level of the state, and at the same time work through the everyday relations of living and working in communities structured on androcentric lines.

This androcentry does not imply that women are marginalized within these communities. Women are well integrated into the local political economy—in a subordinate sense. Women make major contributions to the productive work of the communities, both in public workplaces and in household sidelines and enterprises; women per-

form most of the unpaid but essential work of maintaining households, reproducing the human community (especially, but not only, in
the sense of early childhood care) and caring for the ill and the aged.
Yet women do not have rights comparable to men within their communities in terms of access to or management of resources, nor do they
occupy positions of local political leadership.

The local structures of state power in rural China rest in part on
this basis of gender hierarchy within the political economy. This is entirely in line with the traditional Chinese political pattern of explicit
homology between the relations of ruler and minister and those of
husband and wife, and with the prescription of the "three obediences"
for women. If more recent Chinese polities have not subscribed to the
same ideology, neither have they dismantled either the ideology or the
social relations congruent with it. This is an important dimension in
which the authority of the hierarchical order centered on the nation
derives support and depth from asymmetrical social relations at the base
of the Chinese social order.

Similar patterns may be found in the dynamic area of rural industry. Rural industry and rural economic diversification have a long history in China. Their importance for the shape of the rural economy has
made them an object of state economic policy and one of the main vehicles for state plans for rural development. Many villages in China
have a history resembling Qianrulin's, in which movement toward rural industry was made during the collective era, when a basis was established for the rapid growth this sector enjoyed later, especially in
the early 1980s. Others have benefited, as has Zhangjiachedao, from
special state efforts to promote rural industry in exceptionally poor,
agriculturally disadvantaged villages.

All efforts at promoting rural industry in China operate within a
mixed economy in which the state continues to play a predominant role,
even if less directly in the 1980s than before. And much rural industry,
including all the instances discussed here, has been developed through
the action of various levels of the state, including the village level. Village and township enterprises have been among the most vigorous in
economic development throughout the reform era. They constitute a
major avenue through which local levels of state organization operate
to organize rural economic life. At the same time that the village constitutes the basic level of formal state organization in the countryside,
it is also a formal and effective vehicle of androcentric community life,

and the role it plays is determined by its character *both* as an aspect of the state *and* as an aspect of local community.

The roles of women and men in rural industry are markedly asymmetrical. Women, for the most part young unmarried women working in their natal villages or as temporary contract workers in other villages, form a significant portion of the work force in rural industry. They are, however, concentrated in relatively unskilled, dead-end work and rarely hold responsible positions. Men, in contrast, may occupy similar unskilled positions and may be temporary workers in factories in other villages, but they also have opportunities to enter skilled positions to the extent that these are available in rural industry, and to enter managerial and sales-and-procurement positions. That is, women and men both contribute to the work, although not under the same conditions, but a portion of men, and only rarely women, manage and control these enterprises.

To the extent that rural enterprises are under local state control, the almost total predominance of men at local levels of state government reinforces this gender asymmetry. One of the most important aspects of this asymmetry is partially masked because it is indirect. Benefits accruing from rural industry only partly take the form of direct remuneration to enterprise personnel. A major benefit is the contribution these enterprises make to public accumulation funds at the local level. Funds generated by rural enterprises support the provision of public services and the costs of local government, and also provide investment for further economic growth. In the case of the village enterprises discussed here, these funds accrue to villages. Men working in enterprises in their own villages receive the immediate benefit of remuneration plus deferred and indirect benefits through enterprise contributions to their villages. Women, except for the few working in rural industry in their marital villages, will not enjoy the substantial deferred benefits generated from their own work in rural industry. Customary patterns of social organization intersect with and reinforce the androcentry of local state organization.

Socialist commodity production is also a policy initiative of the national state, one designed to harness market forces in the interests of what is officially described as an updated conception of socialism. The practices involved in making this mixed economy work are predicated on an accommodation with a certain version of state planning and public accountability and with the workings of the variety of market forms present in China in the 1980s.

The partial withdrawal of the state, and especially its higher levels, from the direct management of production and distribution in the countryside early in the 1980s created limited opportunities both for lower levels of the state and for private, including household-based, entrepreneurs to enter or become more active in these spheres. Local state and private entrepreneurs must always do so, however, within a mixed economy still dominated by the state sector. The state—at various levels, extending up to the national level—sets economic policy regarding the role of the private sector, establishes regulatory bodies and practices, levies taxes, sets fiscal and monetary policy, and oversees the state sector of the economy. Much of the very small-scale, household-based activity examined in this study operates on the margins and in the interstices of the state economy, but even it is not removed from the impact of a myriad of state policies and economic interventions. Apart from the initiatives allowing the resurgence of the private sector in the 1980s, the most marked of these have been those accompanying the economic downturn at the end of the decade and the partial retreat from a market orientation since 1989.

Local levels of the state also play a role in the transformed rural market system. A substantial part of their role involves an interface with higher levels within the state sector, in procuring credit, raw materials, investment, or access to markets, as exemplified by all three of the villages examined here. Villages also interface with the private sector; indeed, most economic activity in rural China in recent years has been conditioned neither by state nor private sectors alone but by the management of relations between the two. The role of the local state in determining the activities of the private sector is evident in each of these villages: in Qianrulin, which prohibits private enterprise within the village; in Zhangjiachedao, where private enterprise is permitted, but overshadowed and stunted by the success of the village's enterprises; and in Huaili, which has undertaken the active promotion of small-scale household enterprises within the village.

In the small-scale, household-based portion of the private sector examined in this study, the gender asymmetries are somewhat more subtle and complex than in the other economic spheres examined here. There is no direct allocation of labor to be examined, and households may be quite flexible regarding gender division of labor. Men with skilled training or access to nonrural registration and employment may try to pass these advantages on to their daughters as well as their sons, adding complexities of economic differentiation and political stratification to the problematic of gender difference. Within households and where there is little or no hired labor, as in the majority of household enterprises, division of labor by gender may be less clearly defined than in larger enterprises employing hired labor. The available age and gender composition in the household sets limits on possible arrangements and favors both flexibility in the division of labor and maximal utilization of women's labor, unless and until some or all of the women in the household can be replaced by hired labor.

These circumstances operate in favor of women's exercise of their abilities, and this study, together with comments of women interviewed during its course, suggest that household enterprises provide more favorable conditions for mature women than do extradomestic workplaces, including rural industry. Women appear to be at a continuing disadvantage in managing household relations with outside sources of supplies and markets for their products, and this area remains an almost exclusively male domain. But women can effectively manage local commerce, as in running small shops within their home villages. In contrast with the limits on women outside their households, women are often relatively well placed to manage the portion of the enterprise internal to the household.

The rural Chinese household is an exceptionally clear instance of the realization of state power in everyday life. As I argued at some length in Chapter 5, the household is internally constructed by the regulations and operations of the national household-registration system. The household constructed in this official and administrative sense is not arbitrary or artificial, although it does differ in some specifics from the informal household. In particular, it is constructed on slightly different lines from the informal household and is more clearly bounded. This is most evident in the case of persons who live at least some of the time in a place other than their registered residence—principally those who hold jobs and formal registration at a place separate from the rest of their families but who spend considerable time with their families, and those who are dependents (primarily preschool-age children and some elderly persons) being cared for by relatives in a place other than their formal residence.

These and other ambiguities that constantly arise in the course of everyday life, and the complex negotiations of kin ties, are erased by the requirement of unambiguous registration in one or another household. But the formal household is very close to the informal household in its usual composition, and this also means that it is very close to the narrow sense of the family. The family is a much more elastic concept, but the core of what constitutes a Chinese family, as a multigenerational, co-residential kinship grouping with a shared economy and a joint estate, provides the basis for the household and is often coterminous with it. The critical implication of this connection for the present argument is that the state's construction of the household enters into the critical social unit of everyday life, the family, a unit that is also central to the most intimate aspects of each person's life.

The state works through the household registration system to internally define and to adjust, more or less subtly, several aspects of household and family life. Those mechanisms of population control, in its broadest sense, that require contact or intervention in rural households usually operate through the formally designated household head, who is normally the senior able male in the household. Some exceptions to this arise, for example, in connection with the period of transition while a son is taking on an aging father's role, and this is another aspect of the formal incapacity of the household registration system to accommodate ordinary ambiguities. Exceptions also arise where the man who would otherwise be designated household head holds nonagricultural registration and is therefore not a member of the formal household. The result is that his wife is formally designated household head, a designation that may be relatively empty if his work is nearby and he is in daily residence with his rural family, but also one that may formally recognize the actual role of women who are effectively heading households in which their husbands are rarely present. Whatever the case in each particular household, the designation of a household head—the person through whom the household normally intersects with local authorities—operates to reinforce asymmetries within the household, and by extension within the family, and to link these with the hierarchy of the state.

This entry of the state into household dynamics intersects with asymmetries of gender and generation, which are major structuring principles within, as well as beyond, the household. The marked gender asymmetry of the Chinese household cannot be solely attributed to the intervention of the state specifically through the relatively recent household-registration system. It is worthwhile to consider whether or not there might be a long-standing structure of gender asymmetry operating through a series of historically specific mechanisms and within an ideological and practical framework linking family and state. This would be consistent with Philip Huang's recent suggestions regarding the historical role of the state in shaping the pronatalist values of Chinese society (P. Huang 1990: 225–34).

Gender asymmetry is reinforced by the congruence between state and familial asymmetries. Indeed, the larger social hierarchy concentrated in the state derives force and authority from its connection with the intimate asymmetries of family life. These familial asymmetries are then carried into the wider social domains through both formal and informal gender and generational asymmetries in the dynamics of household boundary management, interhousehold relations, and suprahousehold organization. In all these dimensions, there are informal productive relations of power in everyday life that intersect the minute workings of state power in the household and operate to make it still more diffuse and efficacious. *These relations of power are without exception profoundly gendered.*

Grounded State Power

The role of the state in rural China, and in post–Cultural Revolution China in general, has been an important subject of attention in recent years (see Siu 1989, Friedman et al. 1991). Part of the attention has resulted from the concern of China's top national leadership to restructure the state in order to restore its popular legitimacy, and to devise a form of state more suited to China's economic reform program. The direction in which the state appeared to be moving, prior to 1989, included a withdrawal of direct control over many facets of life, an increasing reliance on market forces to direct the economy, a degree of decentralization of government, at least limited advocacy of a more effective separation between the Party and governmental components of the state, and an increased tolerance for popular initiative and organization. This allowed some comparisons with concurrent dynamics in the Soviet bloc, and scholarly experiments in applying to China the Western model of separate state and civil society. This is not a model readily applied to China, and it has posed analytical and empirical difficulties. There are indications that the reach of the state is not retracting but is becoming more effective through less direct means than those used prior to the reform program (Chevrier 1988, Shue 1988).

Some of the analysis in the preceding chapters is consistent with an approach phrased in these terms. In particular, this includes the analysis of shifts in the structure of the local state, which in these villages resulted in investing the former brigade and current administrative village with enhanced powers. My examination of the mix of local state and market forces in the development of rural enterprises and household-based commodity production is a further instance.

Despite these aspects of the study, I am not satisfied with a conclusion that approaches the restructuring of state power in rural China primarily in terms of direct or indirect government mechanisms, or even in terms of the wider understanding of the state initially employed here—including government, Party, army, mass organizations, and the entire apparatus of ruling centered on the national polity. If one examines the presence of the state internal to the many dimensions of everyday rural life that emerges in this study, a conceptualization of the state as merely penetrating rural society remains inadequate. As normally understood, this suggests such mechanisms as Party membership and organization within villages, structures of local government tied with higher levels of state organization, and the formal workings of the household registration system. All these are present, but more than this is present as well. I suggest a rethinking of state power that no longer conceptualizes it as something "outside" and "above" which then reaches into rural communities, but rather as an aspect of social life that is *simultaneously both diffusely present and productive within everyday social relations, and also present in overt, concentrated form in familiar "state" institutions.* This understanding of state power is closer to the metaphor of permeation, and also closer to the social patterns that appear in this study.

Both aspects mentioned here are essential to this conceptualization of the state. The first underlines the effectiveness and productivity of dimensions of the state that are obscured due to being internal to aspects of social life not ordinarily thought of as integrated into state processes. But to observe this effectiveness and productivity without seeing the connection with overt, concentrated aspects of the state would allow only general statements along the lines of "the personal is political." While this is true, it is not by itself an adequate description of power relations in rural China. The personal politics of family and community described here derive much of their force from the link they have with the institutions of the state, as conventionally understood; conversely, they also operate as a source for the efficacy, legitimation, and naturalization of state power.

The immanence of state power is a key to explicating the dynamics of social life. The state can be viewed as immanent in every sphere of social life, although social life remains a larger and encompassing domain. State power is internal to the definition of such fundamental elements of rural social life as the household and the village. Household and village are created and recreated in structures internally structured by the presence of state power. This structured presence is in no sense inert but is an active part of the dynamics through which households and villages operate in social life. It is not a passive constraint imposed from outside but a productive force operating from within the constituent elements of everyday life. This dimension of state power can be thought of as *grounded state power*.

Grounded state power, as it operates in the material examined here, generates two primary effects. The first is a movement toward hierarchy and hierarchical integration. This is apparent in every aspect of the study presented here: access to and use of landed resources, the androcentric asymmetry of the structure of village communities and village enterprises, the integration of household enterprises in the mixed state-market economy, the structure of rural households, and even internally, in the agency of organized and individual women. In many respects these features are indicative of persistent continuities in the Chinese polity, but each also demonstrates discernible movement or process within rural China in connection with initiatives of the national state. The reform-era state is continuing previous policies of increasing intervention in rural society, and doing so with greater subtlety and potentially greater effect than in the collective era.

The second effect of grounded state power is a movement toward official discourse, explicit rules, and clearly defined boundaries. These are equally evident in all the areas examined in this study, and are also important effects of the activist, if indirect, role of that national state in its effort to centrally redefine rural society and culture. But these effects are not produced by governmental decree or even by a more inclusive conception of policy and its implementation. Rather, they work through intermediate, customary dimensions of rural social life. These effects persist within a larger social dynamic in which hierarchy is not the sole organizing principle and in which much of social life proceeds in implicit and ambiguous practices. There is no requirement in this conceptualization that grounded state power should operate in a wholly unified manner. In common with all other aspects of social life, including the visible operations of the overt portions of the state, there are inconsistencies, contradictions, and conflicts in the play of grounded state power. Conceptualizing state power as grounded can assist in creating a body of social thought adequate to the problems of disjuncture and fragmentation in social life. The operations of grounded state power produce internal fractures within the social field that render ultimate order impossible and that provide the interstices within which disorder and counter-orders can flourish—and within which everyday life is actually lived.

Gender and Power

An understanding of the dynamics of gender and power in rural China requires attention to the intermediate customary mechanisms through which gender and power are constructed. As I have argued elsewhere (Judd 1989), the dynamics of gender in rural China can provide insight into more general questions of structure, custom, and practice. This can be indicated by a return to the issues with which this book began.

Women, unlike men, are barely taken into account in official policies or discourse on the transformation of rural China in the 1980s. The reform program has a dual focus: restructuring the public dimension of rural life, and revising the place of the household in the rural political economy. The reform program and the discourse regarding it are conspicuously silent regarding a role for women in these policies, and regarding the element of gender. The policies are formulated, discussed, and debated *as if they were gender-neutral*. This is pervasive in a program that has had overwhelming importance in rural China throughout the past decade, and that has significantly reshaped the conditions of life in the countryside.

A review of the areas examined in this study makes this clear. Decollectivization and the devolution of primary responsibility for agriculture to the rural household was a policy decision taken on the basis of problems with collective organization, and without specific reference to women. Similarly, the promotion of rural industry is a policy oriented toward diversified economic growth in the countryside, not one explicitly related to the interests of women. The turn toward the market is a product of difficulties with centralized planning and a concern with increasing rates of economic growth, again without consideration of women or gender. Indeed, the role of women in contemporary rural China remains so invisible that they might just as well be "virtuous" women who are lacking in ability and hence irrelevant to the rural political economy (see Chapter 1).

Coincident with this silence, there is a sharply inconsistent set of practices. Women and men are both deeply involved in agriculture, in gender-differentiated ways, and there is a discernible trend toward the feminization of agricultural work both in the three communities studied and in rural China in general. Similarly, in rural industry, there is an unmistakable pattern of activity by both women and men, which is again gender-differentiated and asymmetrical. In household-based commodity production, women and men are both active in gender-differentiated ways, and women's work is often essential to the viability of the household venture. Beneath these commonalities, there are significant differences in the political economy of gender in each of these sectors (the preceding chapters have been largely concerned with tracing those specificities), but each sector would look entirely different if confronted with "virtuous" women as an actuality.

The culture of rural China is marked by *a pervasive devaluation of women that is constantly denied in the practice of everyday life.* People in rural China express both this devaluation and a sometimes implicit, sometimes explicit recognition of women's actual role in rural political economy and social relations. In other words, the devaluation exists and is efficacious—for example, in effectively excluding women from most public roles of responsibility—at the same time that people pursue practical strategies of everyday life in which the abilities and actions of women are significant components. The cultural field is profoundly and pervasively fractured along the line of gender.

The fracturing is facilitated by the partial disengagement of official models of social structure from practical strategies, a disengagement that may be a common structural feature of social fields. This study has been framed within the terms of practice theory, and it may be worthwhile to comment on aspects of the study that contribute to that theoretical orientation. Gender has been the departure point, and, in the process of rethinking gender, it has been necessary to rethink concepts of structure and practice—to locate a space where the practical politics of gender in a fractured social order can be comprehended.

As formulated by Bourdieu (1977, 1990), practice theory prioritized the practical strategies that people use in the course of everyday life. Practice theory situates practice as the critical term between social structure and the predispositions of unconscious habitus. Habitus operates as both a structured and a structuring element generating structure through practice. I have argued elsewhere (Judd 1989) for the utility of an additional conceptual area that can be identified as custom. This is a term common within ordinary Chinese discourse, in which people reflect on their own social patterns. In contrast with comparable concepts in Bourdieu's outline of practice theory, this concept of custom is more clearly, explicitly, and consciously formulated than (unconscious) habitus or (largely tacit) custom or pre-law.

The space occupied by custom in rural Chinese society is located between the official models of social structure on the one hand and the mechanisms of habitus on the other. Custom is consciously formulated and expressed, although it is much more informal and flexible than are official models, and it is not necessarily shared homogeneously by all those in a given cultural field. The elements of the identification of custom as a distinct area are implicit in Bourdieu's treatment of official models, but those elements might be used to greater advantage within the heart of practice theory's theory of practice. The triad of structure, habitus, and practice works most effectively in a homogeneous social field—but that is an abstraction. Where social fields are less homogeneous, and especially where they are fractured by the play of power, custom appears as a useful term lying between perduring structure and the strategies that people create and pursue, consciously as well as unconsciously.

Custom has the flexibility to permit—and to facilitate—disjunctures between official models of structure and actual practices. Through custom, people create and recreate strategies and accommodations with which they negotiate their way in the fractures of the social order. And through custom, the conflicting demands of the official social order are articulated, in however shifting or contradictory a fashion, with the imperatives of everyday life. For example, within the official model, men figure as the primary economic providers in rural China, and their preferred position in rural political economy means that there is some substance to this view. The near silence in the official model regarding the economic contribution of women is more problematic and is not matched by a comparable silence in the realm of custom. Although not elaborated within the official model, there is a substantial and explicit body of custom regarding gender division of labor in the countryside, and this body of custom does give significant weight to the contribution of women. The relatively clear pattern of division of labor by gender and age, even after the end of formal labor allocation, is a clear indicator of the force of custom in this important sphere.

Custom can accommodate shared, and also divergent, views on the part of the people involved. For example, male leaders might dismissively refer to married women active in the public work force as "housewives," whereas women speak clearly of women's domestic work load and never refer to themselves or other women in the same dismissive terms. Divergent views can and do operate within the same cultural field, but they do so at the levels of custom and practice rather than at those of official model or structure. Custom can work effectively in contexts of flux and in the interstices of a fragmented social order. Official perduring models may have a utility (or a liability) in offering coherence or apparent coherence under the same conditions, but they cannot serve as a practical guide for everyday life. The mechanisms of habitus are similarly constrained, insofar as they imply a degree of stability and homogeneity in order to generate structural effects unconsciously. Custom and practice can be effectively realized without any necessity for homogeneity.

I would argue that much of the work that might alternatively be attributed to habitus is actually being done through conscious and provisional custom. The fragmentation and flux of life in modern and contemporary China has required a flexible art of living that can provide the adeptness to handle change and uncertainty. China constitutes a highlighted case of a society characterized over extended periods of time by both official social cohesion and persistent flux and fragmentation. Custom and customary practices provide the cultural resources for living lives in the interstices of such a social order and disorder.

Custom conditions the opportunities available to individuals, the mix of economic resources and possibilities for rural households, the structure of the public work force, and the gendered dimension of local political economy. It is also flexible and, because it is not elaborated within the official model, can be adjusted as situations vary or change. For example, the preference for young unmarried women in the work force of rural industry need not prevent a village from starting to employ married women as well, especially if the alternative is more extensive employment of workers from other villages.

Most important, custom is a privileged locus for state power in its grounded and diffuse form. Here state power unobtrusively and silently meets and meshes with the politics of gender in everyday life. And here grounded state power acquires its gendered dimension. State power, in its more overt and formal forms, lacks the efficacy to structure everyday life but is, in contrast, highly efficacious when it works as grounded state power through the minutiae of custom and customary practice. In the mechanisms through which village land is allocated and through which work on the land is organized, control of the basic resource in the rural political economy is opened to the forces and practices of customary androcentry. In the customary practices through which labor and capital are organized and controlled in village-level rural industry, gender difference operates as a significant factor in capital accumulation and public investment at the village level of the state. The officially promoted revival of widespread commodity production in rural China has utilized some established customary practices in rural business and household activities, as well as contributing to the emergence of new customary practices, such as those involving mature women in specialized households. The construction and regulation of households is perhaps the dimension of grounded state power in rural China that is most obviously gendered.

Although some aspects of the relations of gender and power in everyday rural life go without mention and are either unseen or taken for granted, some have become covert arenas for potentially subversive action within the political margins of women's lives. Throughout rural life, state power is created and recreated as gendered. And gender generates effects of which formal state power is only the most concentrated expression.

There is no differentiating feature in Chinese life that is more profound, continuing, and asymmetrical than gender. Whether located within the habitus, within structure, within custom and practice, or—more accurately—within all of these, gender is a primary productive difference and one that is fundamentally asymmetrical. The reconfiguration of state power in process in rural China draws force and legitimacy from its immanence in the politics and the power of gender.

Reference Matter

Notes

Chapter 1

1. I am analyzing gender and kinship together here, in a manner compatible with the approach of Collier and Yanagisako (1987).

2. For detailed coverage of the earlier stages of the rural economic reform program, see Maxwell and McFarlane 1984 and Howard 1988. Further details on aspects of these and later stages of the program are contained in the following chapters.

3. For further information see "Shandong's Economy in 1986" 1987, "Shandong's Performance in 1987" 1988, "Shandong's Economy in 1988" 1989, and "Shandong's Economic Performance in 1989" 1990. For information placing Shandong relative to other provinces, see Walker 1989.

4. Small daughter-in-law marriage is a form of marriage optionally practiced in China, whereby a family takes in a very young unrelated girl and raises her together with the family's children, with the intention that she will marry one of the family's sons when of age (see M. Wolf 1972). Matrilateral cross-cousin marriage is a form of marriage in which a man marries his mother's brother's daughter.

5. Where patrilocal postmarital residence is combined with surname exogamy in single-surname villages, one implication is that men continue to reside in their natal villages after marriage, whereas women leave upon marriage to join their husbands. This gender difference in postmarital residence is the conventional situation in China because, even in multi-surname villages, most women marry out of their own village.

6. The more specific intellectual debts of this study to the literature in the field are indicated in the substantive chapters.

7. In one of the villages this range was extended, as a result of an offer on

the part of a local cadre and with the explicit advance permission of the individuals involved, to several cases of divorce-and-remarriage or widow remarriage, and a few instances of serious domestic disruption and scandal.

Chapter 2

1. The agricultural figures presented here are derived from official records in Huaili in 1988, 1989, and 1990. The discussions that produced these figures also extended to the problems of arriving at reliable agricultural figures and the official process now used to arrive at estimates of agricultural production. Since the dissolution of the collective, it has been necessary to use indirect methods, such as a survey of a structured sample of village households, combined with experience-based assessment of yields per unit of land and fixed official figures for per unit crop values. Huaili's figures, and those for Shandong Province as a whole, are based on measures of this nature, and there are manuals available designed to standardize reporting of rural production statistics. The figures presented in the text should be read as informed estimates and officially accepted production data. The provincial figure presented here is derived from an official provincial report ("Shandong's Economy in 1988" 1989: 2). For valuable background on Shandong's agriculture earlier in the 1980s, see Sicular 1986.

2. These figures are based on retrospective accounts and extrapolations backward from more precise data provided for 1988, 1989, and 1990. These and all other data presented here are derived from my fieldnotes, unless a published source is cited. The figure of 1,300 mu refers only to agricultural land designated for systematic allocation. It excludes nonagricultural land and land that remained in agricultural group hands for allocation at the discretion of the leadership.

3. By 1989, the upper age limit for women as labor power units had been raised to 50, but this had no effect on land allocation, which was then being carried out according to different criteria.

4. There were specific regulations defining who was required to provide this service and who was exempt. Every five years, all males between 18 and 40 years old who are registered in Huaili are recorded for the purpose of this service and are expected to provide it for the following five years. Grounds for exclusion are mental or physical handicap, status as a state-recognized specialized household, attendance at school, and various kinds of rural public-service work (medical personnel, local [minban] teachers, drivers, electrical workers, and local cadres). One or more cadres lead(s) each village's work team; they are paid RMB 200 for each year they do this work, but are not allocated land for the service. Former servicemen are included in the land allocation but are not required to do the work. Each man who is recorded as required to do the work receives a land allocation for the five-year period, although he will not necessarily be asked to provide the service every year. While the work is actually being done, those doing it are paid RMB 0.30 per day and are provided with food at village expense.

Each year, the county government determines how much labor is required and sends quotas down through township governments to villages. The quotas are framed in terms of the proportion of a village's total population that will be subject to the levy. In 1989, for example, the figure was set at 13 percent, which meant that Huaili was required to send more than 100 men for one month. This was not far below 140, the total number of men required to be available for this work in Huaili. The quota figure was, as always, set high in order to allow for some exemptions to be sold (at the price of RMB 200 in 1989). This is permitted up to a limit of 5 percent of the quota. In the economic conditions prevailing in Huaili in the late 1980s, many men could make more than RMB 200 in a month, and consequently more sought exemptions than were granted them.

I was officially told that replacements are not hired, either by the exempted individual or by any level of government, although I was also told, less officially, that the going rate for a substitute in 1989 was RMB 120–30. This could be attractive for the less fully employed men in the village or the area. Village officials reported that this work was extremely unpopular and that it was hard to meet quotas. According to one unconfirmed but probably reliable report I heard during the flooding of 1990, much of the maintenance of the drainage system had lapsed during recent (relatively dry) years, and the land in some drainage ditches had been cultivated.

5. There are also households of elderly individuals or couples in the village that might, in some sense, be considered to be without land. Although stem families are common in Huaili, there are also many instances of household division leaving elderly individuals or couples on their own, with arrangements made for their allocated land to be cultivated by their divided-out sons, who then provide for their support. These are only apparent cases of landlessness.

6. In the summer of 1990, the highway running along one side of Huaili was closed for upgrading. This hurt local household enterprises that partly depended on highway traffic, especially the restaurants. Local hopes were for increased traffic when the highway was reopened. It is worth noting that the rural economy, in general and in this area, was in trouble in 1990. There had been a general economic slowing in the countryside since 1985, exacerbated by the economic crisis of the end of the decade, and especially by the political and economic crises of 1989.

7. Household land may be freely rented or loaned for limited lengths of time, but it is understood that if this practice continues, the household will forfeit its land allocation in the next land readjustment. Two of the households in Huaili that were without land in 1989 had held land in 1984, rented it out, and given it up in the 1986 reallocation. Long-term private landlordship or patron-client relations based on land resources are not possible under these conditions.

8. The prevalent form of postmarital residence in Huaili is patrilocal. There are a few uxorilocal marriages, but none since 1986. Uxorilocal matches commonly involve men with nonagricultural registration, who would not be eligible for land allocation in any event. In cases of intravillage marriage that have

occurred since 1986, the marrying woman's land remains allocated to her natal household.

9. Despite national legal provisions for inheritance on the part of both sons and daughters, daughters do not inherit in Huaili, on the asserted grounds that they do not assume responsibility for the care of their parents. Yet married-out daughters do customarily assist their natal families, and now have a legal obligation in this respect as well. Huaili's adherence to local custom in preference to national law is a common rural practice. Also see Palmer 1988.

10. This type of "unclear division" (*fenjia bu qing*) is fairly common in Huaili and, I would venture, elsewhere in contemporary rural China. It provides a viable compromise between the younger generation's preference for division into nuclear families and the older generation's need for a mechanism of support in old age.

11. Donkey owners were unanimous in saying that their donkeys were loaned out freely to the entire village, provided they were not needed for work in their own households. They were less unanimous in reporting what I believe was also generally true, that such a loan would be compensated for with fodder for at least the day's work. While the loan was surely generous and beneficial to the recipients, the fodder provided for an otherwise idle animal—fodder costs were high at the time and constantly commented upon—also benefited the donkey owners and provided a solid economic basis for this generalized cooperation.

12. Earlier conceptions of women as being marginal to agricultural labor in north China may have been partly based on too narrow a definition of agricultural work. The most detailed account available for Shandong Province is, unfortunately, not from a cotton-growing region, but is well worth consulting nonetheless (Yang 1945).

13. I am excluding from present discussion a smaller sample of Huaili residents interviewed early in 1988. There were sufficient differences in Huaili's economy in the 18-month interval between these two fieldtrips that the two samples should not be conflated. On this particular subject, I am restricting myself to the more recent data set. In 1990 I visited two additional households, as well as revisiting a number of households in the 1988 and 1989 samples, but I have also excluded these from this discussion.

14. For a broader discussion of the feminization of agriculture and related issues in relation to Shandong Province, see Judd 1990.

15. These 14 do not include the women described elsewhere in the text as carrying a double burden. These 14 (6 of whom are over 50 years of age) reported their main work as unambiguously domestic.

16. The only case of interhousehold cooperation regarding vegetables of which I was informed was that of a young unmarried woman who helped a related household by marketing its vegetables occasionally. This is better conceptualized as part of the multifaceted and often economic help given between related households than as an indication of agricultural cooperation.

17. An exception to this was the case of a few households with land well suited to cotton but not to grain. One other household, where the only man

was elderly, consistently grew only cotton, which was tended by the women in the household, and purchased food grain. In these cases, the relative prices of the different types of crop were irrelevant.

18. I avoid the term "lineage" because it holds more implications than can be substantiated for Huaili. The discussion here is structured around terms used and views expressed by the people of Huaili, and around observed or expressed social relations. I intentionally avoid the language of kinship analysis here, in order not to impose or suggest interpretations that are questionable or that cannot be supported.

19. The implications of this emphasis on size of yuan for the status of women, and for the implementation of China's birth-control program, do not go unnoticed by the local people.

20. Technically, ownership was not and is not at issue, as all agricultural land formally belongs to the state. Under the collective system, effective control was expressed through the term "accounting unit," and this was either the team or the brigade, except in the case of state farms. At the present time, ownership is still held to rest with the state, but households or, in some cases, other units have contracts for use of the land in what is termed a "responsibility system." Administrative levels above either accounting unit or contract unit have, and continue to have, some rights and responsibilities with respect to land, but control and ownership are held de facto by the lower-level units.

21. For an interesting and detailed comparison with Hebei regarding kin and commercial ties in the rural economy, see Wang Sibin 1987.

Chapter 3

1. In characterizing this type of organization as emergent, I do not intend to suggest that the village is an emergent level of organization, but rather that the specific types of village organization now appearing demonstrate some distinctive properties. Also see Duara 1988.

2. The processes of cellularization described by Shue (1988) and Siu (1989) are also relevant here.

3. These observations are based on my reading of the Chinese press at the time, and on personal communications from Chinese fellow students while I studied in China from 1974 to 1977. There was a particular push toward the brigade level in suburban Shanghai in the summer of 1976. I do not have contemporary evidence for a similar push in Shandong Province at the time, but the policies in question were national ones. Developments in places such as Qianrulin may have been in line with national policy while being less closely tied to the more problematic political issues of the mid-1970s.

4. I am referring here to contemporary village enterprises that grew from collective beginnings and that are still closely tied to local state organs. There are also rural enterprises that began privately during the 1980s, which are more independent of the state.

5. Observations made by Huang Shumin (1989) about local cadre resistance to decollectivization may well be pertinent in the case of Qianrulin.

6. For more detail on the "feminization of agricultural work," and comparison with Qianrulin, see Judd 1990.

7. The usual pattern in textile factories in China is that the looms are tended by women while men do the technical, financial, and managerial work. The initial expectation therefore included some job creation for men in the village. The reduction in staff, combined with increased control by the township, resulted in the elimination of jobs for village men and the reduction of jobs for village women in 1990.

8. A Party branch is at a lower level than a Party committee. Chinese usage does sometimes speak of the "two committees" at the village level, but replicating this usage would create confusion since there are, properly speaking, no Party committees at the village level.

9. These benefits include both general community services and individual benefits in cases of particular need. Community services include education (much of the cost of education in rural areas is borne directly by rural communities), health care (to the extent that it has remained available following decollectivization), and any public childcare. Provision for the elderly without children to support them—and care for others unable to support themselves—is provided by the village, to the extent that such individual benefits are available (see Feuchtwang 1987). Additional benefits may be provided at the discretion of any village, such as subscriptions to a magazine for all households (Zhangjiachedao) or organized bus trips to Mt. Tai (Huaili). The quality and range of benefits are important determinants of living standards and quality of life, and are highly variable between villages. The variation is related both to the economic capacity of villages to provide services and to different decisions made at the level of local politics.

10. These observations about women's political participation and Women's Federation policy and actions on this issue are partly derived from discussions that took place as part of the fieldwork reported here. They also represent a summary of research done more intensively with the Shandong Women's Federation in 1990.

11. Skilled workers were referred to in Qianrulin by the term "technician" (*jishuyuan*).

12. Marriage should be interpreted here as an age marker which, in Qianrulin in 1987, separates women of roughly twenty years and older from those younger. The village has very little intravillage marriage, so this also separates women born in the village from those married into it.

13. In the case of women, jobs are also defined in terms of whether they are for a married or an unmarried woman. This is a matter of distinguishing between work for daughters of the village who have not yet married out (even if they marry nearby, they will lose their Qianrulin jobs upon marriage) and wives who are resident in the village of their adulthood.

14. There are men in the village who will never hold leadership positions and may spend many of their adult years in ordinary working positions under the leadership of younger men. Qianrulin's economic growth has opened up a large number of managerial positions for men in Qianrulin but has not en-

sured that every mature man will hold such a post. Qianrulin is a collective community in which hierarchy is manifest, and one of its major manifestations is in the differences between the jobs of men. There is less (but still some) differentiation in this sphere among women, who are more uniformly in less preferred and roughly equivalent positions.

15. These highly skilled workers from outside Qianrulin are referred to as "technicians," as are some slightly skilled local people. There is a clear difference between the two, however, which is indicated by the need to go outside the village to hire these people and to remunerate them at very high levels.

16. The movement of educated and skilled retirees to the countryside is an interesting contrast to the earlier movement of educated youth to the countryside.

17. Retaining urban registration for their children was essential. Parents would not deprive their children of access to urban residence. Also, they will be able to join their children in the cities, even while holding rural registration themselves, if they choose to do so in the future.

18. The outside workers are also outside the influential network of kin ties within the village. At most, some of the workers have used such ties as the basis of introductions when seeking work in the village. The more privileged among the male migrants are recruited from a distance and are already married, so they do not have lineal or affinal ties within the village upon which to draw. Note also that the practice of having all members of a household who are in the nonagricultural work force work in the same enterprise is a measure that keeps lines of authority in the household congruent with those in the workplace.

19. These hats were worn by elderly peasant men and were going out of fashion. Demand for the product had dropped and the factory was on the point of closing in 1976.

20. This was a common occurrence in 1960–62. Both Qianrulin and Zhangjiachedao have a number of residents who worked in cities in the 1950s, whose jobs disappeared in the economic crisis of 1959–61, and who then returned to their home villages.

21. It is possible that the village benefited from political connections after some of these men moved to senior positions. Local people speak with pride of the high positions of some village people now in Fujian Province. There was no mention of assistance from these officials to the village of Zhangjiachedao, and it is difficult to ascertain whether this might have occurred or to what extent it did occur. None of the village's more successful out-migrants was identified as holding a senior post within Shandong Province. The history of this village as a poor one that was a minor base for pre-Liberation Communist Party organizing (in this case running a cadre training school), and that remained poor, is not unusual. Communist bases were typically located in poor regions that continued to be poor after Liberation for the same reasons as before. In the case of Zhangjiachedao, this meant a limited amount of poor quality land and a location far from any urban center.

22. State assistance to rural industry was widely available, in a variety of

forms, in the early 1980s, but had become very hard to obtain only a few years later. By the late 1980s, state policy was to restrict the development of small rural enterprises. The absence of direct state assistance combined with tight money policies made it much more difficult for late entrants to rural industry, such as Huaili.

23. I was conspicuously obstructed in my inquiries about women's educational level during many of my household visits in Qianrulin. A village official who accompanied me on many of these visits consistently interrupted at this point in the interviews, always claiming that the working young women had completed lower middle school. As a result I do not have firm data on the extent to which women's education is being adversely affected by starting work early, but there can be no doubt that this is occurring, and occurring with village knowledge and approval.

24. For a more extended discussion of some of the issues raised in this paragraph, see Judd 1990.

25. I was told that women marrying out of the village would not automatically lose their factory jobs, but I am aware of only one woman who has continued to work in the factory years after marrying out, and she is in long-term residence in her natal home while her husband remains in the army. The problem here appears to be less a matter of policy than a practical problem of shiftwork and childcare, exacerbated by commuting.

26. For a comparison with Taiwan, see Diamond 1979, Gallin 1984, and Niehoff 1987.

27. This was a relatively stable moment in the factory's history. Its period of rapid growth in size had ended by 1984, and future development in the village was intended to take the form of diversification. The factory was working at full capacity.

28. The village must still serve as a conduit for collecting the agricultural and other taxes levied by higher levels of the state.

29. I am, of course, referring here to self-employment in household enterprises. Huaili had few such enterprises that hired any labor. Where they did hire labor, the situation for those hired was no more desirable than in rural industry, although conditions of employment were somewhat different. This might, for example, include receiving room and board in the employer's household. In some cases household enterprises expand to a size comparable to any of the village factories discussed in this chapter, but none of the enterprises in Huaili was on this scale.

I did briefly investigate one such factory in another Shandong village. It was extremely similar to the larger factories in Qianrulin and Zhangjiachedao discussed above, including its reliance on young, unskilled female labor. The chief differences lay in the origin of the factory, the technical skill and entrepreneurial initiative of the household head, and the private ownership of the profits.

Chapter 4

1. For an overview of the situation of women in rural China at the beginning of the rural reform era, see Croll 1987b.

2. For a global perspective on commoditization, see Wolf 1983.

3. I have added the qualifier "relevant" to "capitalist or socialist models" in order to exclude from consideration newer Western models of slower growth. China is determined to attain high rates of economic growth and substantially raise living standards. A model of more limited, sustainable growth may win support in the future but is quite irrelevant to current Chinese controversies.

4. For a discussion of similar issues in the 1970s, see Nolan and White 1979.

5. For a systematic treatment of related issues in an urban context, see Walder 1983.

6. For an illuminating early discussion of models of contemporary entrepreneurship in China, see Solinger 1984.

7. Two of the most widespread forms of disapproved commerce may deserve special mention. One is the practice of buying goods in one locality at a low price and reselling them elsewhere, where they are scarce, at a much higher price. The problem here is that the difference between the two prices may far exceed reasonable returns for transport and other business costs, and so generate inflationary pressures. Within the socialist work ethic, profits earned in this manner cannot be justified as a reasonable return for labor or as contributing the value of additional labor. A second serious practice is the manipulation of price differences between the controlled, planned sector of the economy and the free-market sector. Scarce goods that can be obtained at a low price within the planned sector, through "connections," can be resold at vastly inflated prices on the private market. This practice is subject to the same criticism as the first one, and also raises questions of state cadres' and managers' abuse of positions of trust in the state sector.

8. For a treatment of some negative aspects of the drive for acquiring more money, see Xie Dehui 1989.

9. In 1989, I found cases in which some workers and managers appeared genuinely not to know what their remuneration might be, and expected to find out only when paid at the end of the season or year. Part of this phenomenon was evidently related to the poor and unstable economic conditions at the time, and the uncertain ability of some enterprises to pay their staff. It was evidently also related to an unwillingness, especially on the part of managers, to inquire or appear to be concerned about money.

10. There are interesting comparisons to be made here with household enterprises in Taiwan (see Niehoff 1987).

11. Some questions do arise, and are under discussion in China, about the extent to which the small-scale commodity economy of the present-day Chinese countryside can be integrated with the larger scale of commodity production viewed as necessary for national economic growth (Lin Li 1988). Questions of this nature lie behind the issues of immediate concern here—namely, the prac-

tice of the commodity production economy at the household level, both in ordinary rural households and in specialized households.

12. Putting-out systems are a form of production in which merchants provide ("put out") the inputs to rural households that then supply the product to the merchant. Putting-out differs from simpler craft production in its links with merchant capital.

13. Some other avenues include army service, higher education, and official position, all of which are most effectively pursued by young men, or by others on their behalf. These are possible channels of access to power, prestige, and nonagricultural registration, but are less reliable avenues to economic mobility than direct engagement in the market. Of course, these alternatives are not mutually exclusive, especially when considered in relation to a household, rather than only to an individual.

14. For a comparison of much of the following material with a township in Hebei Province, see Putterman 1989.

15. Huaili is far from the more commercialized areas of Shandong and not close to any city. Dezhou Prefecture, in which it is located, is not especially prosperous, but its economy has responded well to the move toward a commodity economy. Huaili's commercial advantages are distinctly small scale, but they have been sufficient to add enormously to the village's prosperity. Huaili borders on a moderately well-traveled paved highway, and the immediately contiguous village is the site of a rotating standard market. Huaili is one of a cluster of five villages close to the seat of a large township of 61 villages. The township is a thoroughly rural one, does not include any towns per se (nor is this five-village cluster comparable to a town), and is far enough from the county seat (almost an hour by bicycle) not to be in its economic shadow.

16. Households in this third category may, at the larger end of the range, strikingly resemble village-level collective enterprises. Those in Huaili were, with one exception, too small for this comparison.

17. The people of Huaili are constantly watching market trends in order to make crop choices and all manner of other economic decisions. This is typical of peasant and farming societies. It may be somewhat highlighted here because of the transition toward an increasingly commoditized system with which many rural residents are still not wholly familiar, and because of market instability in the late 1980s.

18. The mortality rate for piglets of the size purchased to fatten was not high. A household occasionally reported loss through the death of a pig, but pig-raising was generally regarded as a safe investment, unlike the large-scale raising of chickens.

19. There is a considerable literature on or pertinent to specialized households, although not all of it is relevant to the types of specialized households under examination here. Some of the better sources on the transition toward specialized households as a new socioeconomic form include: Conroy 1984, Song Linfei 1984, Zhou Qiren and Du Ying 1984, Crook 1986, and Croll 1987b.

20. "Key households" were defined by the state as intermediate between

specialized and other households. This category no longer exists and does not seem to have been used in the areas studied in any case.

21. All the households in the sample had at least one member capable of working full time. Dependent households were not included in the sample.

22. Unlike the other highly prosperous households in the village, which tried to varying degrees to hide their wealth, this household was engaged in conspicuous consumption to a surprising degree. The forms of effectively obligatory "social insurance" indicated in the text were supplemented by a pair of guard dogs and a large home safe.

23. Some state-recognized specialized households in other villages do actually run enterprises employing scores of workers in small rural factories, some of which are former collective enterprises that are now being contracted out, and some of which have been independently developed from smaller household-based specialized enterprises. This alternative is well covered in the press and exists in at least one village near Huaili that I visited briefly in 1988. Huaili's initiatives in rural industry have been ones made by the village and have been relatively small scale.

24. Tax evasion is endemic in the Chinese countryside, and its illegality is almost viewed as a technicality. Tax evasion does not meet noticeable popular disapproval, and much of it is quite open, but households do not usually advertise the exact extent to which they have succeeded in evasion.

25. These elements include welfare funds, housing for those rendered homeless by domestic conflict, some machinery (threshing machines), and an organizational infrastructure for job creation (the transport team and, briefly, a weaving workshop). Funds for education are minimal in Huaili, and collective health care no longer exists.

26. Many state-recognized and self-defined households reported building their enterprises step by step from the proceeds of the enterprise, after beginning with modest savings or a loan that was quickly repaid. However, much of the income of these and all other rural households has been going into consumption—improved living standards, new housing, and the now very substantial expenses of weddings. The question of how to channel a larger portion of specialized households' revenue into investment is a national policy concern.

27. Formally, the village head is the top village official, but the continuing practice throughout China is that the Party branch secretary is the actual ranking leader.

28. None of these three villages offers instances of highly conspicuous movements from cadre status to successful private entrepreneur. The most successful enterprises in the three are the village-run enterprises in Qianrulin and Zhangjiachedao, where some cadres have successfully become cadre-entrepreneurs. Huaili, the only village with extensive involvement in private entrepreneurship, is much less affluent. Huaili's current cadres are not, or not heavily, involved in entrepreneurial activity. Some former cadres have been relatively successful, but others have lost their positions due to the reduction in cadre numbers that accompanied decollectivization and have not found al-

ternative avenues for economic success. These men are pursuing ordinary rural livelihoods with distinctly modest success. These three villages to do not illustrate the extremes of cadre entrepreneurship found in some other contemporary Chinese communities.

29. Bookkeeping is essential for rural restaurants to an extent that might not be imagined. Their businesses run largely on credit, and much of this credit is extended to official organs entertaining guests on the basis of official chits that may not be redeemed for a year or more. The financial management of credit on this scale is a major problem for rural restaurants.

30. The one exception to this pattern is Household 21 in Table 4.2, where the key economic figure is the eldest (unmarried) daughter of the household. She is included in these figures in place of her mother and stepfather. This exception to the general pattern holds throughout the following tables and discussion.

31. Another woman, who later became an itinerant watch repairer in rural markets, reported that, when younger, she had also retailed clothing in markets.

32. At the same time, it is important to note that women's participation in the extrahousehold economy in a social context where this participation is the object of disapproval does not place women in a favorable strategic position (see Kandiyoti 1990).

Chapter 5

1. This is strictly the case even for members of one-person households, because everyone is formally included as a member of a household unit in the household registration structure that defines household membership in contemporary China. Members of one-person or partial family households are not well positioned to benefit from household-oriented policies, but they are not excluded from the structure or the discourse to the extent that they would be if the concept of family were the basis of policy and discussion, as in some analogous discourse in Canadian or U.S. society.

2. Suprahousehold forms of organization are vertical, in contrast to interhousehold forms of organization, which are horizontal in character. Interhousehold forms of organization have been promoted in recent years as a solution to the problems of economic scale posed by a household-oriented economy, but have not been adopted to a significant degree in any of the villages I examined in Shandong Province.

3. I did find a case of two women who reported that they were registered simultaneously in two rural localities in two different provinces, but this was technically illegal. The movement from one rural locality to another is not tightly controlled by the government. The constraints on this type of arrangement are those of local government's willingness to accept people as registrants, given that this implies providing access to resources and services. Women married out of their own communities are the people most likely to be in this situation. Women often maintain de facto dual residence for a period following marriage, but there is always a specified date (it may be years after the wedding)

upon which their registration is officially recorded as having moved. Men in uxorilocal marriages have less ambiguous residential status. There is more local concern to restrict their access to resources and their mobility, and they are expected to make a definitive move to their marital village if they hold rural registration.

There are also countless people legitimately living somewhere other than their registered place of residence, either as contract workers or as relatives and dependents of someone registered at that locality. In the 1980s migration was less tightly controlled than in the 1970s, so there are also people whose residence is not legal or not clearly so, but they do not enjoy the access to resources and services that come with legal residence.

4. By this criterion, young married women in Huaili do have the right to be allocated land in Huaili, provided their household registration has been moved to Huaili. This right has not been explicitly denied—the situation is described by all in the village as a matter of waiting for the next readjustment of landholdings. This is a very common situation in the Chinese countryside at present, although the precise details, such as the timing of readjustments, are variable. The actual implication of this situation is that women's access to resources *is* diminished, although access cannot be denied in legal principle.

5. I used this volume to construct the selected sample of households I interviewed in 1989, and to check the accuracy of recorded versus reported information.

6. In Qianrulin the household registration book was drawn upon for information to update older genealogical records available in more conventional form. This process, occasioned by my inquiries of and collaboration with three senior men and a genealogically minded village official, resulted in a current genealogy.

7. Young people working some distance away from their homes as temporary contract workers with agricultural registration may be in a similar situation, although they are more firmly members of the household and do contribute to it. In some cases, however, temporary contract work may be—and be seen and planned as—a step toward nonagricultural registration and potentially permanent departure from the countryside.

8. Small children, especially grandchildren, who belong to other households may well be additional residents. Occasionally a parent or other elderly relative registered elsewhere may also be in residence, although this is more commonly an urban phenomenon.

9. It is not accidental that both these households are, or have been, cadre households and, as a direct consequence, include a number of persons with nonagricultural registration. The earlier pattern of extended households being found more commonly among families of officials and the wealthy has been altered but has not disappeared.

10. These samples overrepresent the proportion of extended families and atypical family or household forms, because they were constructed to explore the range of kinship organization in each village, so atypical households were included to the maximum extent possible. It was not possible to visit or survey

every household, and village records are not sufficiently detailed or current to substitute for direct investigation. The discussion in the text is based on these samples and on extensive discussions with the villagers about households and families in their communities. The samples were constructed in part on the basis of these consultations. In comparison, a study of Jiao County, Shandong in 1986 reported 66.7 percent nuclear families, 24 percent stem families, 1.7 percent extended families, and 7.4 percent other family forms (Zhou Qing 1988: 17).

11. For comparison, see M. Wolf 1972.

12. Shandong houses are characterized by a wall that extends from the house to form a high and solid barrier around the courtyard. All the household's people and possessions, except its agricultural land, are encompassed by this wall. The large wooden front door is closed and locked when nobody is home, and sometimes when people are home. The door often opens to reveal a free-standing "wall" (bimen) with an auspicious character or pastoral scene painted on it. This wall serves to obstruct direct view of the courtyard's interior. Dogs may also be kept to protect the household from strangers, especially if the household is a wealthy one.

13. Isabel Crook (n.d.) has noted the weakness of horizontal ties in a rural community in Sichuan in the 1940s, and this weakness can be related to the social pattern examined here. Chinese culture has more extensively elaborated vertical relations. Mechanisms for controlling access to economic resources within agnatic groups have been widely reported in the south in the form of asymmetrical lineage segmentation and, more recently, in the north in the form of corporate associations (Cohen 1990).

14. Compare Wang Sibin's 1987 study in rural Hebei.

15. For a sensitive and comprehensive treatment of social roles and dyadic relations in rural Shandong, see M. Yang 1945.

16. Daughters can be removed from school or never sent to school at all in order to do income-generating work, to care for younger siblings, or to do domestic work so that their mothers can work outside the home. This pattern has been reported in other, poorer areas of China and appeared often in the histories even of the younger adults I interviewed who were illiterate. However, I met only one older child in one of these villages who for these reasons was not in school and never had been.

17. There is no reason to suppose that there is any reluctance on the part of mothers-in-law to withdraw from income-earning work outside the household, provided neither their own nor their household's standard of living is adversely affected. The work available to rural women is physically demanding, poorly paid, and is not experienced by rural women as liberating. Also see Zhang Juan and Ma Wenrong 1988.

18. The villages discussed here are unexceptionable in terms of recent birth-limitation programs. Each shows much larger sibling cohorts born up to and including the 1970s than in the past decade. None of the villages demonstrates complete compliance with the single-child family policy, but children born in excess of state limits are less numerous than reported in some parts of China.

19. There is actually a nearly universal preference for more than one child, but couples and their parents are to some extent resigned to state birth-limitation policies. For survey data on preferred number of children for a sample of households in Jiao County, Shandong Province, see Zhou Qing 1988: 20.

20. The situation of women in Qianrulin is reminiscent of an earlier argument by Boserup (1970) that the labor of women within a household can be an alternative to hired male labor from outside it. In Qianrulin the choice is between the labor of women in the community who are over 40 years of age and hired labor—female and male—from outside. This may be part of a wider pattern in contemporary China. Daqiuzhuang has attracted attention as a community in which women have chosen to return home to provide domestic labor support for male household members in the extrahousehold work force (Zhang Juan and Ma Wenrong 1988). Daqiuzhuang is also a community with large numbers of workers hired from outside (Jan Wong, oral communication, June 1992).

21. These women may be underrepresented in the sample, since many new brides are not included in their marital household for at least a few months after the wedding, spending some time in limbo between households. During this period they typically do not work, but if their labor is required, they are likely to be included in the household to which they are contributing. The phenomenon of new brides receiving a temporary respite from work as they make the transition to a new household, community, and social status is significant, but it is also a temporary matter and is not directly related to the issues of childcare and married women's work.

22. In interviews, it was extremely difficult to arrive at precise estimates of time spent caring for children. Childcare is not normally viewed as belonging to any category of work or even domestic labor, unless it is an essentially full-time occupation engaged in to the exclusion of other activities.

23. This unusual woman had a history of urban employment and was on her way to recovering her nonagricultural registration and leaving the countryside again. At the time I met her, she was energetically serving as village women's head and considered herself too busy with this work to stay home and care for her infant grandchild. Consequently, her daughter-in-law stayed home.

24. There may be a bias toward the mother, as linguistically suggested, but fathers are not excluded from the niangjia complex.

25. The comparable proportions for men are 66–75 percent participation in the rural economy of north China by a purely agricultural definition and 60–68 percent by a wider definition that includes subsidiary occupations (Thorborg 1978: 585). The same holds true for south China (higher rates for women and lower for men for the more inclusive compared to the less inclusive category).

26. Qianrulin is still collective and still on the workpoint system. Agricultural work is concentrated in a few agricultural work groups, so the issue of agricultural / nonagricultural balance and division of labor is a suprahousehold issue.

27. The two cases of extended family households already cited may be viewed as partial exceptions; however, both households represent the cultural form of the extended family and sensitivity to the wishes and values of parents more than they do economic cooperation. Indeed, each household shows distinct separation between the subunits of each married brother and his respective wife and children.

28. The changes in household and family are connected with changes in rural class structure.

29. For a discussion of family estates in Taiwan, which is pertinent with some adjustment to the present context, see Cohen 1976: 57–85.

30. The premodern practice of parents giving up their own household and moving in rotation to the households of their married sons does still occur. I also came across one case of an elderly man without sons who spent half the year with each of his married daughters. Such arrangements are not wholly a matter of caring for the elderly—the older man tended one daughter's small shop when he lived with her, and "rotating" grandmothers may be just as involved in caring for their grandchildren as are those living in one household.

31. Building a new house for a son may be closely connected with his wedding and may even be necessary to ensure that the wedding takes place. In 1988 in Huaili, a typical cost of wedding and house combined was RMB 17,000. Per capita income for the same village that year was slightly over RMB 700.

32. Cooperation and help are distinctly different categories, although attitudes toward them are in some respects similar. Cooperation implies a mutuality that people sometimes agree to acknowledge, although even that implies some infringement on the ideal of household independence. Help is a much more problematic category for the same reason, and because it implies weakness or dependence and suggests asymmetry. Help is to some extent acceptable in the context of obligatory assistance with rituals and life crises, where the aspects dependency and asymmetry are muted. Even so, help is most acceptable when generalized or when described as being given to someone else.

33. The concept of resources is used here in a broad and not purely economic sense. It includes not only access to means of production but also access to means of influencing political and administrative state processes. This is a necessary adjustment to the features of the Chinese political economy.

34. I did not discover instances of long-term provision of labor to households that were unquestionably dependent, except for reported instances of such help to separate households of parents. Those in need of long-term assistance must turn to the community, and each community is expected to have some resources to help households that are not capable of being self-sufficient. These provisions are locally variable and may be more precarious now than during the collective era (Feuchtwang 1987). The three villages studied all have adequate wealth and village-level administrative structures to provide such assistance. Zhangjiachedao and Huaili each reported a few recipient households; Qianrulin claimed in 1987 to have none requiring assistance.

35. Uxorilocal and intravillage marriages diverge from this pattern. Briefly, some of the divergences are as follows: In traditional uxorilocal marriage, a

woman may be able to activate a wider range of agnatic ties than would otherwise be accessible to her, while her husband almost completely severs his ties with his natal family. In intravillage matches, the husband's agnatic ties are the same as in patrilocal matches, but the wife may retain much closer ties with her family, especially if the marriage was arranged with this specific goal in mind and as an alternative to uxorilocal marriage.

36. In the extreme case, where a man was one of several brothers, he might indicate that virtually all his significant extrahousehold ties were with his brothers.

Chapter 6

1. This comment on the Campaign to Criticize Lin Biao and Confucius is based on my observations and discussions while a student in China during a period (1974–77) that included this campaign, and on discussions with other observers present at the same time.

2. The gender equity provisions of the Inheritance Law are openly ignored in the countryside. It would be a mistake to assume that any of the other legal provisions mentioned here are effectively implemented there either.

3. In the late 1980s, the Women's Federations began to move toward a greater presence in the cities, through organizing women office workers as well as women in the professions and in official service.

4. There is a conflict between customary values and promotion of the state's single-child policy. This women's head reported this conflict as having been difficult in her natal village, where there was substantial resistance to the policy, and less difficult in Zhangjiachedao, where there was more voluntary compliance. This degree of compliance may be related to the relatively high earning capacity of women in Zhangjiachedao and to the village's official, highly visible promotion of intravillage marriage as a solution for the care of aged persons who have daughters but no sons.

5. Although the village level is not formally part of the Women's Federation network, it may be relevant to note here that the Shandong Women's Federation differs from many others in retaining responsibility for preschool education. Indeed, it has been apparent in my investigations and discussions at various locations in the province that a considerable portion of the Shandong Women's Federation's resources, both human and material, are devoted to preschool education. In some other provinces this responsibility has been reallocated to education authorities.

6. Advocacy of "five-good families" is an important element of woman-work at present. Indeed, it is one that is expressed at the central level of the All-China Women's Federation and realized down to the village level in the designation of selected rural households (varying proportions in different villages) as meeting the criteria for "five-good families" (*wuhao jiating*) or the even more demanding criteria for "civilized families" (*wenming jiating*). Achieving either status is considered part of the responsibility of the woman of the household, although it is expressed in nonindividual, familial terms. The criteria for a five-good family,

as posted in Zhangjiachedao in 1986, were: (1) be good in loving socialism, loving the collective, and being law-abiding; (2) be good at daring to reform, being innovative, and fulfilling tasks; (3) be good at developing one's strengths and working hard to prosper, and at leading in helping others; (4) be good at family planning and teaching children, and in civilized manners and hygiene; and (5) be good in respecting the elderly and caring for the young, at democratic and harmonious relations in the household, and at uniting and helping relations with neighbors. This is essentially the same as the 1956 five-good family campaign of the Women's Federations. It can also easily be read as a fairly conventional statement about family relations, most of which would have been traditionally acceptable and advocated. One of the elements that is stressed in discussion is good relations between mothers-in-law and daughters-in-law; this is included but not explicit in the fifth point.

7. Woman-work is official work and is rarely done on a voluntary basis. This is a reason why the women's committees in the villages are commonly inactive or even empty.

8. I am lacking information for 12 other women in the 1989 sample of 40 households in the village of Huaili. Most of the 12 were unmarried young women with whom I did not speak directly. I expect that the lack of information on this point from the household members with whom I did speak indicates that these women were not at all involved with the women's organization, but I have nevertheless omitted them from the discussion that follows.

9. The one exception to this observation would be my own visit to look at and record the Women's Center's displays of woman-work and women's economic activities in the village.

10. This does not have the effect, which might otherwise be expected, of excluding or reducing the number of women employed. Concepts of appropriate gender division of labor reserve many positions, especially tending looms, for women. The effect of this policy therefore runs counter to the current trend of limited educational opportunities for women in the countryside.

11. The notable exception to this pattern is that of women taking on leadership roles where large numbers of men are absent. This occurred in the past mainly during wartime. Zhangjiachedao, for example, in common with many other villages, had a woman as village head briefly at the end of the civil war period in the 1940s. A recent resurgence of this pattern may be occurring in some villages where large numbers of the men work elsewhere and women are taking increasing responsibility for agriculture. However, in the villages studied, and in general at present, enough men are still resident in villages to fill leadership positions.

12. With the term "partially ascribed status" I am referring to the distinction between married and unmarried women. Marriage for women in the countryside is virtually universal, divorce is rare, and age at marriage is quite uniformly in the woman's early twenties. Married status is therefore largely determined by age and gender and is often significant for determining employment opportunities as well as residence and migration ones. A demographic imbal-

ance makes marriage less universal for men, and their age at marriage is slightly more variable.

13. The term "natural division of labor" (*ziran fengong*) is used in intellectual circles in China to refer to presumed biological reasons for customary differences in work between men and women. I have heard explanations in these terms from sources as diverse as male economists and female Women's Federation leaders, although the emphasis is slightly different—on the limits of women doing heavy or dangerous work, or on the demands of childbearing and childcare, respectively. Also see Honig and Hershatter 1988. Similar arguments, expressed in everyday terms, were to be heard in the villages as well.

14. The overwhelming majority of rural military recruits are male. Acceptance for military service is limited and competitive, and only a minority even of the young, healthy male population does serve. Military service has a significant impact on rural leadership because it often includes specialized training or leadership experience and, especially if successful and involving promotion, gives men a valuable political network of fellow veterans with shared military leadership experience. This is one of the channels of upward mobility in the countryside, but it is rarely accessible to women because few women get the opportunity to serve.

15. This woman's position as a kindergarten teacher gave her authority over only one other female kindergarten teacher and preschool children, which did not give her a role in village political or economic decision-making.

16. In areas of China with few alternatives to agricultural work, women are being concentrated in agriculture to a higher degree than in these three villages. In the worst situations, in poorer regions, even this work may be limited in availability.

17. This woman became my assistant as a result of my saying that I would like to hire one male and one female assistant within Zhangjiachedao; the village leaders chose her to replace one of the two men they had already selected. It is part of the gender division of labor in rural China that men normally represent their household or community toward the outside world. My request therefore unexpectedly precipitated the village women's head into a role unprecedented for her.

18. The arguments that follow with respect to freedom were more true of discourse in China before June 4, 1989 than after. Since that time, discussion of freedom has been dangerously open to suspicions of bourgeois liberalism, a serious political taint. It is not clear that the open discourse of freedom can be reduced to bourgeois liberalism, nor is it clear that the more conservative terms of discourse since June 4 signify a shift in aspirations. I have allowed this section to stand as indicative of women's strategies in most of the period in question, while I continue to study the more recent direction of the women's movement.

19. On a national level, this policy of improving the "quality" of women has more complex implications than those which are apparent when it is viewed strictly in connection with rural society and the rural work of the Women's

Federations. The emphasis on quality has become permissible in the reform era partly because of that era's rejection of egalitarianism and its willingness to accept, and even encourage, inequity among individuals and groups. In this respect the Women's Federations are moving in step with larger trends in reform-era China. Within some urban official and professional circles, this has allowed the Women's Federations to become more associated with elite women, potentially opening the door to an element of elitism. But it is not evident that this is the effect of the emphasis on quality in the countryside. Indeed, the reverse might well be argued: In promoting improved education and income-generating skills for rural women, and especially for those without other access to education or economically useful knowledge, this policy and set of activities effectively works to reduce the inequities enabled by reform-era economic policies.

20. This is reminiscent of the Yan'an-period (1937–45) policy of using ideological means to ensure that unified policy was carried out by cadres who were spread through liberated areas that were separated from one another by war zones.

Works Cited

Andors, Phyllis. 1981. "The 'Four Modernizations' and Chinese Policy on Women." *Bulletin of Concerned Asian Scholars* 13 (2): 44–56.

———. 1983. *The Unfinished Liberation of Chinese Women, 1949–1980*. Bloomington: Indiana University Press.

Aubert, Claude. 1990. "The Agricultural Crisis in China at the End of the 1980s." In J. Delman, C. S. Ostergaard, and F. Christiansen, eds., *Remaking Peasant China: Problems of Rural Development and Institutions at the Start of the 1990s*, pp. 16–37. Aarhus: Aarhus University Press.

Babb, Florence E. 1984. "Women in the Marketplace: Petty Commerce in Peru." *Review of Radical Political Economics* 16 (1): 45–59.

Bahro, Rudolf. 1978. *The Alternative in Eastern Europe*. Trans. David Fernbach. London: New Left Books.

Barlett, Peggy F. 1980. "Adaptive Strategies in Peasant Agricultural Production." *Annual Review of Anthropology* 9: 545–73.

Boserup, Ester. 1970. *Woman's Role in Economic Development*. New York: St. Martin's Press.

Bourdieu, Pierre. 1977. *Outline of a Theory of Practice*. Cambridge, Eng.: Cambridge University Press.

———. 1988. "Vive la crise! For heterodoxy in social science." *Theory and Society* 17: 773–87.

———. 1990. *The Logic of Practice*. Stanford, Calif.: Stanford University Press.

Brandauer, Frederick P. 1977. "Women in the *Ching-hua yan*: Emancipation Toward a Confucian Ideal." *Journal of Asian Studies* 36 (4): 647–60.

Buck, John Lossing. 1964. *Land Utilization in China*. New York: Paragon. Orig. pub. 1937.

Burch, Thomas K. 1979. "Household and Family Demography: A Bibliographic Essay." *Population Index* 45 (2): 173–95.

Byrd, William A., and Lin Qingsong, eds. 1990. *China's Rural Industry: Structure, Development, and Reform.* Oxford: Oxford University Press.

Chen Erjin. 1984. *China: Crossroads Socialism, an Unofficial Manifesto for Proletarian Democracy.* Trans. Robin Munro. London: Verso.

Chevrier, Yves. 1988. "NEP and Beyond: The Transition to 'Modernization' in China (1978–85)." In Stephan Feuchtwang, Athar Hussain, and Thierry Pairault, eds., *Transforming China's Economy in the Eighties,* vol. 1: *The Rural Sector, Welfare and Employment,* pp. 7–35. Boulder, Colo.: Westview; London: Zed.

Cohen, Myron L. 1976. *House United, House Divided: The Chinese Family in Taiwan.* New York: Columbia University Press.

———. 1990. "Lineage Organization in North China." *Journal of Asian Studies* 49 (3): 509–34.

Collier, Jane F., and Sylvia J. Yanagisako, eds. 1987. *Gender and Kinship: Essays Toward a Unified Analysis.* Stanford, Calif.: Stanford University Press.

Collins, Jane L. 1986. "The Household and Relations of Production in Southern Peru." *Comparative Studies in Society and History* 28 (4): 651–71.

Conroy, Richard. 1984. "*Laissez-faire* Socialism? Prosperous Peasants and China's Current Rural Development Strategy." *Australian Journal of Chinese Affairs* 12: 1–34.

Constitution of the People's Republic of China [1982]. 1985. *Modern Legal Systems Encyclopedia,* vol. 9: *Asia.* Buffalo, N.Y.: William, Hein and Co.

Cook, Scott, and Leigh Binford. 1986. "Petty Commodity Production, Capital Accumulation, and Peasant Differentiation: Lenin vs. Chayanov in Rural Mexico." *Review of Radical Political Economics* 18 (4): 1–31.

Croll, Elisabeth. 1978. *Feminism and Socialism in China.* London: Routledge and Kegan Paul.

———. 1979. *Women in Rural Development: The People's Republic of China.* Geneva: International Labor Office.

———. 1981. *The Politics of Marriage in Contemporary China.* Cambridge, Eng.: Cambridge University Press.

———. 1982. "The Promotion of Domestic Sideline Production in Rural China, 1978–79." In J. Gray and G. White, eds., *China's New Development Strategy,* pp. 235–54. London: Academic.

———. 1987a. "New Peasant Family Forms in Rural China." *Journal of Peasant Studies* 14 (4): 469–99.

———. 1987b. "Some Implications of the Rural Economic Reforms for the Chinese Peasant Household." In Ashwani Saith, ed., *The Re-emergence of the Chinese Peasantry: Aspects of Rural Decollectivisation,* pp. 105–36. London: Croom Helm.

———. 1988. "The New Peasant Economy in China." In Stephan Feuchtwang, Athar Hussain, and Thierry Pairault, eds., *Transforming China's Economy in the Eighties,* vol. 1: *The Rural Sector, Welfare and Employment,* pp. 77–100. Boulder, Colo.: Westview; London: Zed.

Crook, Frederick W. 1986. "The Reform of the Commune System and the Rise of the Township-Collective-Household System." In *China's Economy Looks*

Toward the Year 2000, vol. 1: *The Four Modernizations.* Washington, D.C.: U.S. Government Printing Office, pp. 354-75.

Crook, Isabel. n.d. *Prosperity Township: A Rural Community in Sichuan in Wartime.* Work in progress, 1987 draft.

Davin, Delia. 1976. *Woman-work: Women and the Party in Revolutionary China.* Oxford: Oxford University Press.

——. 1988. "The Implications of Contract Agriculture for the Employment and Status of Chinese Peasant Women." In Stephan Feuchtwang, Athar Hussain, and Thierry Pairault, eds., *Transforming China's Economy in the Eighties,* vol. 1: *The Rural Sector, Welfare and Employment,* pp. 137–46. Boulder: Westview and London: Zed.

Diamond, Norma. 1975. "Collectivization, Kinship, and the Status of Women in Rural China." In Rayna R. Reiter, ed., *Toward an Anthropology of Women,* pp. 372–95. New York: Monthly Review Press.

——. 1979. "Women and Industry in Taiwan." *Modern China* 5 (3): 317–40.

——. 1983a. "Household, Kinship and Women in Taitou Village, Shandong Province." In Randolph Barker and Beth Rose, eds., *Agricultural and Rural Development in China Today,* pp. 78–96. Ithaca, N.Y.: Cornell International Agriculture Mimeograph 102.

——. 1983b. "Model Villages and Village Realities." *Modern China* 9 (2): 163–81.

Dirlik, Arif. 1989. "Postsocialism? Reflections on 'Socialism with Chinese Characteristics.'" *Bulletin of Concerned Asian Scholars* 21 (1): 33–44.

Duara, Prasenjit. 1988. *Culture, Power, and the State: Rural North China, 1900–1942.* Stanford, Calif.: Stanford University Press.

Ebrey, Patricia Buckley, and James L. Watson, eds. 1986. *Kinship Organization in Late Imperial China, 1000–1940.* Berkeley: University of California Press.

Fazhan Yanjiusuo Zonghe Ketizu (Development Research Institute Integrated Task Group). 1987. "Nongmin, shichang he zhidu chuangxin—baochandaohu ba nian hou nongcun fazhan mianlin de shenceng gaige" (Peasants, markets, and institutional innovation: Deep reforms facing rural development eight years after contracting production to the household). *Jingji yanjiu* 1: 3–16.

Fei, Hsiao-tung [Fei Xiaotong]. 1968. *China's Gentry: Essays on Rural-Urban Relations.* Chicago: Phoenix. Orig. pub. 1953.

Fei Hsiao Tung [Fei Xiaotong]. 1983. *Chinese Village Close-up.* Beijing: New World Press.

Feuchtwang, Stephan. 1987. "Changes in the System of Basic Social Security in the Countryside since 1979." In Ashwani Saith, ed., *The Re-emergence of the Chinese Peasantry: Aspects of Rural Decollectivisation,* pp. 173–210. London: Croom Helm.

Fox-Genovese, Elizabeth, and Eugene D. Genovese. 1983. "The Ideological Bases of Domestic Economy." In E. Fox-Genovese and E. D. Genovese, eds., *Fruits of Merchant Capital,* pp. 299–336. New York: Oxford University Press.

Friedman, Edward, Paul G. Pickowicz, and Mark Selden, with Kay Ann Johnson. 1991. *Chinese Village, Socialist State*. New Haven, Conn.: Yale University Press.

Friedmann, Harriet. 1978. "World Market, State, and Family Farm: Social Bases of Household Production in the Era of Wage Labor." *Comparative Studies in Society and History* 20: 545–86.

———. 1980. "Household Production and the National Economy: Concepts for the Analysis of Agrarian Formations." *Journal of Peasant Studies* 7: 158–84.

Gallin, Rita S. 1984. "Women, Family and the Political Economy of Taiwan." *Journal of Peasant Studies* 12 (1): 76–92.

Harrell, Stevan. 1982. *Ploughshare Village: Culture and Context in Taiwan*. Seattle: University of Washington Press.

———. 1985. "Why Do the Chinese Work So Hard? Reflections on an Entrepreneurial Ethic." *Modern China* 11 (2): 203–26.

Honig, Emily, and Gail Hershatter. 1988. *Personal Voices: Chinese Women in the 1980's*. Stanford, Calif.: Stanford University Press.

Howard, Pat. 1988. *Breaking the Iron Rice Bowl: Prospects for Socialism in China's Countryside*. Armonk, N.Y.: M. E. Sharpe.

Hsu, Robert C. 1985. "Conceptions of the Market in Post-Mao China." *Modern China* 11(4): 436–60.

Huang, Philip C. C. 1985. *The Peasant Economy and Social Change in North China*. Stanford, Calif.: Stanford University Press.

———. 1990. *The Peasant Family and Rural Development in the Yangzi Delta, 1350–1988*. Stanford, Calif.: Stanford University Press.

Huang Shumin. 1989. *The Spiral Road: Change in a Chinese Village Through the Eyes of a Communist Party Leader*. Boulder, Colo.: Westview.

Jiang Zemin. 1989. "Jiang Zemin tongzhi de jianghua (1989.9.29)" (Comrade Jiang Zemin's speech (Sept. 29, 1989). *Guangming ribao*, Sept. 30.

Johnson, Kay Ann. 1983. *Women, the Family and Peasant Revolution in China*. Chicago: University of Chicago Press.

Judd, Ellen R. 1989. "*Niangjia*: Chinese Women and Their Natal Families." *Journal of Asian Studies* 48 (3): 525–44.

———. 1990. "Alternative Development Strategies for Women in Rural China." *Development and Change* 21 (1): 23–42.

———. In press. "Feminism from Afar *or* to China and Home Again." In S. Cole and L. Phillips, eds., *Ethnographic Feminism(s): Essays in Anthropology*. Ottawa: Carleton University Press.

Kandiyoti, Deniz. 1990. Women and Rural Development Policies: The Changing Agenda." *Development and Change* 21 (1): 5–22.

Kang Keqing. 1987. "Jieri tanxin" (Holiday heart-to-heart talk). *Xinhua wenzhai* (April 1987): 3–5.

Kangshi zupu (Kang surname genealogy). 1965. 4 vols. Shentou, China: n.p. (stenciled only).

Lamphere, Louise. 1974. "Strategies, Cooperation, and Conflict among Women in Domestic Groups." In Michelle Zimbalist Rosaldo and Louise Lamphere, eds., *Woman, Culture, and Society*, pp. 97–112. Stanford, Calif.: Stanford University Press.

Li Yunhe. 1985. "Nongcun 'huxue' chutan" (A prologue to the study of rural households). *Xinhua wenzhai* 77 (1985:5): 58–61.

Liang Weiling. 1988. "Guanyu fulian gaige de gouxiang" (Thoughts on the reform of the Women's Federation). *Zhongguo funü* 1: 14–17.

Liang Xuguang, Dong Xiangju, Shang Zhixiao, et al. 1989. *Funü chengcai lun* (On nurturing female talent). Jinan: Shandong renmin.

Lin Li. 1988. "Shenhua nongcun jingji gaige wenti de taolun" (A discussion on the question of deepening the rural economic reform). *Jingji yanjiu* 6: 74–78, 16.

———. 1989. "Wo guo nongye de kunjing yu chulu wenti taolun zongshu" (A summary of discussion on the question of the difficulties and prospects of our country's agriculture). *Jingji yanjiu* 4: 74–77, 73.

Liu Shuzhen. 1988. "Shandong sheng renkou duo yu gengdi shao de maodun yue lai yue jianrui" (The contradiction between the increase in population and decrease in arable land in Shandong Province becomes more and more acute.) *Renkou yanjiu* 2: 50–52.

Luo Xiaopeng. 1989. "The Hierarchical Structure and the System of Ownership in China's Rural Enterprises." *Chinese Economic Studies* 23 (1): 89–99.

Marriage Law of the People's Republic of China [1950]. 1975. Beijing: Foreign Languages Press.

Marriage Law of the People's Republic of China [1981]. 1982. Beijing: Foreign Languages Press.

Maxwell, Neville, and Bruce McFarlane, eds. 1984. *China's Changed Road to Development*. Oxford: Pergamon.

Mies, Maria. 1986. *Patriarchy and Accumulation on a World Scale: Women in the International Division of Labour*. London: Zed.

Nee, Victor. 1985. "Peasant Household Individualism." In William L. Parish, ed., *Chinese Rural Development: The Great Transformation*, pp. 164–90. Armonk, N.Y.: M. E. Sharpe.

Niehoff, Justin D. 1987. "The Villager as Industrialist: Ideologies of Household Manufacturing in Rural Taiwan." *Modern China* 13 (3): 278–309.

Nolan, Peter, and Gordon White. 1979. "Socialist Development and Rural Inequality: The Chinese Countryside in the 1970's." *Journal of Peasant Studies* 7 (1): 3–48.

Oi, Jean C. 1989. *State and Peasant in Contemporary China: The Political Economy of Village Government*. Berkeley: University of California Press.

Palmer, Michael. 1988. "China's New Inheritance Law: Some Preliminary Observations." In Stephan Feuchtwang, Athar Hussain, and Thierry Pairault, eds., *Transforming China's Economy in the Eighties*, vol. 1: *The Rural Sector, Welfare and Employment*, pp. 169–97. Boulder, Colo.: Westview and London: Zed.

Parish, William L., ed. 1985. *Chinese Rural Development: The Great Transformation*. Armonk, N.Y.: M. E. Sharpe.

Parish, William L., and Martin King Whyte. 1978. *Village and Family in Contemporary China*. Chicago: University of Chicago Press.

Perkins, Dwight, and Shahid Yusuf. 1984. *Rural Development in China*. Baltimore, Md.: Johns Hopkins University Press.

Perry, Elizabeth J. 1985. "Rural Violence in Socialist China." *China Quarterly* 103: 414–40.

Potter, Sulamith Heins, and Jack M. Potter. 1990. *China's Peasants: The Anthropology of a Revolution*. Cambridge, Eng.: Cambridge University Press.

Putterman, Louis. 1989. "Entering the Post-Collective Era in North China: Dahe Township." *Modern China* 15 (3): 275–320.

"Quarterly Chronicle and Documentation (July-Sept. 1990)." 1990. *China Quarterly* 124: 760–81.

Rogers, Barbara. 1980. *The Domestication of Women: Discrimination in Developing Societies*. London: Tavistock.

Rosaldo, M. Z. 1980. "The Use and Abuse of Anthropology: Reflections on Feminism and Cross-cultural Understanding." *Signs* 5 (3): 389–417.

Salaff, Janet W. 1981. *Working Daughters of Hong Kong: Filial Piety or Power in the Family*. Cambridge, Eng.: Cambridge University Press.

Scott, James C. 1985. *Weapons of the Weak: Everyday Forms of Peasant Resistance*. New Haven, Conn.: Yale University Press.

"Shandong's Economic Performance in 1989." 1990. *Summary of World Broadcasts*, Part 3: *The Far East, Weekly Economic Report* (25 April) FE/W0125. London: British Broadcasting Corporation.

"Shandong's Economy in 1986." 1987. *Summary of World Broadcasts*, Part 3: *The Far East, Weekly Economic Report* (6 May) FE/W1439. London: British Broadcasting Corporation.

"Shandong's Economy in 1988." 1989. *Summary of World Broadcasts*, Part 3: *The Far East, Weekly Economic Report* (10 May) FE/W0076. London: British Broadcasting Corporation.

"Shandong's Performance in 1987." 1988. *Summary of World Broadcasts*, Part 3: *The Far East, Weekly Economic Report* (22 June) FE/W0031. London: British Broadcasting Corporation.

Shue, Vivienne. 1984. "The Fate of the Commune." *Modern China* 10 (3): 259–83.

———. 1988. *The Reach of the State: Sketches of the Chinese Body Politic*. Stanford, Calif.: Stanford University Press.

Sicular, Terry. 1986. "Recent Agricultural Price Policies and Their Effects: The Case of Shandong." In *China's Economy Looks Toward the Year 2000*, vol. 1: *The Four Modernizations: Selected Papers Submitted to the Joint Economic Committee of the Congress of the U.S.* Washington, D.C.: U.S. Government Printing Office, pp. 407–30.

Siu, Helen F. 1989. *Agents and Victims in South China: Accomplices in Rural Revolution*. New Haven, Conn.: Yale University Press.

Solinger, Dorothy. 1984. "Commerce: The Petty Private Sector and the Three Lines in the Early 1980's." In Dorothy Solinger, ed., *Three Visions of Chinese Socialism*, pp. 73–112. Boulder, Colo.: Westview.

Song Linfei. 1984. "The Present State and Future Prospects of Specialized Households in Rural China." *Social Sciences in China* 5 (4): 107–30.

Stacey, Judith. 1983. *Patriarchy and Socialist Revolution in China.* Berkeley: University of California Press.

Taylor, Jeffrey R. 1988. "Rural Employment Trends and the Legacy of Surplus Labour, 1978–86." *China Quarterly* 116: 736–66.

Thorborg, Marina. 1978. "Chinese Employment Policy in 1949–78 with Special Emphasis on Women in Rural Production." In Joint Economic Committee of the U.S. Congress, ed., *Chinese Economy Post-Mao*, vol. 1: *Policy and Performance*, pp. 535–604. Washington, D.C.: U.S. Government Printing Office.

"Tongfen jiehe xinggongdainong yigongyinong—Zhangjiachedao cun tansuo nongye shengchan zai shang xin jieti de luzi shang de diaocha" (Thoroughly unite using industry to help agriculture and being both worker and peasant—An investigation of Zhangjiachedao Village's explorations in putting agricultural production on the road to reaching a still higher level). *Weifang ribao* (May 17, 1986).

Tu Nan. 1986. "Rural Industry—China's New Engine for Development." *FAO Review* 19 (6): 32–38.

Walder, Andrew G. 1983. "Organized Dependency and Cultures of Authority in Chinese Industry." *Journal of Asian Studies* 43 (1): 51–76.

Walker, Kenneth R. 1989. "Forty Years On: Provincial Contrasts in China's Rural Economic Development." *China Quarterly* 119: 448–80.

Wang Qi. 1988. "Di liu jie quanguo fudaihui de sange rechao" (Three upsurges at the Sixth National Congress of Women's Representatives). *Zhongguo funü* 11: 8–11.

Wang Sibin. 1987. "Jingji tizhi gaige dui nongcun shehui guanxi de yingxiang" (The influence of the reform of the economic system on rural social relations). *Beijing daxue xuebao* 3: 26–34.

Watson, Andrew. 1984. "Agriculture Looks for 'Shoes That Fit': The Production Responsibility System and Its Implications." In Neville Maxwell and Bruce McFarlane, eds., *China's Changed Road to Development*, pp. 83–108. Oxford: Pergamon.

———. 1989. "Investment Issues in the Chinese Countryside." *Australian Journal of Chinese Affairs* 22: 85–126.

White, Gordon. 1987. "The Impact of Economic Reforms in the Chinese Countryside: Towards the Politics of Social Capitalism." *Modern China* 13 (4): 411–40.

Wolf, Arthur P. 1978. "Gods, Ghosts, and Ancestors." In Arthur P. Wolf, ed., *Studies in Chinese Society*, pp. 131–82. Stanford, Calif.: Stanford University Press.

———. 1986. "The Preeminent Role of Government Intervention in China's Family Revolution." *Population and Development Review* 12 (1): 101–16.

Wolf, Eric R. 1983. *Europe and the People Without History.* Berkeley: University of California Press.

Wolf, Margery. 1968. *The House of Lim: A Study of a Chinese Farm Family*. New York: Appleton-Century-Crofts.

———. 1972. *Women and the Family in Rural Taiwan*. Stanford, Calif.: Stanford University Press.

———. 1985. *Revolution Postponed: Women in Contemporary China*. Stanford, Calif.: Stanford University Press.

Wong, Christine P. W. 1988. "Interpreting Rural Industrial Growth in the Post-Mao Period." *Modern China* 14 (1): 3–30.

Xie Dehui. 1989. "Qian, fengkuang de kunshou" (Money—a frenzied, cornered beast). *Renmin ribao*, February 27.

Yanagisako, Sylvia Junko. 1979. "Family and Household: The Analysis of Domestic Groups." *Annual Review of Anthropology* 8: 161–205.

Yanagisako, Sylvia Junko, and Jane Fishburne Collier. 1987. "Toward a Unified Analysis of Gender and Kinship." In Jane F. Collier and Sylvia J. Yanagisako, eds., *Gender and Kinship: Essays Toward a Unified Analysis*, pp. 14–50. Stanford, Calif.: Stanford University Press.

Yang, Martin. 1945. *A Chinese Village: Taitou, Shantung Province*. New York: Columbia University Press.

Yang Yanyin. 1989. "Quan sheng funü tuanjie qilai wei jianshe Shandong, zhenxing Shandong er nuli fendou" (Let all women of the province unite to build Shandong and struggle hard to develop Shandong). *Funü gongzuo* 5: 7–16.

Zhang Juan and Ma Wenrong. 1988. "Daqiuzhuang 'funü huijia' de sisuo" (Thoughts on Daqiuzhuang's "Women returning to the home"). *Zhongguo funü* 1: 8–10.

Zhonggong Shandong shengwei ji nongcun gongzuobu tizhi zhengcechu. (The Chinese Communist Party Shandong Provincial Committee's and Rural Work Department's Constitution and Policy Office). 1985. *Zhuanye hu zhengce fagui zixun shouce* (Advisory handbook on regulations and laws regarding specialized households). Jinan: Shandong renmin.

Zhou Qing. 1988. "Wo guo xiandaihua guocheng zhong nongcun jiating guimo yu leixing jiegou—Shandong sheng Jiaoxian 508 hu nongmin jiating diaocha" (Rural family size and composition in our country's process of modernization—An investigation of 508 households in Jiao County, Shandong). *Renkou yanjiu* 2: 17–21.

Zhou Qiren and Du Ying. 1984. "Specialized Households: A Preliminary Study." *Social Sciences in China* 1: 50–72.

Index

In this index "f" after a number indicates a separate reference on the next page, and "ff" indicates separate references on the next two pages. A continuous discussion over two or more pages is indicated by a span of numbers. *Passim* is used for a cluster of references in close but not consecutive sequence.

Library of Congress Cataloging-in-Publication Data

Judd, Ellen R.
    Gender and power in rural North China / Ellen R. Judd.
        p.   cm.
    Includes bibliographical references and index.
    ISBN 0-8047-2295-1 (cloth : acid-free paper)
    1. Women in rural development—China.   2. Rural women—China—
Social condiditons.   3. Sex role—China.   4. China—Rural
conditions.   I. Title.
HQ1240.5.C6J84   1994
305.42'0951—dc20   93-38862
                                                                        CIP